NSTA Guide to
PLANNING SCHOOL
SCIENCE FACILITIES

2nd Edition

NSTA Guide to
PLANNING SCHOOL
SCIENCE FACILITIES

2nd Edition

LaMoine L. Motz, James T. Biehle, and Sandra S. West

National Science Teachers Association
Arlington, VA

NATIONAL SCIENCE TEACHERS ASSOCIATION

Claire Reinburg, Director
Judy Cusick, Senior Editor
Andrew Cocke, Associate Editor
Betty Smith, Associate Editor
Robin Allan, Book Acquisitions Manager

PRINTING AND PRODUCTION
Catherine Lorrain, Director
Nguyet Tran, Assistant Production Manager
Jack Parker, Electronic Prepress Technician

NATIONAL SCIENCE TEACHERS ASSOCIATION
Gerald F. Wheeler, Executive Director
David Beacom, Publisher

Library of Congress Cataloging-in-Publication Data
Motz, LaMoine L.
  NSTA guide to planning school science facilities / by LaMoine L. Motz, James T. Biehle, and Sandra S. West. -- 2nd ed.
      p. cm.
  Rev. ed. of: NSTA guide to school science facilities / James T. Biehle, LaMoine L. Motz, Sandra S. West. c1999.
  Includes bibliographical references and index.
   ISBN 978-1-933531-08-3 -- ISBN 978-1-933531-69-4 (e-book)
  1. Laboratories--United States--Design and construction. 2. Laboratories--United States.--Furniture, equipment, etc. 3. School
facilities--United States--Planning. I. Biehle, James T. II. West, Sandra S. III. Biehle, James T. NSTA guide to school science facilities.
IV. Title.
Q183.U6B54 2007
371.6'23--dc22

                     2007031616

The information presented in this guide has been compiled by the authors using sources believed to be reliable and to offer the best and most current opinions on the subject. This publication is intended to provide only basic guidelines for good safety practices and does not purport to specify minimal legal standards or to represent the policy of the National Science Teachers Association. No warranty, guarantee, or representation is made by the National Science Teachers Association or the Task Force on Science Facilities and Equipment as to the accuracy or sufficiency of the information contained herein, and the Association assumes no responsibility in connection therewith. It cannot be assumed that all necessary warning and precautionary measures are contained in this publication or that other or additional information or measures may not be required. Readers of this guide should determine the applicable local, state, and federal laws and consult legal counsel prior to initiating any safety program.

Contents

CHAPTER 4

Designing Facilities for the
Elementary School (K–5)   45

CHAPTER 5

Designing Facilities for
the Middle School (6–8)   55

CHAPTER 6

Designing Facilities for
the High School (9–12)   69

PREFACE

For over 50 years, the National Science Teachers Association (NSTA) has been providing information to teachers and schools regarding science facilities and equipment. To provide assistance in the design of secondary school science facilities, NSTA in 1954 published its first book on facilities, *School Facilities for Science Instruction*. This publication was revised and updated in 1961. Although the Association subsequently released several related pamphlets, it became evident by the end of that decade that an updated document was needed.

With new science curricula being published in the 1960s and early 1970s, supported by the National Science Foundation (NSF), a renewed interest and concern for updated and appropriate science facilities was created. In April 1970, NSF approved a grant to NSTA to study exemplary science facilities and identify emerging trends in facility design and use. The publication, released in 1972, *Facilities for Secondary School Science Teaching: Evolving Patterns in Facilities and Programs*, was a result of a project directed by Joseph Novak, of Cornell University.

In 1988, as NSTA president, I established the Task Force on Science Facilities and Equipment. The charge to this task force was to develop a publication or publications on instructional science facilities for elementary and secondary schools and to encourage and assist educational institutions in securing the best facilities possible for science instruction.

The task force was chaired by Ronald Converse, coordinator of K–12 science, Conroe Independent School District, Conroe, Texas. Other members were Dorothy Barton, curriculum coordinator, Beers Middle Elementary Science Program, District of Columbia Public Schools, Washington, D.C.; Tony Beasley, coordinator of K–12 science, Metro Nashville Schools, Nashville, Tennessee; Thomas Gadsden, director of science, K–12, Richardson Independent School District, Richardson, Texas; Ronald Maxwell, independent facilities consultant, Lake Leelanau, Michigan; Ronald Sass, professor of science education, Rice University, Houston, Texas; Victor Showalter, director, Center for Unified Science Education, Capital University, Columbus, Ohio; Jon Thompson, director, Kalamazoo Area Mathematics and Science Center, Kalamazoo, Michigan; Marlin Welsh, director of science, K–12, Shawnee Mission Unified School District, Shawnee Mission, Kansas; and Phyllis Marcuccio, director of publications, National Science Teachers Association.

This task force spent several years studying trends and directions in the design and implementation of elementary and secondary science teaching and learning facilities. They invited school districts to submit videotapes of their exemplary science facilities.

In 1992, a new NSTA Task Force on Science Facilities and Equipment was established, with myself as chair. This group met in Charlotte, North Carolina, and outlined a new beginning and direction for a publication on kindergarten through grade 12 science facilities. The members of this task force were Dorothy Barton, Tony Beasley, and Ray Filipiak, Sheldon Laboratory Systems; Jim Biehle, American Institute of Architects, Saint Louis, Missouri; Thomas Gadsden, Ronald Maxwell, Ronald Sass, Victor Showalter, Jon Thompson, Marlin Welsh, and Phyllis Marcuccio. This meeting produced a pamphlet, *Facilitating Science Facilities: A Priority*. This publication was a checklist for administrators and boards of education, and was disseminated via the NSTA journals and newsletters as well as through various elementary and secondary school journals and newsletters.

During an NSTA Convention in Phoenix, the task force met and established a working outline for the current publication, and several representatives from national science facilities manufacturers joined in the discussion of the outline.

Several task force members were then invited to write recommendations on science facilities for the National Science Education Standards (NSES). The result was the development of guidelines for elementary, middle, and high school science facilities based on NSES Program Standard D: Resources, and published in NSTA's three-volume publication *Pathways to the Science Standards*.

This second edition of the *NSTA Guide to Planning School Science Facilities* includes updated information about planning facilities design, budget priorities, space considerations, general room and laboratory design, furnishings for the laboratory/classroom, safety, ADA, and much more. This edition represents the cooperative input of hundreds of hours and the effort of many individuals.

First acknowledgement and gratitude must go to the NSTA publications staff for all of their efforts and assistance in completing this guidebook. Special thanks go to Andrew Cocke, who guided us through this project, and whose expertise in editing assured us a fine product.

A number of interested people submitted suggestions and references, and provided valuable reviews of the manuscript.

A deep sense of gratitude is extended to James T. Biehle, AIA, and president, Inside/Out Architecture, Kirkwood, Missouri, for his untiring support, interest, and tremendous contribution to the writing of the publication. A special thank you is also extended to Sandra West for her outstanding contributions to the development of the manuscript, especially in the areas of science safety and safe laboratory designs, and to Juliana Texley for her contributions to the inclusion of

ADA guidelines as they relate to the planning and designing of school science facilities. Additional thanks goes to Da-Shawn Coleman for her outstanding technical assistance in orchestrating the format and layout of this publication.

This second edition could not have been completed without the ideas and support and assistance from various manufacturers of science facilities and equipment. Our special thanks to the late Raymond Filipiak, of Sheldon Laboratory Systems, for whom this edition is dedicated.

The support and encouragement of many teachers, supervisors, curriculum directors, and other administrators of science education kept our task focused and moving toward completion of this second edition.

To Gerry Wheeler, David Beacom, and Claire Reinburg, thank you for the contributed counsel and ideas, as well as the administrative and editorial assistance.

To all of these and many others, the authors owe much for their valuable contributions.

LaMoine L. Motz
White Lake, Michigan
March 2007

DEDICATION

Dedicated to the memory of Raymond E. Filipiak, whose knowledge, insights, and contributions to school science facilities were exemplary and are greatly appreciated. He directly and indirectly made significant contributions to this book.

INTRODUCTION

Through the National Science Education Standards, our profession has called for learning environments in which students explore, inquire, and construct their own knowledge about the physical world. Good science programs require the uniquely adaptable learning space we call a laboratory, as well as access to both indoor and outdoor space for research, environmental studies, and reflection. Yet the vast majority of communities moving toward the Standards will find their progress limited by the facilities available in their schools.

Today, across the country, large numbers of school buildings are in disrepair. The General Accounting Office (1996, 3.1) reported that over one-third of our schools, serving over 14 million students, need either extensive renovation or reconstruction, and another one third have at least one major structural flaw, such as a leaky roof, outdated electrical systems, or dysfunctional plumbing. Many of the remaining schools were planned without any consideration of what we consider as the requirements for effective science education. The National Clearinghouse for Educational Facilities reports that more than 122,000 public and private school buildings in the United States are, on the average, more than 45 years old. More than a quarter of them were built before 1950, and 73% date from before 1970. American school districts spend between $20 billion and $30 billion each year on new school construction. Renovations add even more to this expenditure (National Clearinghouse for Educational Facilities 2006).

Numerous studies confirm that the school environment strongly affects student performance. One such study found that students in the best-designed schools scored between 5 and 17 points higher on standardized tests than kids who attended class in substandard buildings (Lyons 2001). Good school design also includes outdoor areas, which offer space for group activities and environmental studies. Innovative schools use their buildings and grounds as giant science labs—"three-dimensional textbooks," the American Architectural Foundation (AAF) calls them—that teach lessons in biology, Earth science, and physics.

Sustainability is emerging as an overriding principle in architecture and design, and is greatly informing school design and construction. Sustainability is about meeting current needs without depleting resources or harming natural cycles for future generations. In school science design, this means paying attention to the kinds of materials used in the construction, how the building is positioned on the grounds, how waste gets handled, and also the ease with which renovation might occur in the future.

A laborartory/classroom

Over the past few years, many school communities have experienced growth in student population, and have had to add to or expand their existing facilities.

In the eight years since the first edition of this book was published, the authors have toured hundreds of schools with new or newly renovated science facilities. Many were planned using the recommendations outlined herein and the students and science teachers using them are benefiting from safer, more flexible and functional spaces. However, many new facilities are still being planned as new versions of long-outdated designs with little flexibility and a lack of the space and equipment needed to make hands-on, inquiry-based science education a safe reality.

As we move toward the National Science Education Standards, we must accept the challenge of revitalizing both our science teaching and our facilities. Just recently legislation was introduced under bills being considered by both the U.S. House of Representatives and Senate to upgrade high school science classroom/laboratory facilities, increase training in laboratory safety, better integrate lab lessons with other academic science content, and use labs to encourage students to pursue science study in college. The National Science Foundation would oversee this new program.

NSTA believes that the science facilities in our nation's schools deserve a strong commitment and continuous attention. It is in science classrooms that students work, learn, and experience real science, using the tools and practicing the skills and habits of mind that encourage science learning. Students form their first and most lasting impressions of the importance of science there. The attention that our communities pay to good science classrooms is a measure of the level of our regard for science education.

The ideas and guidelines for remodeling and replacing facilities presented in these pages are compatible with the principles of the National Science Education Standards, which detail expectations for teaching and programming at all school levels.

Those who are planning facilities for science education will want to weigh their plans in relation to the requirements of the Standards and to trends in science teaching. The resulting facilities should serve both the present and the evolving science programs of the future.

The purpose of this book is to familiarize educators, administrators, and citizens with the stages of the process of planning for new and renovated science facilities and to provide specific, detailed information on many items and aspects of the planning and design phases. This information will also be useful to facilities planners and architects.

Regrettably, in some cases, teachers asked to join a planning committee serve only as token members. Yet, the active participation of science teachers and leaders is key to a successful project.

This book is designed to provide teachers, curriculum leaders, and administrators with a broad vision of the role of facilities in science teaching, as well as the background they will need to become valuable contributors to any facilities project team. It also reflects the most up-to-date research on best practice and environments for science learning. We hope that the book will help planning teams design effective spaces that meet their objectives for teaching and learning science.

LaMoine L. Motz

Reference

American Architectural Foundation and Knowledge Works Foundation. 2006. Report from the National Summit on School Design: A resource for educators and designers.

General Accounting Office. 1996. *School facilities: America's schools report differing conditions.* GAO Report No. HEHS-96-103. (June 14). Washington, DC: Author.

Lyons, J. B. 2001. Do school facilities really impact a child's education? CEFPI *Issuetrak* (November).

National Clearinghouse for Educational Facilities. 2006. Average construction cost for elementary, middle and high schools in 2005.

CHAPTER 1

Advocacy and the Planning Process

Key ideas in this chapter:
- Appropriate facilities must be available and maintained to support quality science programs.
- The philosophy and mission of the science curriculum and instruction dictate the shape of the science facility.
- Good planning involves good communication with all stakeholders (teachers, administrators, architect, contractor, science facilities consultant, parent representative, and others).
- Include all stakeholders in the process, do thorough research, and solicit expert advice.
- Determine the needs of the learning environment, which should drive the design of the facility.
- Stakeholders must work together to develop a realistic timeline for new construction or renovation.
- Curriculum must shape the science facility, or, thereafter, the facility will shape the curriculum.
- At every phase of the planning process, all participants must be budget conscious.

Empowering With Information

Science educators believe that students construct their knowledge of the natural world best in safe, secure, and stimulating learning environments. In order to achieve these goals, teachers, researchers, and planners must become advocates for the school facilities in which they work. The program standards of the National Science Education Standards (NSES) provide a strong foundation for advocating improvements in school science.

National Science Education Standards

National Research Council, National Academy of Sciences

Program Standards (Excerpts)

All elements of the K–12 science program must be consistent with the other National Science Education Standards and with one another and developed within and across grade levels to meet a clearly stated set of goals.

The program of study in science for all students should be developmentally appropriate, interesting, and relevant to students' lives; emphasize student understanding through inquiry; and be connected with other school subjects.

The science program should be coordinated with the mathematics program to enhance student use and understanding of mathematics in the study of science and to improve student understanding of mathematics.

The K–12 science program must give students access to appropriate and sufficient resources, including quality teachers, time, materials and equipment, adequate and safe space, and the community.

All students in the K–12 science program must have equitable access to opportunities to achieve the National Science Education Standards.

Schools must work as communities that encourage, support, and sustain teachers as they implement an effective science program.

SOURCE: National Research Council, *National Science Education Standards,* National Academy Press, Washington, DC, 1996.

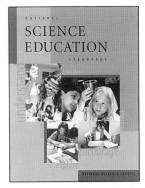

The *National Science Education Standards*

A high school lab/classroom

This publication is a tool for teachers, science specialists, school teams, school boards, architects, and others concerned who plan, design, and build exemplary science facilities for the youth of today and the future. The information in the chapters that follow is intended to empower teachers, schools, and communities to meet the challenge set by the National Science Education Standards.

Support for Good Facilities

One of the earliest, and often hardest, steps in the process of renovating or developing new science facilities is to convince the school community that change is needed. Given the tremendous pressure to expand and improve all kinds of educational facilities, it is up to science teaching professionals to become advocates for the resources and classroom environments they need. And while administrators, school board members, and parents may initiate building programs based on their perceptions of space needs, it is important for educators to promote an understanding of the relationship between facilities and curriculum. This is best accomplished with an understanding of the National Science Education Standards and

An elementary science classroom

their significance and an effort to integrate these Standards into the decision-making process.

NSTA's Task Force on Science Facilities and Equipment (1993) suggests that we might begin our advocacy by helping our boards and school communities recognize the following rationale and philosophy:

Our nation must have a scientifically and technologically literate citizenry that is prepared to understand and deal rationally with the issues and opportunities within a scientific and technological world.

American schools should give science a central role in K–12 instruction where each student should have the opportunity to be engaged in science each day of each school year.

Science and technology occur in many different settings: schools, universities, hospitals, business and industry, as well as government, independent research organizations and scientific organizations. Work places include classrooms, offices, laboratories and natural field settings.

Hands-on laboratory experience is integral to the nature of science and must be included in every science program for every student.

Laboratory experience is critical to the student's cognitive development. Therefore, appropriate facilities must be available and be maintained to support quality science programs.

An Interpretation of the Standards

Evaluating current programs and the facilities that support them is an important part of planning. Does the school district have clearly stated goals and outcomes? Is science an integral part of these goals at all levels? Have the National Science Education Standards impacted these goals and outcomes? Such a review serves both to clarify the direction of the science program and to help to raise the school community's awareness of the importance of the program.

Science facilities must support today's curriculum and tomorrow's, too. In order to ensure that happens, it is useful to consider the following goals suggested by the principles of the Standards:

- The facilities are capable of supporting all of the objectives of the science program.
- Science facilities are available to all students all of the time. At the elementary level, this may mean providing large, self-contained classrooms that have ample access to water; pairing science-friendly classrooms with those that lack the needed resources; or maintaining discovery rooms that provide reasonable access to all teachers when they need them. At the high school level, this means ensuring that enough combination laboratory/classrooms are available to enable every student to study a laboratory science every year.
- The facilities and equipment provide a wide selection of experiences appropriate to the learning potential and interests of students with varied capabilities and learning styles.

We should continue to seek a deeper understanding of how students at each level learn and to provide facilities that enable us to respond to those needs.

- The science facilities provide lab/classrooms and outdoor space for investigations, demonstrations, and research, including access to natural settings for outdoor science activities.
- The facilities are adaptable. Team teaching, integrated curricular activities, and flexible grouping are well supported by the physical plant.
- Science lab/classrooms are provided with science supplies; instruments and equipment; and ample, secure space to store these items.
- The arrangement of furniture and utilities in the lab/classroom is flexible so that the teacher is able to direct activities easily while providing supervision and maintaining maximum control. At the same time, students are able to move around and exit without encountering obstacles.
- Provision is made for easy access to audiovisual resources for individuals and groups under conditions controlled by the classroom teacher.
- Educational technology is within reach, bringing information, data, instrumentation, and research into the classroom, enabling students to explore the world.

The Planning Phase

How do we translate our philosophy, mission, and curriculum into the bricks and mortar of a science-learning environment?

Participants

Because the science program and science facilities are so interconnected, the active participation of the teachers, with their extensive experience at the grade level and understanding of the National Science Education Standards and best practice, is crucial to any planning team's success. Since there are many steps along the way between initial planning meetings and the completed facility, the science teachers should be integral members of the team from start to finish.

There are also many other important participants in the planning process, whether in leadership roles or as valuable sources of input concerning the specific needs of the school, district, curriculum, or program.

For public school projects, members of the school board and the administration usually determine and communicate the community's fiscal constraints and legal requirements and ensure that educational programs and facilities standards are incorporated. Administrators also bring to the team their comprehensive understanding of how the various sectors of the school community interface with each other. Curriculum coordinators present the needs of the program and the requirements of the instruction plans, while community members can contribute essential input into political and family needs. Often, a science supervisor or other science education leader is instrumental in a variety of roles, including coordination, communication, evaluation, and research. Local and state facilities planners and consultants assume various functions and provide important information, perspec-

tives, and ideas. The local facilities planner may coordinate the planning process.

The best planning teams capitalize on the unique characteristics of their communities. Parents and community members should be represented in planning at every step of the way. An experienced science facility architect is essential to translating the needs of the science program into design concepts. Business consultants, especially those in science -related corporations, can review equipment and facilities design to determine school-to-work potential; furnishings and equipment consultants will provide specialized advice. Also useful are the school's custodians and maintenance staff, who are aware

An aging science lab

of maintenance problems and the value of specific products and can contribute ideas to the design decisions.

Important, but sometimes forgotten, contributors from the school community are the students, whose experience and opinions should influence decisions regarding space requirements and other aspects of facilities use. Students seldom attend formal meetings, but their input should always be considered.

Whether the project involves remodeling existing space or creating new space, the most important design expert will be the architect, who also provides expertise in engineering, structural requirements, building codes, and safety. The architect should be involved in the earliest of planning stages to evaluate existing spaces, ensure that the appropriate amount of space is allocated, and that sufficient funds are provided for that space. Later, a construction manager or general contractor will also join the team.

Working on a multidisciplinary project team is often a highlight in a teacher's career, but it takes a great deal of time. Teachers are often the team members with the least flexible schedules and most limited time to devote to planning. It helps for other participants to provide the support the teachers need to be able to participate in the process. Schools are encouraged to provide release and/or summer planning time to ensure that their faculty input is thorough, ongoing, and not rushed. Finally, curriculum analysis and facility development will require the efforts of many employees, who should be compensated for this valuable work.

When teachers and curriculum educators assume the major responsibility for planning renovations and new construction, the resulting facilities will be successful in meeting the instructional and developmental needs of the students. Their expertise and experience are the foundation for providing many years of exciting education.

Planning Committee

The planning committee includes a variety of individuals, each with a slightly different perspective on the objectives to be achieved. The committee commonly includes the principal, science teachers, science supervisor, superintendent or assistant superintendent, and repre-

sentative parents and students, and may include other school administrators, science specialists, other instructional specialists, facilities planners, a school board member, an architect, construction management, estimating experts, science facilities consultant, school support services personnel, and community and business leaders. For maximum effectiveness, the planning committee should be kept small, or little will be accomplished.

Planning committee at work

The planning committee normally begins to prepare a statement of needs. From these needs, the team will move to determine educational specifications that provide the basis for decisions on design development. Educational specifications describe the science curriculum and instructional strategy and summarize educational program needs, approximate or specific space needs, and other information to be used in determining the physical requirements of the facility.

Because large numbers of people may be involved, the planning committee can be grouped into two or more subcommittees.

Curriculum Subcommittee

The curriculum subcommittee should include science teachers from all levels as well as the district's science supervisor and curriculum coordinator. Other potential members are students, parents, a school board member, the assistant superintendent in charge of curriculum, and local business and industry leaders. The curriculum subcommittee evaluates the school district's entire program, determining how well the sequence of instruction progresses from kindergarten experiences through advanced placement courses in high school, and how this sequence might be modified to accomplish the goals of the National Science Education Standards. It is also charged with ensuring that decisions concerning space, building, landscaping, and other factors meet curriculum requirements. This subcommittee should probably begin its work before the facilities subcommittee gets started, so that the facilities group has some direction with which to evaluate existing facilities.

Facilities Subcommittee

The facilities subcommittee includes the district's facilities administrator, the science supervisor or coordinator, science teachers from each discipline, and an architect with experience in school science facilities. It may also include students, parents, a science facilities consultant, and a school board member.

Furniture and equipment consultants and suppliers, business and industry representatives, and other community leaders may also participate.

This subcommittee's responsibility is to evaluate any existing science facilities with respect to the curriculum guidelines established by the curriculum subcommittee, and to analyze the physical needs of the district's science program based on the anticipated curriculum, enrollment, and other factors.

Project Oversight

The planning process is sometimes made more efficient by selecting a small decision-making team whose job it is to keep the others up-to-date and receive their input, but which has the power to make decisions. Such a project oversight committee might, for example, have three voting members, who follow the project from beginning to end and work directly with the architect and construction manager or a general contractor. The school principal, superintendent, representative parents, and a few other key figures can be included in regular meetings with the architect and later with the construction team, but the decision-making responsibility in such cases rests with the three representative voting members. This can eliminate the need for much of the large-group consensus work.

The Planning Process

The planning committee, in consultation with the superintendent, school board, and other participants, must consider every aspect of project development, ranging from the nature of the science program to budgetary constraints. These aspects also include such factors as the number and nature of science facilities needed, clustering facilities, safety requirements, technology needs, adaptations for students with disabilities, government regulations, and maintenance requirements.

The usual sequence and approximate timing of the various steps and stages of planning and construction are expressed graphically in sample timelines later in the text. These include the following:

- define the science curriculum
- select the architect
- evaluate the existing facilities
- use good data to predict future enrollment needs
- "program" the science space needs
- review and approve program
- present to the board of education
- obtain financing
- develop and approve the schematic design
- develop and approve the final design
- specify the furnishings and equipment
- solicit and evaluate bids
- construction and project oversight
- fabricate and install the furnishings and equipment
- inspect, develop "punch list" of imperfect construction situations, and remedy each
- move in

Students suggesting ideas

While the traditional timing of selecting an architect often follows financing, the architect should be selected at the beginning of the process, so s/he can add expertise and experience in the rest of the steps, including evaluating existing facilities, programming space needs, and determining the budget. This may require that some funds be set aside for the architect's fee prior to the step of obtaining overall financing.

Defining the Science Curriculum

Sir Winston Churchill said, "We shape our buildings; thereafter they shape us." The science facility corollary to that is "Curriculum must shape the science facilities, or, thereafter the science facilities will shape the curriculum."

The first major step in the planning process is curriculum review. The curriculum subcommittee evaluates the school district's science program to ensure that the curriculum has been defined. In some cases, a standing or special committee will devote months to developing the curriculum. To make certain that facilities will not become outdated quickly, the staff should have opportunities to review current trends and directions in curriculum and instruction. Many districts are studying integrating science education with career technical programs; such analyses should be conducted during the curriculum review process as they may have a significant impact on the requirements of the physical facilities for science.

Educators touring other schools

Later, periodic mid-design review meetings will ensure that this valuable input from the faculty is not lost as the project develops.

Planners should consider consulting with teachers of prekindergarten, extended day, fifth-year high school, and other special programs. Even though the science team is not responsible for the curriculum of these programs, the committee can provide a service by designing spaces that are science-friendly.

Evaluating Existing Facilities
An inventory of current facilities can be a powerful tool for advocacy in the early stages of planning. It is often useful for the science supervisor, teachers, administrators, and perhaps the facilities director or other interested participants to conduct an early walk-through with the architect of a school's facilities for a preliminary quick assessment, using a checklist as a guide. The resulting, relatively brief, inventory may be used to help alert administrators, parent groups, and the school board to the school's greatest needs as part of a larger needs assessment process.

The architect, consulting engineers, and members of the facilities subcommittee will conduct a more extensive and detailed evaluation later, to use in preparing materials to be presented to the school board.

The three sample checklists in Appendix E may be expanded and adapted to reflect the needs and goals of individual schools and programs. The lists are not meant to be complete or exhaustive. Appropriate guidelines may be selected using the detailed suggestions and recommendations found throughout this book. Consult Chapter 3 for information on questions of safety and accessibility, and Chapters 4 through 6 for most other topics. See also the safety survey in Appendix B.

Determining Future Enrollment
Determining your facility's space needs requires more than a calculator and a crystal ball. You have to have a good understanding of the nature of your community, and the trends in curriculum.

To project the number of students your school will serve 5, 10, or even 20 years into the future often requires expert help. It just doesn't depend on the number of housing units, but their size and cost. Parents of young children often choose the lower priced housing in a community; as a subdivision gets older, it goes through cycles. Children grow into their teens, families move to larger homes and younger couples take their place. Larger condos may attract singles or senior citizens. All of these changes become factors in a professional demographic projection. From the educator's standpoint, the only certainty is change. Get expert help in predicting your community's demographics before you build.

A second prediction your team will have to make is what sort of courses those students will take. Will your school's graduation requirements in science be increased? Will special education courses be merged with general education offerings? Will disciplinary courses be integrated? Some curricular trends can be inferred from the National Science Education Standards. But in many cases, that means developing factors that would support many possibilities. Flexibility is the key to developing effective facilities.

For science educators today, the planning process must be creative, indeed. Tomorrow's biology will look more like chemistry, physics will be required for most, and more students will take additional courses to meet graduation requirements.

Determining the Nature of the Facilities
"Programming" is the initial step in developing a plan for the physical facilities. Its purpose is to determine what types of spaces the science program will require, how many of each type of space are needed, how the spaces should

relate to each other, and what special needs each space will have, including dimensions. These decisions are made in response to the science program's instructional and educational requirements.

To maximize students' hands-on science experiences, a combination classroom\laboratory space has been shown to be the most effective, allowing the teacher to move the instruction from a classroom or discussion arrangement to a laboratory arrangement and back again during a single class period. To estimate the amount of space needed, planners should imagine the most generous amount of lab/classroom space available for each student today and multiply that by the number of students expected in the lab/classroom in the future. The trend is toward an increasing need for more space to conduct safe and effective science programs.

In order to predict future science enrollment, planners should consider the projected growth in the school population, changes in demographics, neighboring feeder schools, and other factors such as local business growth.

The National Science Teachers Association recommends a maximum class size of 24 students in elementary, middle school and high school lab/classrooms, in rooms large enough to accomodate them.

Clustering Facilities

The desired relationship between the science facilities and all other school areas should be determined early in the planning process. In middle and high schools, for example, this might include providing easy access to the media center, technology education area, computer center, or to the home economics, agricultural science, fine arts, or graphics rooms. Since science facilities are very costly, providing access to and from applied science areas can help ease the budget and contribute to students' understanding of the interrelationship of disciplines.

The location of science facilities within a school has an important impact on how well the science program works. If the elementary school science discovery center is far from the general education classroom, time will be lost during class changes and the facility will be used less frequently. If the location of a facility is essential to the program, this element should be built into the planning process. In many elementary schools, locating the science center adjacent to the art, music, or physical education rooms should be considered. Traffic patterns along the halls leading to these rooms and the noise generated by students and equipment are additional factors to be analyzed.

In middle and high schools, the relative location of the science lab/classrooms is also an important planning issue. Should the biology classrooms be next to the chemistry room? As you will see in later chapters, locating classrooms next to the appropriate, safe storage rooms is a crucial safety step. In some large high schools, the division of the school population into semi-autonomous houses or pods may result in decentralized science facilities, which can lead to additional construction and operating expenses as well as the duplication of equipment and the fragmenting of the science faculty. Further, isolating physics or advanced biochemistry lab/classrooms may be counterproductive to the curricular objectives of the department.

Completely separate science facilities for each house or pod increases first costs and long-term operating and maintenance costs and lessens the serendipitous exchanges

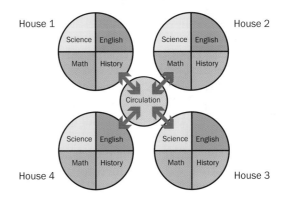

"House" Adjacencies (Before)

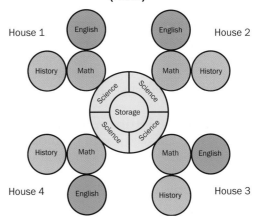

"House" Adjacencies (After)

among science faculty colleagues and between science faculty and students, since the science faculty is now broken into smaller, separated groups. First costs increase because separate, disbursed storage of equipment and supplies often requires duplicating equipment that might have easily been shared in a more centralized arrangement (one science chair related that their new school had spent $100,000 the first year in duplicated equipment). Science facilities have expensive plumbing, electrical and ventilating (HVAC) requirements and resulting costs that can be minimized when centralized, but increase with duplication when decentralized. Long-term operating and maintenance costs increase because, with multiple HVAC systems, more energy is expended in heating, cooling and ventilating the science areas, and multiple machines increase the need for maintenance.

The house concept can still be implemented with centralized science facilities. Individual houses can radiate outward from a science core. Individual science facilities for each house can still be directly connected to the house they serve, but storage, expensive utility systems, prep areas, and faculty offices can all be adjacent to one another, saving both first and long-term costs and increasing collegial contact among colleagues and with students.

Planning for Future Change

For science leaders and teachers, participating in a design team is both a challenge and an opportunity, as it requires them to consider what they really want to accomplish educationally and to decide what types of physical facilities will enable them to reach their objectives.

A high school biology lab/classroom

However, teachers must also bear in mind that they will not be the only instructors to use the facilities they are planning. Because most classrooms outlive the careers of those they first serve, teachers must think about the science teaching of the future and how to design space today that will serve their successors for decades.

For example, in the seventies, many schools were built around an "open classroom" concept, with teaching stations clustered around a media area without complete walls to separate the stations. By the next decade, schools were rebuilding enclosed classrooms as teachers moved "back to basics" and wanted private spaces. In the eighties, the movement toward integrated curricula caused schools to begin incorporating more science-friendly equipment into all classrooms. What will the future bring?

Obtaining Approval and Financing

Once the programming has been completed and the result reviewed by the planning com-

mittee and approved by the board of education, the remaining steps involve funding, detailed architectural design, construction, furnishing, and, finally, occupancy.

The process for getting legal approval for major construction projects varies from state to state. While a small renovation may be accomplished by a simple vote of a board of education, most construction work will require public votes and the issuance of bonds.

Thus, advocacy does not end with the planning process. To achieve community approval of the request for new school construction, planners use their expertise and the experience of others, networking with the staff of newly constructed schools in similar communities with the help of the team's architect or construction manager. Accurate and consistent estimates of the total cost of the project should be made available in order to maintain the public's confidence.

Selecting the Architect

Ideally, to take advantage of the architect's expertise in programming and planning, the architect should be selected prior to the initial planning process. In many public construction programs, an accurate estimate is necessary before public referendums or state approval. This can only be done by working with an architect and an experienced estimator. Once funding has been approved, the architect will create the detailed design and administer the construction contract.

While architectural training promotes understanding of construction methods and human needs, architects differ widely in their style and sensitivity to student issues as well as their experience in dealing with science facility design. Careful interviews and visits to the architect's previous projects are vital—and planners should not forget to interview the teachers who work in these facilities.

The Design Phase

An experienced school architect will address the educational needs when designing the facility to meet the objectives of the planning committee. It is important to realize that like doctors or teachers, architects often have specialties. An architect who builds outstanding office buildings may not know the relationship between structure and function in a school building.

The architectural design phase can take as little as three months for a simple renovation to six or eight months for a large addition. It begins with the creation of a schematic design and concludes with the final design documents that serve as building instructions for the contractor.

Professional laboratory consultants and other experts can contribute to the design team. Equipment consultants and suppliers are happy to provide information. The fire marshal or state fire inspector is a frequent source of advice, either on site or via off-site review. Civil engineers for soil and foundation work, mechanical engineers for HVAC and plumbing systems, and electrical engineers for power and technology will each be essential to some aspects of the project. Building inspectors and historic preservation commissions may make contributions, and interior designers can add to the appearance of a project and the quality of the learning environment.

The construction phase of the project and various construction-related topics, including the budget, are discussed later in this chapter.

The Role of the Science Education Leader

The science supervisor, science coordinator, or other science education leader plays a key role in the design, planning, and development of science facilities. The leader ensures that the design will create learning environments that support curricular improvements, appropriate assessment, educational change, excellence, and equity. The science education leader's work starts long before the planning stage, because of the amount of information that will be required.

A major task for the science education leader is to make sure that curriculum improvement drives the design process. He or she serves on or chairs the curriculum sub-committee and functions as the curriculum consultant on the planning team.

In this role, the science education leader must be prepared to answer the following questions:

- What science curriculum will the students be following?
- How might this curriculum change in the future?
- How might graduation requirements change with the curriculum?
- What curricular improvements must be supported by the new facilities?
- What types of facilities and equipment will be needed to implement these curricular improvements and facilitate learning activities?

- Will the proposed design of the facilities help to implement the curricular improvements?

One important objective is to support the recommended designs and equipment by
- presenting research evidence that they have been used effectively
- describing how they will be used to enhance and improve the curriculum, instruction, and assessment, and why alternative options will not
- explaining how they will resolve difficulties in teaching and learning science
- building confidence by showing how they agree with national and local standards and by obtaining the teachers' support.

Hands-on science

Supervisory Roles

The various functions the science education leader performs in the course of assisting the planning team in its mission include the following:

Planning and coordination. The science education leader plans needs assessments and workflow analyses, organizes tours of exemplary science facilities, facilitates meetings between teachers and administrators, and may serve as the liaison between instructional staff and architects.

Information and communication. The science education leader tracks and disseminates information on innovations and anticipated trends in curriculum and instruction. This includes

- identifying guidelines and expectations for improving the facilities
- supplying the planning team with model floor plans, room designs, and equipment lists
- describing specific requirements for casework, furniture, and equipment
- informing administrators and teaching staff about specifications for the facilities.

Evaluation. The science education leader reviews architectural plans, specifications, and drawings for the facilities to strengthen instructional options; analyzes, updates, and issues safety requirements in compliance with state standards and accepted educational practices; and plans the safe use of chemicals, electric power, biological materials, equipment, and safety devices.

Promotion and representation. The science education leader participates in fundraising for the facilities project and for promoting educational improvements. Other duties include representing the planning committee at educational events at schools, science centers, PTA and community meetings, professional development workshops, and local and national education meetings.

Addressing the School Board
Although school board systems differ significantly across the country, in almost every state, the first step to getting approval for renovating or building a science facility is winning the approval of the board of education. In 40 states, the approval process for major construction projects begins when voters endorse the board's request for a bond issue or an increase in the millage. In other states, a simple majority vote of the board can provide the capital to construct new facilities. Learning how the board operates and how to communicate with it are essential skills, and presenting an effective case for a facilities project may be the defining moment in the concept's progress toward realization.

Usually, the planning committee prepares the case, which is reviewed by the superintendent before the superintendent or assistant superintendent, the science education leader, or a teacher presents it to the board.

Communicating With the Board
All communications with the board should be coordinated through the superintendent or his or her designee. Because most board members serve part-time, they rely heavily on the information gathered by the administrative staff and presented to them by the superintendent. As a result, the relationship between the board and the superintendent is crucial, as is the superintendent's support of the proposed project.

Communication with board members is best done through the appropriate channels and chain of command, rather than through informal conversations with individual members. A phone call or conversation with a board member may be counterproductive if it catches the superintendent off guard. Similarly, working with a single member can backfire, as the best boards prefer to work through committees to reach consensus.

The Presentation
The most successful presentations are those that acknowledge the board members' point of view. Members must weigh their desire for academic excellence against their responsibilities for fiscal restraint. The clear majority must be able to see the cost effectiveness of the proposal and be confident that they can communicate the program's value to their constituents.

Planning committee presentation

Important questions to address in a presentation to a board include:

- Why should we approve the project?
- What evidence is there that the project will be successful?
- How will students benefit?
- How many students will benefit?
- How will the project promote equity?
- How long will it take to complete the project?
- Is the project cost-effective?
- Will the project have lasting value?

The proposal should be compatible with the district's mission statement and strategic

Example of a Timeline for New Construction
(Durations Shown in Months)

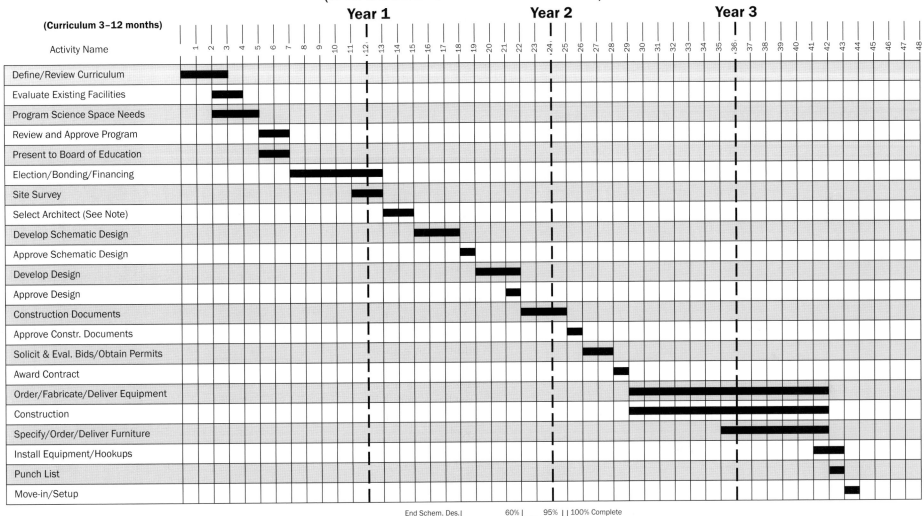

Notes:
1. Curriculum development may take up to 12 months; a review, approximately 3 months.
2. Evaluation of existing facilities includes reviewing the hazardous materials survey.
3. Timing and length of the bonding/financing process vary considerably.
4. The architect may be selected at the start (if funds are available) or at the end of the bonding process. An architectural consultant often works with the planning team from the beginning.

5. Cost estimates are calculated when the schematic design is completed and again when the construction documents are 60% and 95% complete.
6. Movable equipment (including furniture) is sometimes purchased separately from the construction contract. Some items must be ordered early, and items such as computers should be ordered as late as possible.

7. Construction time includes routine delays due to weather.
8. It is usual to build a contingency into the schedule for unexpected delays.
9. A punch list, made by the architect or the contractor, shows incomplete or faulty work.
10. The warranty period may continue for up to 12 months after occupancy.

Example of a Timeline for a Renovation
(Durations Shown in Weeks)

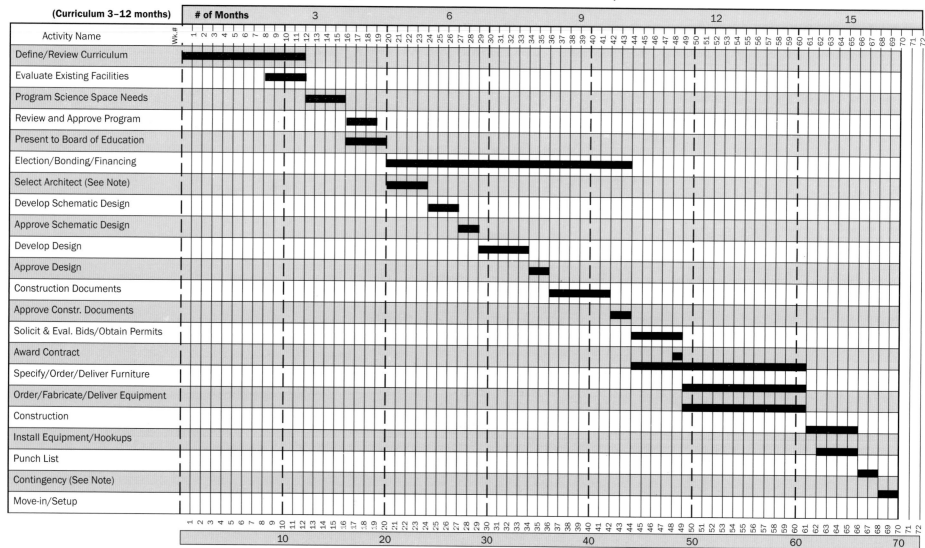

Notes:

1. In this example, funds are available to select the architect at the start of the bonding process.
2. Fixed equipment, which includes science lab casework and lab tables, is normally part of the construction contract.
3. If a renovation is planned for the summer months, bidding for equipment must be conducted early to ensure timely delivery. The architect and owner may choose to solicit bids early for the casework.
4. Furniture and other movable equipment are purchased separately from the construction contract.
5. The contingency time allowance helps compensate for unexpected delays throughout the project.

plan, and its ideas consistent with the long-range thrust of these policies. It helps to show that all possible alternatives have already been explored and to cite similar projects that have been successful. Data from educational sources will support an explanation of what the facilities will need to meet the objectives of the National Science Education Standards and conform to the requirements of the construction industry.

When it is time to address the board, the presenter should work with the superintendent to plan the time and format of the presentation, which will most likely be at a public meeting. The speaker should address the board through its president (Mr. or Madam President), refer to colleagues and administrators by their formal names, and, finally, remember to thank the board for its time.

Building the Science Facility

Charting the Path

How long will it take to renovate the science facility or build a new one? The answer is usually much longer than we think, given the requirements of obtaining approval and financing, the detailed planning and competitive bidding that precede all public works, and a variety of possible unknowns and delays of construction.

Attention to scheduling and communication is critical to the success of the project. Even the wisest purchases and most skilled contractors cannot compensate for the havoc that inadequate project coordination can cause. The facilities planner or another coordinator should

consult with the members of the planning team and make sure that all parties are in agreement with the rationale and design program.

Timeline

The two sample timelines shown—one for a renovation and one for new construction, such as a science wing—indicate some of the basic steps involved in the planning, designing, and construction phases of a project.

Each of these examples illustrates one way the steps might fit together in a particular context and given a particular set of factors. In practice, the sequencing of many of the steps will vary considerably in different situations, as will the time required for each step.

The architect may be selected before or after the bonding or financing process, depending on the circumstances. In fact, an architect often works with the planning committee from the beginning and may be chosen for the design contract as well.

Construction

Construction will be the responsibility of either a construction manager (CM) or a general contractor (GC). Many school districts have facilities planners who are responsible for communicating with the architect. Otherwise, the architect will be the primary communicator between the planning team and the construction team and be charged with seeing that the philosophy and requirements defined by the team become a reality. It is important that the team make its wishes and needs known to the architect.

Construction managers conduct on-site supervision of projects for a set fee; they have extensive expertise with codes, estimating, bud-

geting, and labor regulations. When a school employs a CM, the contracts for electrical work, mechanical work, masonry, etc., are issued by the school district and sequenced and supervised by the construction manager. The use of construction management firms in renovations and school projects has been increasing.

A general contractor is usually selected through an all-inclusive, lump sum, competitive bidding process. The GC assumes responsibility for completing the construction, supervising all phases of the work, and issuing all of the subcontracts to trade contractors.

Each system has its own benefits. In general, the "one bid" structure provided by a general contractor places most of the risks for change orders and last-minute redesigns on the contractor. This may result in a higher initial cost. The construction manager acts as the agent of the district to minimize the cost of changes when they occur. So while the initial cost may seem lower with a construction manager, the planning team must be well prepared and well disciplined to avoid needless changes late in the process. The construction manager or general contractor should work in concert with the school representatives as overseers of the project.

Paying the Bill

At all stages of the planning process, every step must be budget conscious. Whether the project is a small one financed by an endowment or general operating funds, or a major effort financed by the sale of municipal bonds, the scope of the work to be undertaken must always be determined with the advice of experts on the funds available.

A Budget for a High School Addition

Building Construction Cost (10,000 square feet x $185/square foot)	$1,850,000.00
Science Casework and Equipment (4 lab/CRs @ $50,000 and 2 prep/storage @ $20,000	240,000.00
Site Development Costs	175,000.00
Off-Site Construction Costs	100,000.00
Landscaping	15,000.00
Movable Equipment	150,000.00
Subtotal A	$2,530,000.00
Design Contingency (10% of Subtotal A)	253,000.00
Construction Contingency (5% of Subtotal A)	126,500.00
Subtotal B	$2,909,500.00
Architect and Engineer Fees (7% of Subtotal B)	203,665.00
Surveying	2500.00
Geotechnical Investigations	5,000.00
Building Permit	7,500.00
Owner Miscellaneous Cost Allowance	15,000.00
Technology Allowance	45,000.00
Furniture	25,000.00
Subtotal C	$3,213,165.00
Inflation (5% per year)	160,658.00
Total Building Costs	$3,373,823.00

To planners whose usual responsibilities do not include such major expenditures, the cost of construction can be numbing. The work done for public entities involves the services of registered architects and engineers, a variety of technical consultants, and contractors or construction managers—whose combined fees can add between 15% and 20% to the cost of construction.

When schools must raise a bond by public referendum to finance construction, the process of determining how much a project will cost can be complex. The district can seldom afford to do complete designs and estimates before the project is approved. So the school team must go to the voters with only an estimated value for a partially designed plan. After the voters give their approval, the team completes the planning process, adhering to the strict financial limits imposed by the public.

Participating in a planning process often places a new kind of challenge on educators. Responsibility for developing and meeting budget is different than living within one in the classroom. It's important to constantly evaluate each choice from the standpoint of pre-existing priorities. There are often choices between short-term savings and long-term maintenance expenditures, or choices between appearance and functionality. It takes a well-coordinated committee that communicates well to make these decisions effectively.

Developing a Project Budget

The following example illustrates the types of costs that should be considered in determining an overall project budget, and of their relative magnitudes. The costs of this project are taken from a real example. Of course, the budget for any project must be individually developed, because construction costs, fees, and scope vary widely from project to project, from one location to another, and at different times.

In order to develop a budget for a new science facility it is important to know how many science spaces will be needed and how many teachers will be needed to staff these spaces. (See "A Budget for a High School Addition.") It is also important to remember that science spaces are generally larger and more expensive than standard classrooms; just how much larger will be dealt with in later chapters.

In this example, a high school science addition of 10,000 square feet is being constructed with an overall project duration of two years, from the beginning of planning and design, not counting curriculum review, to final occupancy. The base construction cost per square foot of $185 was taken from the Means Building Construction Cost Data 2005, for a 3/4 cost-level (the book's term for higher-end cost) high school. To further modify this average cost for a complete high school so as to more closely reflect the costs of a purely science addition, the mechanical, electrical and plumbing costs for the typical high school were increased to those for a research laboratory (an additional $49 per square foot). Such a 10,000 square foot addition might include four lab/classrooms and associated prep and storage spaces. The basic construction cost listed above does not include a sufficient allowance for the types of fixed casework and equipment typical of science spaces, so an additional figure of approximately $50,000 per lab/classroom and $20,000 per prep/storage space should be added. A design/bid/build approach was used, without a construction manager.

Note that these are not the only costs associated with a project. The budget doesn't include costs of the purchase of land or costs related to a bond election and payment of interest.

In renovations, any costs of hazardous material abatement such as asbestos or lead-based paint must be added, as these are generally not included in the construction costs and fees.

In a budget,

- the construction cost is generally an estimate of the general contractor's bid for the building.
- science casework and equipment includes cabinets, fume hoods, counters, laboratory tables, and carts, but not glassware, microscopes, and other smaller items.
- site development costs include such items as grading, roads, and retaining walls.
- off-site construction is the construction that needs to be done on the property of others, such as extending water lines, sewers, and roads to the site.
- landscaping includes new trees, shrubs, and other plantings.
- the contingencies are figures to cover unpredictable costs.
- the costs of most engineering consultants are generally included in the architect's fee.
- surveying, generally required for a new building, and geo-technical investigations to evaluate soil conditions are usually contracted for by the owner.
- technology infrastructure is often performed by a separate contractor.
- furniture is often purchased separately from the construction contract and includes design and specification costs. For a science building, furniture generally consists of student and teacher chairs, desks, and filing cabinets.
- inflation is considered, because the construction market will probably change by the time bids are taken; the effects of inflation average out to one half the annual rate of inflation over the construction period. Here, it is calculated as one half of 5% over two years, or .025 × 2 × the final subtotal.

Relocation

When doing a renovation, it is important to determine and plan for the financial consequences of any "swing time"—moving into temporary quarters—as well as the disruptions to the school.

Limiting the construction period to the summer vacation may greatly increase the cost of a job, due to overtime charges and, often, because construction contractors may be busier during the summer. It is worth finding out whether it would be possible to have the work continue during the school year. Can fences, barriers, and temporary relocations make construction safe? Other factors to consider are noise, odors, dust, blocked access, and strangers in the building. This situation requires careful analysis. For any project that is estimated to last longer than two months, very serious consideration must be given to vacating the construction area. The extent of hazards and disruptions caused by coexisting with construction are rarely well understood until they have been experienced.

Controlling Extra Costs

It helps for planners to acquire a background in some of the mysteries of the construction process, such as pricing and collecting competitive bids. In almost all public construction, the contractors are chosen by a closed, competitive bidding process after the design has been completed.

One budget category is *general conditions*. The fence that separates the project from the school, copying plans, express deliveries, builders' cellular phones, and

A through-the-wall aquarium

even the portable toilets are general conditions items. They are not formally part of the construction, but the job will not get done without them.

Change orders are often a dirty word to school districts that may expect that the project will be completed for the amount of the lowest bid. Quite simply, a change order is a written instruction to the contractor to change something that is shown in the construction documents. Change orders are an inevitable part of any project and may range from something as simple as changing the color of a wall to a major cost to alleviate some unanticipated condition behind a wall in a renovation.

There are ways to keep change orders to a reasonable level. For example, an appointed representative from the district might be authorized to approve every change order up to a certain limit as long as the total does not exceed the budgeted contingency; this person must have a clear understanding of those estimates, expressed in dollars, which will need formal action by the board.

Another budget item that may be unfamiliar

to the planning team is the contingency fund. This is a figure, amounting to between 10% and 15% of the estimated total cost that is added to the budget to cover unforeseen events. The percentage for the contingency figure for a renovation project should be higher than for new construction, because of the greater potential for hidden adverse conditions. In renovation projects, the builders often find surprises behind the walls, and even the best-drawn plans will require changes. In new construction projects, unforeseen problems with the condition of the soil can require corrective measures. In these cases the builder will seek authorization to add charges to the original estimate. These are some of the reasons why it is almost unheard of for the final bill to be the same as the original quoted price.

A good architect designs within budget limits and communicates with the planning team to set priorities. At the same time, a professional estimator from the architectural or construction management firm can keep track of market conditions and make good estimates of construction costs. But even with all of this professional help, it is the planning team that must manage the budget—while bearing in mind that initial construction costs, life-cycle costs of maintenance and operations, and aesthetics are important factors. If cuts must be made, the educators must make the calls. Deciding between two desirable features is often a task best left to people with classroom experience.

One or two cost estimates should be performed early in the design process, before the final documents have progressed to a point where making changes is time consuming and costly. Usually, these would be performed at

An undesired construction change

the completion of the schematic design and at the 60% document review stage.

If an estimate suggests that a project is over budget, the architects and their consultants should engage in *value engineering*, the process whereby a list of alternative ways to achieve the same design goals within the budget is prepared and evaluated. These alternatives may include making changes in the brands of materials or equipment, simplifying design elements, or even making small alterations in the drawings to change the sequence of installation of materials. This process increases the chance that bids will come in within the budget. Sometimes, merely changing the mix and timing of tasks can make the difference. For example, a contractor who has to wait while other skilled craftsmen do a small job will add the cost of that time to the bid.

Architects and construction managers have adopted the value-engineering concept in an effort to stretch the value of a construction dollar. This term has two distinct meanings in the building industry. When it occurs early in the planning process, value engineering is a valuable tool. It is a way of imbedding your priorities into choices you make. But in some projects, "value engineering" has also been used for the process of salvaging a budget when bids come in way too high and the specifications must be retroactively changed. In this kind of decision-making, education seldom wins. So early planning is always the best way to achieve "value" in your engineering. It can produce greater savings if it is performed early in the planning and design of a project, when the time and cost implications of making a change are lowest. The longer one waits,

the higher the cost of making the change and the lower the resulting life cycle cost changes. Waiting until the bids are in before seeking less expensive ways of constructing the building indicates that the design and construction team has not been completely effective during the planning and design stages. Suggested changes after bids are received are more likely to reduce the quality of the project, and the value as well.

Throughout the budgeting process, the key concept is prioritization. The overall goals of the project must be kept at the forefront. It does not hurt to post them in the meeting room, to remind everyone to stay on target. When the facilities are completed, the weeks and months of decision making and work will be rewarded with many decades of great educational environments.

Avoiding Surprises

To make sure that the science facilities that were envisioned in the early stages of the planning process are the science facilities that the faculty walks into when the building opens, science teachers need to maintain their oversight of the project throughout the design and construction process. Because, things change....

From the initial planning meetings to the final walk-through of the completed spaces, there are many possible opportunities for change. During the initial planning stages science educators are asked to define their ideal science teaching spaces, without regard for budgets or available space. This is an important step, because, unless the ideal is defined, it is highly unlikely that even a small portion of that ideal will be achieved. Once the ideal spaces are defined and the entire project is programmed, the total estimated cost might well exceed the budget initially conceived. School administrators and board members must then determine if the budget can be raised and, if not, where priorities lie. Adjustment to the ideal spaces will be likely—science teachers need to participate in this discussion.

As the architect produces a building from the approved program information, the shape and arrangement of the various spaces will be defined. A nearly square physics lab/classroom may become longer and narrower. The location of the chemical storage room may become more remote from some of the chemistry lab/classrooms. Faculty offices, if provided, may not be centralized in the science department. Science faculty need to participate in these discussions to make these changes to the ideal as acceptable as possible. Architects are good problem solvers and enjoy a challenge, so science faculty should not hesitate to express concerns throughout the design process.

The construction procurement process is another opportunity for unwanted changes to the ideal. Most specifications allow the bidding contractors and equipment suppliers several options for obtaining the most competitive prices. There are a number of very capable science casework and equipment manufacturers who can furnish excellent products; however, not all of them offer the same range of products and what may be a very attractive product for one manufacturer may not be available from another. Further, the competitive bidding process often leads contractors to suggest alternate products or materials to those specified at a cost savings. Science teachers need to participate in the evaluation of these alternatives to avoid having products of significantly inferior quality substituted or the elimination of features that are important to the teaching of science.

Once construction begins, incorrect installations, incomplete or inaccurate drawings, unforeseen field conditions (especially in renovation of existing buildings), and changes required by the local building official as con-

struction proceeds may impact the usefulness or completeness of the ideal science facility. A couple of examples: The exhaust duct from a fume hood in a chemistry lab/classroom was stainless steel at the hood, but the ventilation contractor connected this to a galvanized steel duct running above the ceiling, through the roof, to the exhaust fan. The chemistry teacher, walking through the building as it neared completion, caught this error and notified the administration who had the duct changed to the specified stainless steel throughout. On another project, the local fire marshal interpreted the chemistry prep room as a separate lab and called for a second exit from this space. The only available way to create this second exit was through the chemical storage room—not an ideal or safe arrangement. The architect was able to convince the fire marshal that the prep room was a secondary part of the main chemistry lab/classroom, not a separate lab, and the change was not required. Science faculty need to gain access to the construction as it proceeds and keep a lookout for similar shortcomings.

CHAPTER 2

Current Trends and Future Directions in Science Education: Breaking Down the Walls

Conducting scientific inquiry requires that students have easy, equitable, and frequent opportunities to use a wide range of equipment, materials, supplies, and other resources for experimentation and direct investigation of phenomena.

—National Science Education Standards, p. 220

Key ideas in this chapter:

- Both inquiry—a research proven effective strategy for learning content—and direct instruction—an effective way for learning process—require adequate space and flexible science facilities.
- Awareness of Standards, recommendations, and codes is crucial to effective facility planning.
- The essential elements in school technology are communication and flexibility.
- Technology occurs in a seamless environment and has become smaller and more personalized.
- Various learning platforms now allow students to learn at their own time, pace, and place.
- School technology includes not only computers for teaching and learning, but also technology that keeps the science facility and building secure.
- Many assistive technologies are available for science classrooms for all students, and many more are on the horizon. Plan ahead to incorporate new technologies.

One of the most exciting aspects of the planning process is the opportunity to plan for the future. Foresight in planning can expand the potential of science learning environments for decades to come. This brief outline is intended as a summary of some of the changes that are occurring in science education. To understand the likely extent of these changes and their implications for school facilities design, attention to the Standards and a review of relevant research are recommended.

Standards-Based Programs

The simplest educational concept—and perhaps the most significant—to consider in designing tomorrow's science programs is inquiry. In keeping with the Standards' strong emphasis on inquiry-based programs, students increasingly will be exploring the world inside and outside the classroom. The move toward inquiry will mean that more space and greater flexibility will be needed in science facilities. There will also be a need for more extensive storage space because of the increased need for equipment and the greater emphasis on student projects.

Research supports the use of inquiry as an effective strategy for students to learn content. On the other hand, research supports the use of direct instruction as an effective strategy to learn process whether it is the process of experimental research design or a skill of using a piece of equipment. Interestingly, both inquiry and direct instruction require adequate facilities during science activities and investigation.

Many other trends and changes, including some that are discussed below, are likely to be sustained because of the support given in the Standards.

A flexible design with movable tables for both laboratory and classroom instruction

Integrated Curricula

Science no longer stands alone, especially in kindergarten through grade 8. While many elementary schools are still building specialized science or discovery rooms, the trend toward teaching science every day and linking

"Window Into Science"—corridor side

it to social studies, mathematics, and language arts has created pressure to make every classroom science-friendly. Where this is not possible due to space limitations, some schools have paired versatile multiple-use classrooms with classrooms geared to language arts in order to encourage sharing of the facilities and thereby make space for running investigations available to all students.

A major issue in elementary science education is whether the greater portion of the program will be taught by the general education teacher or by a specialist. If it is to be the classroom teacher, who will help manage shared supplies and equipment? Or will supplies and equipment be duplicated in each classroom with the associated secure storage that science materials require? While a specialist has a deeper content knowledge, the general education teacher is sometimes more able to link ideas and take advantage of authentic real-world situations from which science concepts can be derived. This is an example of how curricular issues can affect the use of facilities, with decisions varying in different communities. The solution lies in building facilities that have great flexibility.

Many middle schools have been moving from departmentalized programs, with all laboratories taken together, to an interdisciplinary teaching approach, with one science teacher for each team, creating problems where current facilities do not allow easy access for each cluster of students. Similarly, some large high schools are also dividing their student bodies into smaller "houses." The U.S. Department of Education and the Gates Foundation have sponsored landmark programs to explore the effects of "smaller communities of learners" on education, with dramatic results. But whether a team designs a smaller school or a smaller unit within a school, this integrated approach requires more sections, more storage, more equipment and creative solutions to classroom design.

Finally, as science curricula in middle school and high school become more integrated, increased space and flexibility of facilities, as well as the relative locations of the classrooms, become more important. As readers will see in the chapters that follow, it's not only important to design what's in the science classroom but what is near it—from other classrooms, to storage, to outdoor learning spaces, design and technology, and career-focused education spaces. So in the planning process, science educators always need "a little help from their friends" in other departments.

Co-Teaching and Inclusion

Students who are challenged or at risk are seldom separated from the general education classrooms, and special-needs teachers usually work in the general education environment. This situation demands more space and more flexible classroom arrangements for small-group work. Regulations require wider aisles and other adjustments and modifications for students with disabilities. Class size guidelines include both student-adult ratios and student space ratios. Adding extra supervision for students of special needs can help the former, but exacerbate the latter problem. The newer trends toward inclusion and co-teaching have challenged buildings and classrooms that were once built for separate or noninclusion type classrooms.

Some students need intensive, separate assistance at certain times, such as during the administration of a test. The ease of access by these students to a resource room is also a factor for the planning team to consider. Excluding science students with disabilities from authentic laboratory facilities is unthinkable, and a violation of state and federal laws.

Independent and Small Group Projects

Today's students have more opportunities to follow their own curiosity. Small group and independent projects often last several days or weeks and require extensive space for work and for storage. Because of the constraints of liability law, teachers need to have constant access to those students who are working independently. This may mean providing separate glassed-in spaces for planning and execution of projects, or some other means of supervision, so that teachers can manage several spaces at the same time. In early elementary classes, overhead mirrors and appropriately sized room dividers create spaces for independent explo-

A small group meeting area

ration without compromising accessibility or supervision. There are also trends in technology that require separated spaces, especially for students with special needs. For example, students with special needs often require more space to learn.

Secondary Courses

Although secondary courses change slowly, they are taking on a different appearance as we move toward the future, creating the need for more space for lab/classrooms and storage. The most important change relevant to facility needs is that more students are studying science, partly because the requirement that high school students take a minimum of three years of laboratory science is becoming more common with many states requiring four credits of science for advanced diplomas. While some coursework may involve distance learning or early college enrollment, the increase in face-to-face enrollments must be considered in demographic projections.

The move to inquiry-based programs further increases space needs with investigations that may last for several class sessions and require space to leave apparatus in place for more than one class group. Such programs may also require the flexibility to group work surfaces in a variety of ways, requiring movable work surfaces and the additional space in which to move them.

Biology and Earth science courses are changing dramatically, with both including more chemistry and physical science investigations than ever before. The movement toward integrated courses at the middle and high school levels has already been mentioned.

Finally, there is increased demand for programs, such as applied physics, that have become more popular with students because of the integration of design and technology and engineering applications into the programs. These programs often involve the sorts of equipment for construction and modeling that may once have been associated with design and technology courses.

Instructional Methods

Perhaps the most difficult aspect of facility planning is accommodating individual instructional styles, especially at the secondary level. Despite the trends toward more active student participation and increased cooperative work, some teachers still prefer lecture-style instruction, and most instructional models include at least a short, 20-minute, period for lecture or discussion. Should the new science rooms accommodate lecture-style seating arrangements?

Some of today's teachers prefer the sound-absorbing characteristics of cinder block walls, while others prefer the folding walls that allow

Technology in the classroom: Plan ahead

team teaching. Can and should both be accommodated? Some expensive postconstruction remodeling has been undertaken in the past when teachers discovered that they could not function in some open classroom or other nontraditional facilities that well-meaning planning teams had designed for them.

Laboratory/classrooms should not just be designed for the old-fashioned "cookbook science" approach in which all students follow the same recipe, use the same ingredients, and are expected to achieve the same results. The science facilities should be flexible to accommodate multiple teams of students implementing investigations that they have designed to answer a

Lots of technology within a poorly planned space

specific question or questions posed by the teacher or themselves.

While there is not necessarily a set answer to issues raised in response to instructional preferences, two guiding principles are useful. First, make a firm commitment to adapt the facilities to the Standards' recommendations. Change may be slow, but it is coming and most construction projects are built for decades of use. Secondly, do not expect the new facilities to result in change in methodology overnight. While they may present an appropriate environment for newly trained teachers and can remove barriers for teachers who want to change, they will not motivate those who have little inclination to do so.

Technology comes in smaller packages

Technology and Tomorrow's Curriculum

No paper publication could hope to keep pace with the cutting edge of school technology. In fact, technology is changing so rapidly that it is highly likely that technology planned today will be obsolete by the time the new facilities are ready (see "Hitting a Moving Target," p. 27). Nevertheless, the trends and implications of technology in school programs are major considerations for every planning team. The keys to ensuring that learning spaces will not become outmoded quickly are a good understanding of the general direction of the changes to come and a commitment to flexibility in everything that is installed.

The essential element in school technology is communication. The global village may be a cliché, but the global classroom is a real-

ity. New facilities should be designed with multiple access points to the Internet and the world. Phones for voice communication, appropriate media for video and data, and computing devices for data processing, are all essential. Although the newest communication access systems combine phone, voice, and data in a single wireless system, the most important part of the communication system is still the basic equipment used for accessing outside telecommunications systems. Today's facility project teams do not debate whether to put a computer in the classroom area or in the laboratory area; both require them.

No space planned for computers

A second element is flexibility. When the budget is tight, adequate wiring should be installed in the walls during the construction stage and the plans should include fiber optics and cable wiring accessible from almost everywhere. This will save money by allowing the installation of additional lines in the future.

Planning to address the need for computers in the lab/classroom means creating a comprehensive list that includes processing

speeds, amount of memory, hardware, software, software training, delivery times, installation, and service.

In addition to computers, scientific instruments and many other kinds of technological

Technology in the physics lab/classroom

equipment are also needed in the science lab/classroom. Wide counters equipped with separate circuits for power are necessary to accommodate the equipment. Easy access to shared equipment, such as copiers or scanners, is also necessary. Lots of technology keeps being added to the science classroom, requiring more space and increasing safety problems with overcrowding and more wires and extension cords that are possible fire, electrical, and trip hazards.

In just a few months during 1997, the delivery of state-of-the-art video moved from cable to digital data video streaming. Every year, the capacity of processors to access data doubles. The task of the planning committee becomes harder when it is realized that the state-of-the-art may change from the time of the groundbreaking ceremony to the dedication of the facility! Whether the planning committee is able to achieve its goals easily or faces difficult choices, it is imperative to make decisions that will not preclude the adoption of current and future advancements.

Breaking Down the Walls

As a part of a book about building great science facilities, that may seem an odd title. But in fact, today's technology is truly "breaking down the walls" of schools and expanding science-learning spaces into the world around. Both literally and figuratively, the sky is the limit for today's science students because of the use of technology.

Asked what tomorrow's learning technology will look like, many experts simply throw up their hands. In two- and three-year building programs, the process of designing technology for the facilities is often delayed until the very last minute in order to take advantage of falling prices and rising expectations. Consultants won't predict more than a few years in the future. But there are many things we *do know* about the technology component of tomorrow's classroom:

- Technology will occur in a seamless environment without borders or limits. In practical purposes, that means wireless environments that minimally cover the entire campus, with the ability to link virtually everywhere. This will create tremendous challenges with respect to security, control, and liability.
- Technology hardware will be smaller and more personalized. It's not unreasonable to expect that every student will have their own, small digital devices in tomorrow's schools. In the short term, expect highly flexible laptops rather than space-eating desktop workstations in science classrooms, with accessory hardware like personal digital devices and computer probes to enhance their reach.

Portable technology

- "Learning Platforms" (specialized digital environments that create virtual classrooms in cyberspace) will expand the space and time limits of every classroom. They will no longer be used only for specialized classes, but will be normal components of the curriculum in almost every classroom.
- Distance learning will replace some of the scheduled face-to-face instruction, making the precise space requirements of the day-to-day program more difficult to predict. At the same time, there will be increases in graduation requirements in science, so demographics will be more difficult to pin down.
- Antennas and receivers for students to receive data directly from professional (often government) sources.
- Lifelong learning will bring far more, and more diverse, students into the building at times other than the traditional school day.

Hard or Soft, Large or Small

For the past 20 years, computers in science classrooms have challenged planners. How much space will they take up? How much electrical power? How can they be situated so that they don't interfere with hands-on laboratory exploration? Kept away from water? How can they be secured? What physical and/or software systems can ensure internet safety?

As technology has grown, the planning challenges have actually decreased with the diminishing sizes of the equipment. Most of the new facilities being built today are incorporating very small "notebook" sized computers, which are either assigned to students or stored and charged in rolling banks by the instructors. The trend in such hardware is toward even smaller equipment in the future.

A laptop computer storage and recharging cart

But as the physical size of computers has decreased, their potential to create virtual hazards has increased. The virtual world represents a web of risks to students and teachers—not just the easily recognized dangers of inappropriate content, but the tempting hazards of undocumented and unvetted pseudoscience that can tempt students.

Even the best filtering software can't ensure that students will use technology appropriately in the classroom. While desktop stations can sometimes be arranged so that the teacher can constantly monitor use, laptops and personal digital devices can't be so easily supervised. So facilities planners may need to work with instructional technology experts to build in additional software and hardware filters and blockers to make supervision easier.

Even if schools construct and maintain secure wireless networks with good software to record student access, that may not solve the problems. In many places, a student with a good laptop can reach more than one wireless network from the school system. With appropriate subscription services, they can even access satellite services from the school. Some municipalities have taken the step of making wi-fi available across their areas. Those networks are also available to students. Even cell phones have internet access within schools.

The best solution for these internet security challenges is in discipline and good student contracts for appropriate behavior, not in facility design. But it remains worth noting that it is probably not worth the expenditures to design any school connectivity environment on the assumption that it will be the only one to which students have access.

Hitchhike the Universe

NSTA's position statement on laboratory science recognizes that tomorrow's students won't just "experiment" with the data they collect in their classrooms, but with real-time data they can access from all over the universe. With specialized receivers, students today can collect data on weather, astronomy, or biological phenomena directly. They can also download amazing amounts of real-time data from the National Aeronautics and Space administration (NASA), the United States Geological Survey (USGS), and the National Oceanic and Atmospheric Administration (NOAA) from internet links to satellites. They can even analyze random radio signals from the ends of space.

Often, the inclusion of specialized receivers or antennas depends on the advocacy of one enthusiastic teacher. That's unfortunate, because retrofitting a learning space to make provisions for a weather station, astronomical lab, or stream monitoring station is far more expensive later than at the start. The prescient planning team will make space for special dish antennas and measurement equipment, with a conduit for direct wiring to the classroom.

Because these kinds of data analysis projects don't fit into the old-fashioned 55-minute time frame, they take place most easily in the "project space." That's just one more reason to reject the traditional box classroom of the last century.

The Virtual Classroom

Virtual learning classrooms (platforms) were first developed for distance learning coursework. WebCT, Blackboard, Angel, and other software systems enable a teacher to interact in either a synchronous or asynchronous manner with any number of students. While critics first panned these courses as "impersonal," they have become increasingly popular. They may incorporate two- or three-way real-time audio and video for more personal contact among students, and almost always incorporate access to the internet, to preprogrammed web and hypermedia presentations.

Learning platforms enable students to learn at their own time and pace. They allow students who reside in remote areas, with family obligations, or with disabilities that limit commuting to all have more opportunities for greater access to coursework. And the choices that platforms provide—when to study, how fast, how intense—can entice students with learning styles that aren't ideal or frequently observed in the traditional classroom.

Today, the choice is no longer "face-to-face" or "distance learning." Teachers of real-time traditional courses are finding many uses for learning platforms in and out of their brick-and-mortar classrooms. These platforms can be used to

- provide synchronous chat and response during formal class time, when students input answers to discussion boards or online quizzes while they are at school;
- expand classroom discussion to out-of-class times;
- provide a documentable environment for group work in or out of class time, with a record of each student's contributions;
- invite guest speakers into the classroom;
- take students on virtual field trips to research sites or museums; and
- provide an anonymous virtual environment in which students can safely meet and interact with other students in other places.

The inclusion of distance learning as a component of almost every course has implications for facilities. Projection and sound equipment (detailed below) must be available, as well as facilities for students to be recorded for transmission. When a small subset of students participates in distance learning, they may not need the full-time supervision of a teacher but will need supervision. That requires a space (like the project spaces described in other areas of this guide and below) for them to work in semiseclusion.

A final advantage of distance learning platforms is to invite others. Independent schools have pioneered the concept that parents should be given access to lessons, homework, and even grade books for younger students. This sort of public access is often uncomfortable to teachers at first, but it's inevitable in the classroom of the future. Distance learning systems can also invite the natural world into the classroom. There are schools doing 24–7 quantitative observations of zoo animals, volcanoes, and even deep-sea vents using their distance-learning platforms. In the classroom of tomorrow, there's no limit to where your students can go—and only you can limit who can visit.

There's one application of the older model of distance learning that's not likely to disappear, the "special event." Use of video (through a distance-learning platform or a direct system like cable) to invite a special speaker into a classroom is still a great way to expand students' imagination. To accommodate special events, tomorrow's schools will still build mini-auditorium rooms (sometimes called kivas or conference rooms) in which two or three classes can meet to see special presentations. These spaces should be equipped with the best of the projection equipment described above, plus adaptive technologies (below) and microphone and recording equipment for feedback.

Lights, Camera— Where's the Action?

Another set of planning specifications that was once very significant to architects involved projection of media (movies, videos) and images (transparencies.) These technologies have very little application today, and will probably disappear within a few years. While some veteran teachers might lobby design teams for the sorts of darkening shades and projectors that enable ancient technology, it's always important to see those expenditures as choices that might exclude a more modern purchase.

At the same time, projecting clear computer (digital) images is a constant need. Overhead digital projection equipment should be the norm in all classrooms and meeting rooms today. Normally, the instructor or student will attach his/her own laptop or PDA to the system. It's not recommended that a large desktop system be attached because that will become dated far too soon.

Digital projection systems don't require the same level of room darkening that the old-fashioned projection systems did. But their sound systems are often less high-tech and flexible than the visual components. Many classroom computer projectors blare or reverberate through ceiling tiles. Make sure a good sound engineer takes a look at the systems before they are bolted into the classroom structure. This process requires a good understanding of the shape of the room, the types of wall and floor coverings that it will contain, and the furniture that will be installed. There's nothing as frustrating as trying to teach while your walls vibrate from the DVD being played next door!

Finally, today's science classrooms regularly incorporate the development of movies, animations, and multimedia presentations as part of the curriculum. That requires specialized equipment, but the cost drops each year. Planning committees may need to take these options into consideration when allocating spaces. The traditional "project room" where students can work on extended or advanced projects will often include space for video production today. Tomorrow's project room may include the development of physical and virtual models that scientists and engineers use in research today. These spaces can also serve as the site for small group distance learning, described above. If they can be sited in an "L" shaped space off a larger classroom, or separated from the workstation of a certified teacher or media specialist by a glass partition, they can provide good sound environments, and secure spaces at the same time.

A perimeter computer station

Adaptive Technology

When an educational plan is developed for a special education student, the potential value of assistive technologies must be considered. But the specialized technologies that enable students to maximize their abilities aren't just for students with documented disabilities. They are often worth considering for all students—and far less expensive when they are built in from the start.

It's impossible to list all of the creative assistive technologies that might be available in tomorrow's science classroom. But here are a few examples:

- Auditory field systems are specialized speaker systems that surround students with modified sound. These systems may not just amplify sound (pump up the volume) but enhance higher frequencies to make sounds clearer. As many as 50% of primary students have temporary, fluid-induced hearing impairments at high frequencies some of the time (due to the shape of their ear canals.) Older adults often have the same limitations due to the normal hardening of the otoliths inside the middle ear. An electronic field system costs less that a thousand dollars to install if it's done when a room is built, but many times that much if it has to be retrofitted after the room is complete.

- Lavaliere microphones help teachers as well as the students they serve. Voice injury is an occupational hazard to teachers. Combined with a field system (above) a tiny microphone costing a thousand dollars or less can save a career.

- Electronic "smart" whiteboards enable teacher drawings and writing to be converted to electronic images. When these boards are linked to wireless networks, visually impaired students can retrieve the images in a larger, more detailed form.

Safe and Secure

School technology includes not only computers, but also the technology that keeps the building secure. In the school of tomorrow, metal keys will be relegated to the museum cabinet with the slide rules.

Keypads enable schools to constantly monitor who is where, when and why. They are ideal to provide temporary, cancelable access to substitutes and maintenance workers, as well as to provide a lasting record of who has access to supplies or equipment. At the end of a workday, a quick glance at a control panel can assure an administrator that everyone is safely out of a lab or storeroom. An electronic keypad system can also be modified to record how often and during what time frames rooms are used most frequency, or to ensure that the ventilation system is on when it's needed.

Security may also include cameras and sound alarm systems. Of course, this requires appropriate (legal) notification and board-approved guidelines for the persons who will use the spaces. But this is well worth the effort. With such systems becoming very easily affordable and more commonplace, the school design teams who opt to skip these expenses may sometime face the question "Why not?"

Finally, electronic security can include inventory control systems. There are many good programs that are available from major supply vendors. Bar coding can reinforce the need for teachers to keep track not only of what they have, but how old the stock is, and how often it is used. These programs can also be used to quickly print labels for smaller classroom containers. But all of this requires preplanning, making space for computer equipment, printers and scanners at the entrance to the storeroom for teacher use.

"Hitting a Moving Target—Planning for Technology in New Science Spaces"

by James T. Biehle, AIA

Planning to provide technology for new or newly renovated science teaching spaces is like trying to hit a moving target with a peashooter. Technology is changing so rapidly that anything we plan today will be obsolete in the one and a half to two years that it generally takes to get a building designed and built.

In 1999, when we published the *NSTA Guide to School Science Facilities*, we recommended providing desktop computers on rolling carts. We suggested adding 15 square feet per computer to the space to accommodate these carts. We also noted that some schools were moving toward using laptop computers. Schools spent thousands wiring their buildings so that computers could talk to each other and, eventually, to the internet.

At a recent planning session for a new middle school science facility, Mark Kesling, the Orchard School's technology coordinator, suggested that we assume that there would be technology in the new spaces, that it would be wireless, and that we would make up our minds about what it would be when we were about six months out from occupancy. Based on what I see in the schools I visit and at the trade shows at NSTA conventions, this makes perfect sense.

In 1999, most school computers were desktop units and most data networks were hard-wired. Today, most school computers are laptops and most new installations have wireless networks. The NSTA trade shows include more and more applications that utilize PDAs (personal digital assistants) and before long I suspect the PDAs will be replaced by blackberry enabled cell phones.

A number of classrooms are now equipped with interactive electronic white boards that act as a pro-

jection screen for digital projectors and allow input to an attached computing device via special markers. A more recent iteration of this technology is the portable interactive whiteboard which attaches to a typical marker board with suction cups and scans the surface as a person writes or draws with special markers. Surely just around the corner is the thin plasma screen described in Bill Gates' book *The Road Ahead* that covers an entire wall and needs no projector.

A science teacher at a middle school in St. Louis envisions herself walking around the science classroom with a tablet PC, writing information on it that will be projected on a large screen using wireless technology to connect the PC to the projector as well as the network. The media technology coordinator at the New London, Connecticut school district is already planning to be able to project holographic images in a classroom that would allow students to be inside a virtual human heart.

How, then should we plan for technology advances that we don't have now, but probably will by the time our buildings are completed? Mark Kesling uses the following process:

1. Establish a "place holder" for technology in the overall facility budget for purposes of funding. He does this by adding to what he knows today an additional cost factor based on interactions. "What interactions do we wish to create in the new space with technology for all users: teachers and students?" Since the cost of a computer and digital networking is actually decreasing, a school should be able to "get more bang for the buck" when the technology is installed.
2. "Stay on top of what's coming down the road, but keep the brakes on until you are sure it will work." At

the same time, use your imagination: Projecting a holographic image of the human heart may seem pretty far-fetched until you think about what a wonderful teaching tool this might be.
3. Adapt the technology plan as the new building and its spaces evolve and as the professional development of the teachers progresses. "The role of the tech person is to listen and then make recommendations throughout the process." All potential users should be queried, including students (who are usually further up the technology learning curve than we are). Listen to "unlikely advisors: parents, construction workers, and custodians." Allow yourself the luxury of saying "I don't know" and ask for help when needed.
4. Communicate the technology plan and its adaptations to all affected parties throughout the process. "A small, seemingly insignificant decision at the time can later turn into a huge political nightmare if you don't communicate properly throughout the process."
5. As the final finish work of the construction nears, the new technology equipment should be ordered. "Money needs to be reserved for change orders like hanging brackets, cabling, and jacks that were missed or unanticipated during the planning process."

The technology target doesn't stop moving, but following an imaginative, yet disciplined plan such as Mark suggests can help assure that most of the technology you install will serve the needs defined by the users for at least the foreseeable future (who knows, that might be as long as 10 minutes).

CHAPTER 3

Safety Guidelines

Key ideas in this chapter:

- Building for safety is the first line of defense.
- Laboratories are often too few and too small.
- The single most critical safety factor is adequate space.
- Research links increased accidents with overcrowding.
- Increased state science requirements to meet global competition call for more laboratory/classrooms.
- The formula for calculating how many laboratory/classrooms your school needs can be used for planning.
- National, state, and local codes have requirements for many safety features.
- Professional science safety experts, science facility consultants, science education associations, and independent research provide guidance with "Best Practice" recommendations.

In order for students to inquire confidently, we must create safe classroom environments. Safety is not just a set of rules but a state of mind, and perhaps, most importantly, it is an attitude and a set of skills that carry over into a student's daily life. But research also shows that the space in which students inquire is vital to their safety and security. This chapter summarizes some of the important factors that contribute to safe laboratory environments.

"Best Practice" in the design of safe facilities is derived from research and from the guidelines produced by professional associations.

What is considered safe today—or tomorrow—is not the same as what we once might have been satisfied to build. Safety guidelines that are appropriate for your building project will derive from not only best practice but from your curriculum and projected enrollment.

Many science educators look for safety guidelines in the realm of litigation. This isn't the best source of information. While there has been a long history of tort litigation involving safety in school facilities, the vast majority of lawsuits that are filed against ("deep pocket") schools never reach court. It is often the loss reduction arms of school insurers who have the best record of these suits.

While the first line of and best legal defense for school districts, boards, and employees, architects, and contractors is to build safe facilities, purchase appropriate furniture and equipment and follow safety guidelines and requirements, that isn't why we stress safety. We know that safe, secure students learn best. So building safety into the facility from the outset also fosters excellence in science instruction. Proper facilities provide safe environments for science education and minimize litigation.

Building for Safety

School laboratory design can support safety in many ways, such as providing an adequate number of laboratory/classrooms (West 2006), ample work space, facilitating the supervision of students, incorporating safety features, and avoiding hazards (Biehle, Motz, and West 1999). There are a variety of federal regulations and local and state codes and standards that apply and can have a significant impact on design decisions. But there is a good deal of variability in which codes apply. OSHA protects workers, while fire safety organizations stress prevention of combustion and explosions. Some states regulate school construction at the state level, while in other states the local municipality's codes apply. Information about the various codes that might apply to your construction will be available from your architect, school science safety consultants, school district officials, local government building officials, state and local fire marshals, and the relevant federal agencies. Planners also need to know what the research says about the links between facilities and increased accident rates (West et al. 2003).

Safety Guidelines

The best practice recommendations from science education professional organizations should be followed. Organizations such as the NSTA, the Council for State Science Supervisors (CSSS), the National Science Education Leadership Association (NSELA), and other national and state science education associations have valuable information for designing science facilities that will enhance learning and provide a safe learning environment.

Adequate Space

The single most critically important factor in designing safe science facilities is adequate space. Research shows that overcrowding due to lack of space is the factor that correlates most closely to an increased rate of accidents in a classroom (West et al. 2003). This guideline is distinct from parallel lines of research on links between increased student performance and the teacher/student ratios. A significant increase in science accidents occurs in the science laboratory/classroom when space is inadequate.

Overcrowding can be the result of not building an adequate number of laboratory/classrooms initially (see section on Calculating an Adequate Number of Laboratory/Classrooms, p. 32). There are a number of different guidelines for space-per-student. State fire, building and occupancy codes such as the International Building Code (IBC) and the National Fire Protection Association (NFPA) Life Safety Code 101 all call for educational occupancies (laboratory and shop) to provide 50 square feet/occupant net. This figure is used in determining the minimal number of occupants for which means of egress must be designed. The IBC and NFPA standards are used to determine the number and size of exits for safe egress. The standards are specific for the type of room; for example a classroom is 20 square feet net/occupant. Note the 50 square feet net is for laboratory space only, not the classroom/lab, and the teacher is counted as an occupant.

NSTA guidelines recommend 60 square feet/occupant for a combined laboratory/classroom. These guidelines assume that the learning space will be used for both classroom instruction and laboratory investigations—a model we recommend. Often the most effective learning occurs in an environment where there are regular transitions between laboratory and classroom activities. And they also assume that there will not be a great deal of space used for fixed computer stations (See rationale in Chapter 2). Requesting an adequate number of laboratory/classrooms and adequate space is often difficult for the science planners, but the evidence supports the need for both effective instruction and safety. Overcrowding affects safety in two ways: (1) inadequate individual workspace and (2) too many students for the science teacher to safely supervise.

Here is some of the research:

Room Size

Rooms that are too small are linked to higher accident rates. West et al. (2003), in an analysis of accidents, reported 68% of the accidents occurred in rooms that were less than 1,000 square feet. A pure lab should have at least 1,200 square feet (50 square feet/student with a maximum of 24 students). A combination

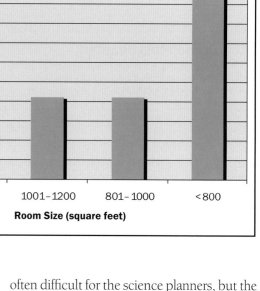

Number of Accidents Increases as Room Size Decreases

P = 0.05

Minimum Recommended Floor Space per Student, in Square Feet

	Elementary School	Middle School	High School
Science Room	40		
Multiple-Use Classroom	45	60	
Combination Lab./Classroom		60	60

Minimum Room Size for a Class of 24, in Square Feet

	Elementary School	Middle School	High School
Science Room	960		
Multiple-Use Classroom	1,080	1,440	
Combination Lab./Classroom		1,440	1,440

laboratory/classroom should have at least 1,440 square feet (24 students at 60 square feet/student). Note the chart, which shows how dramatically the accident rate increases as the room size decreases.

Space per Individual Student

Laboratory/classrooms must be built to accommodate the number of students likely to be assigned to them. Crowded laboratory/classrooms cause students to have to work too closely together, preventing them from escaping hazards and hampering teachers' ability to circulate and supervise students. Besides adequate floor space, students need their own work areas, ample work surfaces along with a sufficient number of shared sinks, and heat and electrical sources in order to be able to work safely. (See Appendix B.)

Students need adequate individual workspace to do science safely. Several studies report increases in accidents when students do not have sufficient personal lab space. Young (1972) was the first to report an increase in accidents when there is inadequate space. Although NSTA no longer recommends building pure science laboratories because it does not allow the smooth integration of laboratory investigations within the daily science instruction, a minimum of 50 square feet per student is needed for a pure lab design. West et al. (2003) reported 66% of the accidents occurred in rooms where students have less than 60 square feet/student. Note the graph showing the spectacular increase in accidents when there is less than 60 square feet/student (West et al. 2003).

Instructionally, science teachers report

doing twice as much "hands-on" science when students are in a combination laboratory/classroom rather than having to go to a pure lab to conduct science activities (West, Biehle, and Motz 2000). Research provides

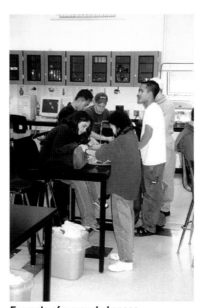
Example of a crowded space

evidence that use of integrated lab/field activities improves students' understanding of subject matter, development of scientific reasoning and increases their interest in science (National Research Council 2005, pp. 3–12). A minimum of 60 square feet per student is needed for a combination laboratory/classroom to meet best practice recommendations for scientifically literate graduates who can compete globally.

If any one class size is going to be greater than 24 students, then the lab should be increased

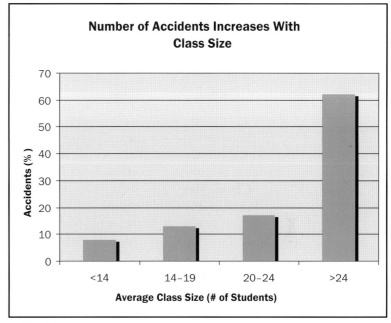
P = 0.05

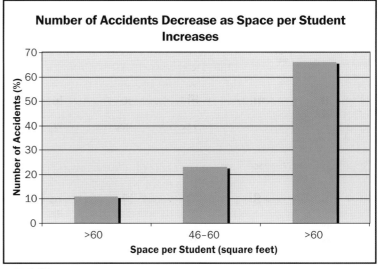
P=0.05

by an additional 60 square feet/student. For example, if the district plans to put in 28 lab stations (four more than recommended), then the lab room size should be increased from 1,440 square feet to 1,680 ($4 \times 60 = 240 + 1,440 = 1,680$) square feet to ensure adequate individual workspace. However, supervising an overcrowded laboratory/classroom of 28 students increases the risk of increased accidents. (See next section.)

Class Size
Class size is another critical safety issue because two safety factors are at work: lack of adequate space per student and too many students for a teacher to properly supervise. Teachers report overcrowding is their primary safety concern. West et al. (2003) reported that 61% of the accidents occurred when classes were larger than 24 students. NSTA recommends that every science class size (not average) be limited to 24 if there is adequate space (1,440 square feet for a combination laboratory/classroom). The potential of another person (a paraprofessional or co-teacher) in the classroom will add to the space needed. Although a class size should never exceed this level, even with adequate space, it is wise to make allowances for future accommodations that may cause laboratory/classrooms to be larger in the future.

Note the chart on the preceding page that shows the dramatic increase in accidents when the class size is greater than 24 students.

Space for Technology
Science was the first academic discipline to use technology extensively in schools. Historically, electronic equipment such as microscopes, balances, hot plates, computers, printers, calculators, and chromatographs have long been a staple in conducting scientific investigations. Planning for exemplary science facilities must include space not only for traditional technology such as those previously listed, but also for technology not yet known. While computers are getting smaller and more portable (see Chapter 2), more diverse types of technological equipment are taking their place: probes, satellite receivers, gauges, and meters. Even with constant miniaturization, the need for space for new technology will always be present. It is important to consider that portable equipment might temporarily block access to a shower, eyewash, or exit. Changes in science programs and instructional methods may result in a need for increased laboratory/classroom and support space.

Space for Accessibility
Requirements for compliance with the Americans with Disabilities Act (ADA) and Individuals with Disabilities in Education Act (IDEA) have increased the amount of space required for a safe science environment. In addition to the normal amount of floor space allotted per student, additional space may be needed to comply with ADA guidelines for an adapted student workstation. One ADA workstation requires the same amount of space as two non-ADA stations. Extra space may be needed when some students with disabilities have aides to assist them. See Chapter 9, Science for All.

The Occupational Safety and Health Administration (OSHA), CFR 1910 defines the term "laboratory" as "a facility where the labora-tory use of hazardous chemicals occurs. It is a workplace where relatively small quantities of hazardous chemicals are used in a nonproduction basis." Science classrooms fit both of these definitions. However, there has been some misuse of these terms, particularly by architects and administrators, when they did not want to abide by the "occupancy loads" required for school science laboratories (Roy 2002). Science laboratory/classrooms have been labeled "classsroom" to avoid meeting science space requirements.

Calculating an Adequate Number of Laboratory/Classrooms
Competition in a global economy requires a scientifically literate population and workforce. A response has been a national call to improve high school education including increasing the science requirements for high school graduation. Some states have already moved to requiring four years of science, which means that some schools that did not previously build enough science laboratory/classrooms find themselves with an even greater shortage of science facilities needed to have an adequate science program for their community. Below is a real example of how a district properly determined how many science laboratory/classrooms are needed.

High School "X" has a stable population of 1,400 students in grades 9–12. They want 80% of their students to take four years of science and 20% to take three years of science. They wisely limit the science class size to 24 with each teacher having his/her own laboratory/classroom and each teacher teaching five classes per day. To accurately calculate the number of laboratory/classrooms needed a school needs to identify the following:

- total enrollment
- target % of students taking four years of science
- target % of students taking three years of science
- number of classes/sections each teacher teaches daily
- class size limit of 24 students

Here's how high school "X" calculated the number of science laboratory/classrooms needed in the new science wing after identifying the above data.

1. Calculate the number of laboratory/classrooms needed for the 80% who are taking four years of science.
   a. The district's goal is for 80% of their graduates to take four years of science. 1,400 × 0.80 = 1,120 students taking four years of science.
   b. With a class size of 24 and each teacher teaching five sections, that equals 46.7 sections 1,120/24 = 46.7 classes (say 47).
   c. 47 classes divided by 5 classes/teacher = 9.4 teachers and/or labs.

2. Calculate the number of laboratory/classrooms needed for the 20% who are taking three years of science.
   1,400 × 0.2 = 280 students taking three years of science
   280/24 = 11.7 classes
   11.7 classes/5 classes for each teacher = 2.3 teachers/labs

3. Total the number of teachers and laboratory/classrooms needed for steps 1 and 2.
   9.4 + 2.3 = 11.7 = 12 laboratory/classrooms needed for 80% of the students to take four years of science and 20% to take three years of science with a class size of 24 and teachers teaching 5 classes daily.
TOTAL = 12 laboratory/classrooms

A simple way to quickly determine the number of laboratory/classrooms needed is to refer to the chart in Appendix I, p.139.

A few schools are planning around the assumption that some of their future classes will occur online. But, research supports the use of more hands-on, minds-on lab and field investigations, not fewer. Furthermore, even these courses will regularly meet face-to-face, and it is likely that an expanded vision or increased science requirements (or required credits for graduation) will encourage more students to take more classes. So it is always wise to plan for more students and more courses, not just what you need to get by now, especially when the world is moving toward more, not less science and technology in the future.

Emergency Exits

Another crucial concern is the ability to exit safely from laboratory/classrooms during emergencies. Students of all ages and adults must be able to find their way out of a school in a prompt and orderly manner.

The NFPA Life Safety Code (2006) requires a minimum of two exit access doorways in rooms that are greater than 1,000 square feet. For any building, two or more exits are recommended for every laboratory and preparation room.

These should be at opposite ends of the room, with doors opening outward. In some schools, ground floor windows can be designated as emergency exits. It is important that these exits be unobstructed and labeled so that they are never inadvertently locked or screened.

Electricity

Access to electricity and its associated safety issues must be considered from the beginning of the design process. Ground-fault interrupters (GFI) protect people against major shock and electrical fires by preventing short circuits, and should be installed on all circuits in the laboratory/classroom. Even with this protection, outlets should not be located within several feet of water sources. All outlets in the school must be grounded, as required under Occupational Safety and Health Act (OSHA) regulations, to prevent electrical accidents. Surge protectors are used to protect computers and other electronic devices from power surges, which may be random or induced by lightning.

Sufficient electrical outlets should be provided to avoid the need for extension cords, which present significant electrical, fire, and trip/fall safety hazards. For example, plans should include at least one duplex outlet per two lab stations in addition to the minimum of three duplex outlets on the instructional wall(s). Outlets should NEVER be placed near a sink.

Outlets placed underneath the counter edge of a lab station put the electrical cords hanging over the edge at risk of being caught by some movement pulling the electrical device off the counter. Outlets servicing a perimeter pier are best placed at the head of the

Not enough outlets— a real safety hazard

peninsula with the sink placed for easy access at the end of the aisle or end of the peninsula. This placement of outlets allows the electrical cords to lie down the middle of the counter and out of the work area. When considering alternatives to wall outlets, it is important to investigate their pros and cons with respect to safety. Floor boxes, if used, should comply with Underwriters Laboratories (UL) water exclusion requirements and should never be located close to water sources or areas where water is used.

Manual shut-off switches should be located so that the teacher can easily access them and shut off the electricity, gas, or water in different zones when not needed for science activities. Emergency shut-off controls for electrical or gas service should be highly visible, clearly labeled, and available to the teacher, but not easily accessible to the students. They are normally located near the teacher's station and not far from the hallway exit, but not immediately adjacent to the hall door. The placement should be such so that students are not able to hit the switch as they exit the class each period causing repetitive problems. Lastly, DC lines should not be used.

Refrigerators in a prep room are useful for storage of lab or field materials, but should never be used for storage of food and/or drink. The refrigerator must be labeled "Lab Materials Only—No Food or Drink." If a flammable needs short-term cooling, consider doing so in an ice bath rather than an expensive spark-fee refrigerator. Any long-term cold storage of flammables requires a spark-free refrigerator. Electrical devices with a source of ignition, such as a thermostat or a light switch, should not be used in an area housing flammables such as the chemical storeroom.

Heat Sources

All sources of heat present potential safety problems. The decision to use gas or alternative heat sources in laboratories depends on instructional and preparation needs, and the procedures for minimizing hazards. In general, educators are no longer recommending gas service below the high school level in science laboratory/classrooms. As hot plates tend to draw large amounts of electrical current, it is essential that a science laboratory/classroom have several 20-amp circuits. Water can be heated in microwave ovens or hot pots. Small bottle butane gas units might also be used in place of a central gas system to feed Bunsen burners; safe and secure storage of the gas cylinders must be addressed. Alcohol burners are not recommended nor should they be used, as they pose unnecessary hazards and have been responsible for some of the worst laboratory accidents reported (Texley, Kwan, and Summers 2004, p. 39).

If gas is required, the manual control valve for shutting off the gas in the laboratory when the teacher is not present or when lessons do not require gas should be accessible only to the teacher. If a preparation room has shut-offs for several laboratory/classrooms, these must be clearly labeled to indicate which lines they control.

The clearly labeled emergency gas shut-off valve should be activated by pushing a highly visible button, with a keyed reset mechanism to turn the gas supply back on when the emergency is over. This keyed reset feature can also be used by the teacher to shut off the gas when it is not needed in lieu of the control valve mentioned above. Models that have red shut-off buttons recessed into a metal frame minimize the possibility of an inadvertent shutoff. All emergency controls in the laboratory/classroom should be in a location that is readily accessible by the teacher, but not too easily reached by students.

Hot Water

For sanitary reasons, hot water is needed in all science laboratory/classrooms and general elementary classrooms where science is taught.

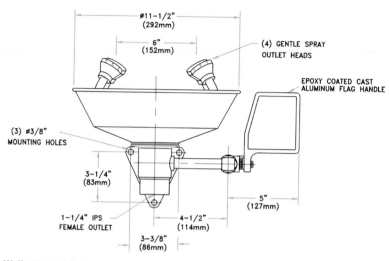

Wall-mounted dual eyewash

Schools need to be mindful of the maximum temperature of the hot water and keep it well below the scalding point. Sanitizing chemical-splash goggles, washing glassware, washing hands after working with chemicals or living specimens, and cleaning equipment for reuse all rely on the use of hot water. While some schools use alcohol gel for sanitation purposes, it is important to remember that these gels are highly flammable and in general, are not a substitute for hot, soapy water.

Eyewash and Safety Shower

The American National Standards Institute (ANSI) sets the standards for eyewash and shower equipment. An eyewash and a shower that can be accessed within 10 seconds (ANSI Z-358.1-1998 or newer), both clearly marked, must be installed in every science laboratory/classroom and preparation room where hazardous chemicals are used. They must have sufficient water pressure to operate properly, tepid water temperature (78–93°F) to avoid scalding, and be kept free from obstructions at all times. Although not necessarily required, the floor should have a drain and a trap with a trap primer so that the eyewash can be flushed weekly to wash out physical and biological contaminants. The eye/face wash and shower should be separated sufficiently so that both can be used at the same time. The shower should be activated weekly to verify proper operation (ANSI Z358.1). If there is no drain in the laboratory/classroom design plan, then the eyewash and shower must be plumbed to allow weekly flushing into a container.

One accessible eyewash and shower is required in each room and they should

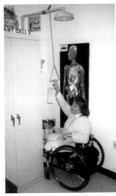

An accessible safety shower/eyewash

also accommodate persons without disabilities. For example, there must be enough room for a person without disabilities to bend over to use the eyewash. This can be accomplished by modifying a standard safety shower/eyewash so that the hanging shower pull rod is not more than 54 inches above the floor and the nozzles of the eyewash are not more than 34 inches above the floor (Biehle, Motz, and West 1995).

One or more ANSI standard eyewash is required for any laboratory/classroom and preparation room where hazardous chemicals are being used. The device must be able to wash both eyes simultaneously. Squeeze bottles and body drenches are not sufficient. The eyewash should provide an instant supply of fresh, aerated, tepid water with tempered flow for at least 15 minutes. The device should be able to stay in the open position, leaving the user's hands free. Instruction should be provided to alert the user to hold the eyelids open during flushing because a person normally closes their eyes when water is splashing into them.

The shower should be large enough to accommodate both an injured person and the person who is helping to wash the chemicals off the injured person. It should have a fixed

valve handle or a chain or rod with a large ring handle. Instruction should be provided for proper use (Texley, Kwan, and Summers 2004, p. 34).

For more information on eyewashes and showers, see the American National Standards Institute (ANSI) standards for eyewash and shower equipment (Z-358.1-1998 or newer) and Appendix B.

Storage Facilities for Students

Individual storage facilities for students can be safety hazards. Separate, locking drawers for students, once the norm, can be more of a problem than a benefit. Students can store dangerous materials in them and separate locked storage spaces take a great deal of time to search in an emergency. Larger storage areas with separate bins are preferable.

Student backpacks can also create safety hazards ranging from a tripping hazard when left of the floor to an opportunity to transport dangerous items into or out of the science space. Backpacks on a work surface can disrupt activities and limit the available surface area for an investigation; when left on the floor they can block accessibility to persons with disabilities and egress in case of a fire. The appropriate place for student backpacks is in the students' lockers. When this is not an option, individual open storage cubbies or wall-mounted hooks near the entrance door

Cubbies for student backpacks can be built into laboratory/classroom storage shelving

should be provided to keep the clutter away from the working areas of a laboratory/classroom (Texley, Kwan, and Summers 2004, pp. 61–62).

Storage of Hazardous Chemicals

Secure storage of chemicals is a major safety and legal consideration in science facilities design. Best practice includes having an entirely separate and secure chemical storeroom that is vented to the outside of the building (NFPA 45).

Security of Chemicals

Many serious accidents occur when unauthorized persons steal chemicals. Chemical storage rooms should have lockable, fireproof doors that open outward. Chemicals should never be stored in prep rooms, laboratory/classrooms, or areas where students or other unauthorized persons frequent or have access, even accidentally. Walls surrounding chemical storerooms should extend from the floor to the bottom of the floor or roof structure above for both safety and security reasons. Many accidents in which people are seriously hurt occur after chemicals that were stored in insecure areas were stolen. Tort law tends to hold schools liable for not providing security for chemicals, because it is negligent to fail to provide secure and safe storage for chemicals. Planning safe and secure chemical storage is relatively easy to do during the early phases of the design process.

Separate Chemical Storeroom

The chemical storeroom is to be used for chemical storage only and not as an occupied space such as a preparation/equipment storeroom

(West 1991). As such, no one should be in the chemical storeroom except when obtaining or returning chemicals. Chemical storerooms should never be used as preparation rooms. Student assis-

Well-designed chemical storage facility

tants should never work in chemical storage rooms. Adequate space for safe storage of chemicals should include at least one (1) square foot per student, which is included in the 10 square feet minimum per student recommended for support area (preparation and storage space). For example, each laboratory/classroom designed for 24 students should have approximately 240 square feet of support area, including at least 50 square feet for a separate chemical storeroom to meet the minimum wheelchair turning radius required for any room.

More chemical storage space may be needed in schools where advanced chemistry is taught. Support areas for other science disciplines such as Earth science may not use enough chemicals to need a separate chemical storeroom, but will also need to store their chemicals in a secure storeroom. However, such courses still need the space to store large and unusual shaped equipment such as stream tables. The area needed for lab prepara-

tion and equipment/materials storage can be one large room.

A dedicated and properly designed storeroom is the best way for hazardous chemicals to be secure. Chemicals should also not be stored in the preparation room or in the equipment storage room or where sensitive equipment or electrical shutoffs are located. Prep rooms that are designed to also store chemicals are a liability. They endanger the teacher, and cannot be secured to allow only those with a specific need for access to enter. Student assistants should not be allowed to work in the prep room if there is any possibility that a chemical might be available.

The chemical storeroom must have enough space to allow the storage of chemicals in compatible groups and with sufficient distance between incompatible chemicals. For example, containers should be stored not more than two deep and a hand's width apart. Some chemicals are incompatible, such as nitric acid that must be stored separately from organics. Commercial chemical supply companies can supply various compatible storage arrangements.

Storerooms should be sited as close to point of use as possible. Chemicals should never be taken through the halls during change of classes. Newer school designs have created back or private hallways in order to create safe pathways for the transport of chemicals. Storage rooms should have separate key systems. Keypad systems, with codes that can be invalidated when substitutes or other staff no longer have a need to enter, are recommended. Temporary codes are also valuable for maintenance persons and contractors who might have a temporary need to enter a storeroom. It should be rare that a custodial, maintenance or contract person should need to enter a chemical storeroom.

Specialized Cabinets

Commercial companies have developed storage systems designated for proper chemical storage. Secure, specialized storage units for acids, flammables, and corrosives are available for purchase and are to be placed in the chemical storeroom, not in the prep or equipment storeroom. An Underwriters Laboratory (UL) approved, grounded, and dedicated flammables cabinet for safety must be provided. Corrosives must not be stored in a metal flammable or any other type of metal cabinet. Any chemicals not kept in a separate chemical storage area must be kept in a dedicated, lockable cabinet that is specially designed for storage of chemicals and not in a general storage cabinet. Storing chemicals alphabetically, instead of by compatibility, is hazardous.

Shelves and cabinets for chemical storage must be attached to the wall for stability. Wooden shelves, plastic shelf supports, and other materials that resist corrosion will prevent the collapse of shelves loaded with chemicals. The supports must be spaced closely enough to prevent the shelves from sagging. The shelves should be no more than 12 inches deep, so that the chemicals will not be stored more than two containers deep. Space chemical containers so that each one can be removed easily without knocking over adjacent containers. Lips on the edges of shelves help prevent the containers from falling and any spillages away from a person standing in front of the shelf.

Shelving should be constructed of sturdy materials that will not sag over time. No chemical storage shelf should be more than 60 inches from the floor so that the average person can read the labels on the containers and reach items easily without the risk of an item tipping or falling to the floor (Texley, Kwan, and Summers 2004, p. 56).

Different courses need specialized storage. Lack of attention to these details can cause safety problems. For example, if thought is not given to where the telescope or skeleton is going to be stored, either can become a trip hazard as well as damaging expensive instructional equipment.

See the Electricity section earlier in this chapter concerning a spark-free laboratory refrigerator. The long-term storage of certain flammables is a major safety issue and should be carefully considered before including their use in the curriculum.

It is vital and required in many areas to place chemical inventories and material safety data sheets (MSDS), which list the properties and hazards of the chemicals, in accessible locations outside chemical storage rooms as well as inside them. The school nurse and administrator will also need copies. The local fire marshal may also want a copy of the MSDS data sheets. These records inform fire and safety personnel concerning what is being stored, so that they can assess the potential for combustion ahead of time. Most jurisdictions require that MSDSs can be available either as paper copies or electronically. However, they must be easily accessible to users to promote frequent usage.

Ventilation

The ventilation system is another major design consideration, particularly for a renovation. Generally, older school buildings were not air-conditioned and often relied on gravity ventilation and open windows for cooling. Public buildings are not heated and cooled as closed systems. Their constant intake of approximately 15% outside air contributes to a healthy environment, though it adds to heating costs. An architect or HVAC engineer will calculate the percentage of outside air that needs to be brought in continuously and how long it takes to circulate all of the air in the classroom.

Room exhaust fan

Forced ventilation at a minimum rate of eight changes of air per hour for occupied science laboratory/classrooms and preparation rooms per NFPA 45 and continuous-forced ventilation at 12 changes per hour for chemical storerooms and rooms used to house animals is required. There should be a minimum of four exchanges/hour in unoccupied laboratory/classrooms. Standards including OSHA 29 CFR part 1910, p. 3332, 4 (f) specify outdoor air exchange rates (ASHRAE *Laboratory Design Guide*. 2001, p. 32). All exhausts should be vented to the outside of the building away from an intake duct, not recirculated in the building's ventilation system.

Fume hoods should never be used as part of the science facility's general ventilation system. Fume hoods use the most energy in the science facility and are often left running to overcome the inadequacy of a building's ventilation system. This practice adds significantly to the cost of operating the building as it draws air from the rest of the school and exhausts it directly outside. Fresh air required to make up for this exhausted air must be heated or cooled and humidified or dehumidified to maintain the comfort level of the entire school, using still more energy. The exhaust fans in a fume hood system are not designed for continuous operation and will break down much more rapidly if misused in this fashion, adding still more costs to the operation and maintenance of the building.

Chemical storerooms need separate systems that vent directly outside, usually to the roof and away from fresh-air intake pipes. Storage cabinets for flammables are generally not ventilated unless local code requires it; however, corrosives cabinets should be ventilated to the outside. Exhaust grilles in chemical storage rooms should be located both at the ceiling and at the floor level to remove vapors that are heavier than air.

Every science room should be equipped with a purge system with exhaust fans designed for the rapid venting of excessive fumes, smoke or bad odors created by an investigation. Purge systems in chemical storerooms and laboratory/classrooms must also vent directly outside, again usually to the roof, and away from fresh-air intake pipes. These small units often replace a windowpane and are controlled by an on/off switch on a nearby wall. They should be equipped with fan guards.

For more information on ventilation, see the ANSI standards for laboratory ventilation (Z-9.5-2003) and consult the American Society of Heating, Refrigerating, and Air-Conditioning Engineers (ASHRAE) standards. See Appendix B for more information.

Fume Hoods

Fume hoods require make-up air systems to replace the room air that they remove. The systems can be an integral part of the building's ventilation system or part of the installed hood. They should operate automatically when the hood fan is turned on and provide the appropriate amount of make-up air at the right time. The hood must exhaust directly to the outdoors, preferably through a stainless-steel duct that runs to the roof of the building and vents at a sufficient distance from any air intake to prevent the recirculation of exhaust air. The correct separation distance depends on the physical configuration of the building and should be calculated by an HVAC engineer. See the Ventilation section concerning the energy and operations cost of using fume hoods for general ventilation.

The hood should provide a minimum of 80 linear feet of airflow per minute at its face with the sash open 6 inches above the bench or counter. The sash level should be marked for 100 linear feet of airflow per minute, with the date of the last measurement. A hood with a fixed sash opening height may not provide adequate working space for tall users.

There are various types of hoods that can be selected depending on the need. A freestanding hood with three transparent sides, only one of which is operable, may be used to enable students to work in small groups or

Fume hood with transparent sides

gather around an investigation. These hoods are often known as "demonstration hoods." Some schools install individual downdraft fume hoods at each student workstation, but these tend to have poor ventilation and fume-removal capabilities, and the loss of working space is a disadvantage. Some recently developed, movable or ductless fume hoods have impressed science safety experts with their ability to serve the needs of a school science program by recirculating air through a series of filters designed for the specific use of the program. The advantages include the ability of one hood to serve several lab/classrooms if the curriculum does not require heavy fume hood use, no ductwork installation, and lower energy costs. However, the filter packs are specifically defined for the chemicals and quantities to be used, and must be periodically replaced and properly disposed of as hazardous waste.

At least one hood should be designed to be accessible for persons with disabilities. This includes lowering the deck to 34 inches above the floor, providing a protected knee space beneath the hood, placing the controls within reach of a person in a wheelchair, and

Ductless fume hood

modifying the controls to eliminate the need for twisting the wrist.

A fume hood is required for every chemistry, physical science, and other science laboratory/classroom or prep room where hazardous or vaporous chemicals are used. Advanced chemistry and biology classes generally need at least two hoods, and they should be separated by several feet, with adjacent countertop for support area. Best practice places fume hoods away from walkways or doors so that the proper airflow is maintained. Fume hoods are not needed at the elementary level and only rarely at

A fume hood designed for wheelchair

the middle school level. However, most middle schools need a fume hood in the preparation room.

For more information on fume hoods, see sections 5.6.1 and 5.6.2 of the ANSI standards for laboratory ventilation (Z-9.5-2003) and Appendix B. Consult the ASHRAE (ANSI/ASHRAE) 110-1995 standards and be sure that all hoods meet the 4.0 AU 0.10 standard for testing fume hoods. Also refer to the NFPA 45 for further information on fume hood ventilation.

Fire Protection

When science facilities are built, walls between the laboratory/classrooms and hallways are usually extended above the ceiling to the bottom of the floor or roof structure above, providing effective fire protection for the hallways for as long as an hour. Fire-rated corridor doors are generally required. In many jurisdictions, current building codes require school buildings larger than 20,000 square feet in area to have a built-in fire-sprinkler system that may replace the requirements for fire-rated doors. Dead-end hallways should be no more than 20 feet long. Fire alarm systems that use visual signals in addition to auditory alarms to aid hearing-impaired persons are usually mandatory.

Sprinkler systems are recommended for laboratories and for preparation and storage rooms. Fire protection in chemical storage rooms is usually achieved by maintaining careful practices and installing sprinklers, as well as smoke and heat detectors and monitoring systems. If sprinklers are present, separate, protected storage must be planned for water-reactive materials and chemicals. See NFPA Standard 45 (2004 or newer) guidelines.

Local government building and fire officials can provide information on the need for sprinklers, smoke detectors, and specific types of fire extinguishers, and have discretion when codes don't specify requirements for science laboratory/classrooms. Local and state fire codes should be met or exceeded.

Other safety gear, including personal protection, fire blankets, safety shields, and a first aid kit, should be provided for each laboratory/classroom. Appropriate signage should be posted to alert and guide users in using safety gear. Post signage on state and local requirements for personal protection such as chemical-splash goggles. Appropriate eye protection includes chemical-splash goggles for use with chemicals, heat or glassware and safety glasses for projectile protection. Both the chemical splash goggles and the projectile protection spectacles should meet the ANSI Z87.1 impact standard. See Appendix D for a more complete list.

Housekeeping

Good housekeeping is a safety issue, not a lifestyle choice. Cleanliness and

Good housekeeping is essential, as clutter like this can lead to accidents.

orderliness as safety factors are intuitive and logically appropriate as well as an OSHA criteria which refers to housekeeping in several standards included in 29 CFR part 1910. All places of employment, passageways, storerooms and service rooms are to be kept clean and orderly and in a sanitary condition. Good housekeeping reduces injuries and accidents, improves student discipline and employee morale, reduces fire potential and accidents due to falling items or items in aisles and can even make operations more efficient. Avoid stacks of papers and other junk on countertops and desks and in sinks or cabinets, and on tops of cabinets. Daily housekeeping involves cleaning and replacing all materials and equipment to their proper storage place, returning chemicals to the chemical storeroom. Students should be a part of the daily maintenance by cleaning their individual areas.

Other Factors

Additional factors that contribute to safety include adequate lighting, emergency lighting, suitable areas and furniture for dispensing chemicals safely, and the provision of safety guards on equipment. The laboratory layout should be conducive to the supervision of students. Windows in offices, preparation rooms, and student project rooms will facilitate visual supervision of the students. Good communication systems, such as telephones, two-way public address systems, and emergency call systems, are essential for maintaining a safe environment.

Special Precautions for Seismic Areas

Designing or renovating a facility in an area subject to earthquakes, poses additional prob-

lems. The Northridge, California, earthquake in 1994 demonstrated that vertical ground motion could have a devastating effect. Items on shelves bounced up and down and fell off, which means that lips or low guardrails on shelves, which are mandatory in seismically active areas and normally increase safety, did not succeed in keeping the items in place. Beakers and storage canisters should be stored in recessed cabinet frames so that they will be held in during vertical motion. This motion may also cause sliding doors on cabinets to fall out of their tracks unless the top and bottom guides are deep enough to prevent it.

In areas of potential seismic activity, it is particularly important that heavy items not be stored on open shelving or on top of wall cabinets. Expensive equipment such as computers and countertop apparatus should be clamped or bolted down, and tall storage cabinets should be bolted to the walls to prevent their overturning. Cabinet doors should have latching mechanisms that create a positive latch; magnetic catches and roller catches are not sufficient to prevent cabinet doors from opening during an earthquake. Light fixtures and other items that hang from the ceiling must be suspended separately and braced diagonally above the ceiling.

Particular attention needs to be paid to the strength of the walls and the weight-bearing capacity of the floors when heavy rolling shelves are used in seismically active areas. In an earthquake, these shelf units can generate enough momentum to roll quickly in one direction, crashing into the stationary end unit. If the walls are built of metal studs and drywall, or of un-reinforced masonry, the rolling units can

crash through them. The shelves should be kept clamped to their rails at all times, except when they are in use.

Connections for gas lines in seismically active areas should be flexible.

Problems Specific to Renovations

When science facilities are being designed or renovated, the three most important elements to consider are safety during science activities, protection from fire, and easy evacuation from the laboratory/classroom.

These objectives may be difficult to accomplish. Older buildings, most built without adequate number of laboratory/classrooms nor adequate lab/classroom space, sufficient exits, fire barriers, and storage areas, will be subject to the latest occupancy, building, and fire codes as soon as structural alterations are started. The designer should keep in close contact with government building officials, fire marshals, and state fire inspectors to ensure that the proposed alterations and additions conform to code and to best practice in fire safety.

Renovating older buildings may bring to light hazards not anticipated when construction plans were made. For example, asbestos may have been installed in an old building before it was considered to be a hazardous material, and it may not yet have been removed through an abatement process. Asbestos removal is extremely expensive. Raising a carpet or a layer of tile only to find asbestos tiles, or opening a wall and discovering asbestos-wrapped pipes, always results in increased construction costs. Time is also a concern, as the abatement process must be supervised by trained consultants and cannot be carried out while students are in school. Finally, when schools plan for renovation, they inevitably find materials that they have stored for years but have not used in recent memory. It is wise to budget money for a bonded disposal company to remove all those materials that have not been used in the past year.

States are beginning to adopt school facilities standards that will impact the design of both the total facilities and have specific impact on the science area. Adequate number of laboratory/classrooms nor adequate laboratory/classroom space for doing science safely, separate chemical storerooms, fume hoods, supplemental purge systems, and ventilation are frequently addressed in these state standards.

All stakeholders should be aware of both the requirements and the recommendations based on the safety research and the profession's best practices. If heeded, this information will enable the design and building of safer and more instructionally effective state-of-the-art science facilities.

Minimizing Litigation

We began by stating that minimizing litigation should not be the primary motive for building a safe facility. But it is still a reality of life in the 21st century. So it should be one of the factors that planning teams consider.

A key word in litigation is "reasonable": To avoid litigation, a reasonable effort to provide an environment that is safe for teachers and students is required. This effort must be based on current best practice, not on what has worked in the past. It is not necessary to de-

sign for protection from a worst-case scenario. For example, we would not eliminate electrical outlets because a student could stick a piece of metal into one, but we do restrict their placement to appropriate locations and provide the necessary GFI on circuits. It is our responsibil-

Billboard near Detroit

ity to ensure that space is adequate to promote safety, that class size is in the desired range, that an adequate number of laboratory/classrooms have been built to prevent teachers from "floating" from room to room and students meeting in nonscience rooms, and to provide for increased state science requirements, and that the architectural design enables teachers to exercise close supervision.

Tort Law

A tort is a wrong or injury to a person or property not involving a breach of contract. The standard of proof is a preponderance of evidence. The burden of proof rests with the

plaintiff, who must establish that the preponderance of evidence shows that the defendant occasioned the damage. A person is expected to reasonably foresee possible injury arising out of the foibles of human nature and to be able to anticipate difficulties.

- *Negligence* is defined as conduct that falls below a standard of care established by law to protect others against unreasonable risk of harm. Educators are expected to minimize risk of harm. The law requires only that reasonable and common sense decisions be made to promote safe working and learning conditions for the staff and students. There are levels of risk in the school environment, as in all areas of everyday living, that have to be tolerated, yet that permit reasonably safe, positive, and optimum learning. The goal is to promote maximum safety in order to prevent injury to people and damage to property while promoting effective science instruction.

A finding of negligence usually involves one of the following:

- *Misfeasance*—Performing a legal action in an improper way. This term is frequently used when a professional does his/her job in a way that is not technically illegal, but is nevertheless mistaken or wrong. Examples include:
  - Principal assigns a science class to a non-science classroom
  - Posting an exit sign over a closet door by mistake
  - Installing a safety shower and forgetting to turn on the water

- *Nonfeasance*—Failure to do something that is legally obligatory or what should be done. In schools, failure to take the necessary action to protect students, providing inadequate facilities, allowing a lack of proper facilities, and mandating curricula when facilities are inadequate for them can result in a finding of negligence, as in *Bush v. Oscoda*. (See box.) Other examples include deliberate:
  - Failure to provide safe science facilities
  - Failure to provide an adequate number of science laboratory/classrooms
  - Failure to use good housekeeping standards
  - Failure to provide proper eye protection
  - Failure to provide a separate secure chemical storeroom

- *Malfeasance*—Doing something that is wrong or illegal. This term is often used when a professional commits an illegal act that interferes with the performance of his/her duties, misconduct, committing an unlawful act, or doing what should not have been done—in this case, the performance of an act that places students or employees in danger. Other examples include deliberately:
  - Designing science rooms that are too small
  - Not installing an eyewash in a science room
  - Not turning water on for eyewash or shower
  - Forcing student or employee to assume an unnecessary risk, use defective equipment or unsafe methods

The following are additional examples of litigation involving school facilities:

Maxwell v. Santa Fe Public Schools, 1975. A school board, but not the teacher, was held liable for a student injury because eye protection was not available.

Reagh v. San Francisco Unified School District, 1953. A school district was held liable for injuries that resulted from chemicals being kept on an open shelf rather than in a secure area.

Allowing poorly designed science facilities that do not provide a safe learning and working environment due to any of the following causes may result in litigation:

- inadequate space/overcrowding
- lack of separate, secure chemical storeroom
- poor ventilation
- conditions that lead to poor supervision of students
- lack of safety eyewashes or showers, or alarm systems
- lack of adequate number of or unsafe electrical outlets

Asking teachers to work in unventilated spaces, violating the Occupational Safety and Health Act (OSHA), and forcing a student to take an unnecessary risk, such as moving chemicals from room to room because of inadequate chemical storage facilities, are some of the acts that might result in a finding of negligence. The newspaper story "Teacher Falling Into Acid" (1989), shows how a failure to provide a safety shower led to a serious injury that might easily have resulted in litigation.

Best Practice

In the end, the question that all planning teams must consider is: "How do we limit risks without unduly limiting science learning? Fortunately, an abundance of information is available on this subject from research, and some guidance from the records of tort law cases.

The Research Base

Planning teams and designers need to be well informed about the research base regarding accidents. Newspapers often publish reports on accidents in laboratory/classrooms, since the accident rate in schools is 10-50 times higher than that of the chemical industry (Kaufman 2002). School science accident rates seem to be increasing (Gerlovich, Wilson, and Parsa 1998). Overcrowding is the greatest concern of science teachers and links with increased accident rates (West et al. 2003). Research goes beyond the headlines to look at the factors that accompany school accidents, which include

- overcrowding
- inadequate or poorly designed working space, and too few work/lab stations
- teachers with inadequate content preparation

- teachers who are teaching more than two preparations at the same time
- poor school discipline
- inadequate safety training

It is important to remember that many research studies were conducted before the greatly expanded use of technology in the classroom and the passage of the Individuals with Disabilities Education Act of 1997. The significant impact of these two factors on the amount of space required for a safe and effective science learning environment should be taken into consideration when planning facilities.

No facility can be completely accident-proof. The way to minimize risk is to follow the precepts of best practice and safety research. School districts and planning teams should consider recommendations found in professional publications concerning designing facilities that provide the safest working and learning environments for teachers and students. The expectation is that planners will have a reasonable awareness of student behavior and anticipate the difficulties that might arise, so that they can design facilities that do not present unsafe environments. Besides reviewing the research base, consulting with experienced school science safety professionals, school architects with experience in designing science facilities, suppliers, and other consultants should prove helpful. Above all, the principles behind creating safe and effective instructional spaces should be given priority in the budget and the planning process.

References

Biehle, J. 1995. Complying with science. *American School and University* (May).

Biehle, J., L. Motz, and S. West. 1999. *NSTA guide to school science facilities*. Arlington, VA: National Science Teachers Association.

Bush v. Oscoda Area Schools, 109 Mich. App. 373, 311 N.W.2d 788 (Mich.App. 1981).

Emergency Eyewash and Shower Equipment (ANSI Standard Z358.1-1990). New York: American National Standards Institute.

Fire Protection for Laboratories Using Chemicals (NFPA Standard 45). 1996. Quincy, MA: National Fire Protection Association.

Gerlovich, J. A., E. Wilson, and R. Parsa. 1998. Safety issues and Iowa science teachers, *The Journal of Iowa Academy of Science*, 105(4): 152–157.

International Code Council (ICC). 2006. *International building code*, 5203 Leesburg Pike, Suite 600; Falls Church, VA 22041-3401.

Kaufman, J. 1989. *Laboratory safety guidelines*. Natick, MA: Laboratory Safety Institute.

Kaufman, J. 2002. International Science Safety Conference Proceedings. Sacred Heart University, Fairfield, CT.

Laboratory Ventilation (ANSI Standard Z9.5-1992). 1992. New York: American National Standards Institute.

Life Safety Code (NFPA Standard 101). 1977. Quincy, MA: National Fire Protection Association.

Maxwell v. Santa Fe Public Schools, 87 N.M. 383, 534 P.2d 307. 1975.

Method of Testing Performance of Laboratory Fume Hoods (ANSI/ASHRAE Standard 110–1985). 1985. Atlanta, GA: American Society of Heating, Refrigerating, and Air-Conditioning Engineers.

National Science Teachers Association. 1990. Laboratory science. In *NSTA handbook 1998–99* (194–197). Arlington, VA: Author.

Reagh v. San Francisco Unified School District, 119 Cal.App.2d 65, 259 P.2d 43. 1953.

Roy, K. 2002. International Science Safety Conference Proceedings. Sacred Heart University, Fairfield, CT. Laboratory Safety Institute, Natick, MA.

Teacher Falling into Acid. 1989. *Lubbock Avalanche Journal* (March 3) 4C.

Texley, J., T. Kwan, and J. Summers. 2004. *Investigating safely: A guide for high school teachers*. Arlington, VA: NSTA.

West, S. 1999. Lab safety. *The Science Teacher* 58 (9): 45–51.

West, S. 2006. *Science facility standard for excellence in scinece education*. Austin, TX: Texas Association of School Boards.

West, S., J. Biehle, and L. Motz. 2000. *Building state-of-the-art science facilities*. Paper presented at the National Science Teachers Association national convention.

West, S., J. F. Westerlund, A. L. Stephenson, and N. Nelson. 2003. Conditions that affect secondary science safety: Results from 2001 Texas survey, overcrowding. *The Texas Science Teacher* 32 (2).

Young, J. R. 1972. A second survey of safety in Illinois high school laboratories. *Journal of ChemEd*, 49 (1): 55.

For additional resources, see the bibliography.

"Teacher Falling Into Acid"

A science teacher, working alone after school to prepare chemicals for the next day's instruction, dropped a bottle of concentrated sulfuric acid, slipped on the spilled acid, and fell backward onto a large piece of broken glass and into the puddle of acid. She called for help, and a colleague carried her to a gymnasium shower because there was no safety shower in the entire science area. She suffered severe burns to her head, back and arms, made worse by the delay in rinsing off the acid.

CHAPTER 4

Designing Facilities for the Elementary School (K–5)

Elementary school science programs vary widely, but are important in laying the foundation for secondary science programs. Some schools prefer using teams of teachers, whose members can specialize, while others stress the integration of subjects by offering all content instruction in the self-contained classroom. Whichever of these approaches is taken will influence decisions concerning the settings for instruction. Because trends will always change, even within the same school system, the challenge to those charged with creating elementary facilities is to plan for the present with an eye toward flexibility in the future.

The most basic decision at the elementary level is whether to build separate science facilities or to make all classrooms—or one of each shared pair of classrooms—science-friendly. Most schools that have the resources opt to do both, putting the basics for science in every room, while creating a special place for more in-depth discovery. This approach facilitates science's integration with other subjects, while stressing the unique characteristics of the science environment.

The essential facilities for science, including hot and cold running water and flat work surfaces, are reasonable for every general education classroom, while the specialized storage and instruments that support special adventures can find a home in that special science area.

Whether science is taught in the general classroom or in a dedicated science room, there are some similar guidelines that must be followed. Space, flexibility, and safety are among the most important considerations. The following sections offer detailed suggestions and information for designing and equipping these learning environments and for providing the other resources that a good science program requires.

Space Requirements, Room Design

To accommodate current technology needs and teaching practices,

• a good science room will require a minimum of 40 square feet of floor space per elementary student, or 960 square feet for 24 elementary students.
• a multiple-use classroom in which science is taught will require a minimum of 45 square feet of floor space per elementary student, or 1,080 square feet for 24 elementary students.
• an additional 10 square feet of space per student will be needed for preparation space for the teacher and separate storage space (240 square feet for a class of 24).
• an additional 24 square feet minimum should be added to a multiple-use classroom to accommodate two 4-foot-wide, tall storage cabinets for science-related storage in the classroom.

The 2006 NSTA Position Statement on laboratory science recommends a maximum class size of 24 students in an elementary school.

If fixed computer stations are used, an additional 15 square feet is needed for each desktop computer station or equipment such as an electronic marker board. However, fixed stations are not recommended for tomorrow's classrooms. (See Chapter 2 on Technology.) Add 15 square feet for a laptop computer storage cart and approximately 20 square feet to accommodate a student with disabilities.

For safety and flexibility, a rectangular room at least 30 feet wide, without alcoves, is recommended. A ceiling height of 10 feet is desirable. The science room should have two locking entrances, doorways and a lab station that accommodate persons with disabilities, and adequate ventilation. It should also have projection equipment rather than suspended televisions, for both safety and accessibility.

The Multiple-Use Classroom

To maximize the relevance of authentic science experiences to young children, it is important that science can happen in self-contained classrooms. In the early years—prekindergarten through grade 2—science should be integrated with other subjects and activities throughout the day. The self-contained classroom will require plenty of tables and uncarpeted floor surfaces where messy activities can be conducted easily. Sinks and counters at student-height are also needed, so that frequent hand washing and cleanup can be accomplished with minimal assistance. It is also important that every classroom have hot and cold running water and soap.

In the upper elementary grades (3–5), the classroom should have a greater capacity to accommodate science activities, even if some of those activities will be performed in a dedicated science room. Provisions should be made to integrate science into classroom projects by providing hot and cold running water with soap, flat surfaces, electricity, connectivity ports, and provisions for overnight storage of projects in the classroom. Specialized storage for chemicals should be considered, even though the recommended stock of chemicals in the elementary level is very limited.

Furnishings

All multiple-use classrooms used for science will need:

- movable, flat-topped tables of appropriate size for the students;
- a large sink (15 × 25 × 10 inches) with hot and cold water, mounted at student height, with an attached, hands-free tepid water eyewash;
- additional sinks or "wet areas;"
- counters, base and wall cabinets, and adjustable shelves of various depths to house science-related equipment and materials;
- some form of lockable storage;
- tote-tray storage units or carts;
- a marker board and tackable wall surfaces for displaying charts and posters, photographs, and maps;
- a projection screen and digital projector;
- electrical outlets with ground-fault-interrupter (GFI) protection; and
- connectivity, preferably wireless.

Many of the suggestions and ideas presented below for room arrangements and furnishings for specialized science classrooms apply to multiple-use classrooms as well.

The Specialized Science Classroom

See Table of Critical Dimensions in Appendix C for specific dimensions.

As enthusiasm for science grows, so do expectations of students and teachers. Some schools are lucky enough to have a science specialist, but even if such a staff member is not available, the existence of a special space for extended exploration is always desirable. The elementary science laboratory, often called the "discovery room," is a large, well-equipped, and well-lit classroom with 4–5 sinks and extensive storage for science equipment and kits. These materials may be used in the room or checked out for follow-up activities in the homeroom. This specialized room should be accessible to those with disabilities. While a discovery-room approach requires cooperation and schedule coordination among the elementary staff, most teachers feel that the academic advantages of this specialized science room outweigh any administrative requirements. Discovery science rooms have the unique capacity to reflect the school community and the environment, by incorporating local weather monitoring and astronomy equipment and collections from local strata and native plant gardens.

Because of differences in both the students and their science programs, there are advantages to having separate science classrooms for kindergarten through second-grade students and for third- through fifth-grade students, although the facilities are very similar. The furnishings for each are described below.

A specialized science classroom

Furnishings (K–2)

The type and arrangement of space desirable for students in kindergarten through second grade requires great flexibility. Fixed student workstations should be avoided in favor of flat-topped movable tables. For safety reasons, there should always be a minimum of 4 feet between the perimeter counters and the tables. It is important for planners to verify that the floor space will be suitable for small-group arrangements around a central, movable teacher's table or cabinet, as well as for traditional classroom seating and other arrangements. Allow at least 4 feet on all sides around each grouping of tables. In the classroom-type arrangement, provide a minimum of 8 feet from the front wall of the classroom to the first row of tables. The teacher will then be able to move around

A multiple-use classroom planned for science

easily, have the use of a table, instruct at the board, and use a projector.

Sinks (K–2)

Several sinks with tall, swiveling, aerated faucets should be inset in the student-height, perimeter countertops. The number of sinks depends on the number of students and the types of activities that are expected to require sinks. A good rule of thumb for kindergarten through second grade is one sink for every four to six students. Standard stainless-steel kitchen sinks are acceptable, but they should be large—15 × 25 inches, for example—and have fairly deep (10 inches) bowls. It is best to provide hot and cold water and soap (not alcohol gel) at all sinks, for safe hygiene. A drinking fountain and dual hands-free tepid water eyewash can be provided at one sink and a hand-held, pullout body drench shower at another.

The teacher will need a portion of counter space at least 6 feet long and an adjacent sink at the standard adult standing height of 36 inches.

Work Space (K–2)

The height of counters along the classroom perimeter should be 24 inches. It may be necessary to provide some variety of counter height to accommodate students of different heights. Watch for sharp corners, especially at this primary level.

In order to allow the flat-topped tables to be level when they are pushed together and to compensate for variations in students' size, adjust the tables to the same height and order chairs or stools of various heights. A good height for the tables is 20 inches. Square tables, 30 inches on a side, work well, as do rectangular ones that are small enough to be moved easily, yet large enough to permit students to spread out their work. Chairs or stools can be used for seating. Many teachers prefer stools without backs, because they can be pushed under the tables when not in use, freeing up floor space.

The teacher should have a movable table or cabinet in which materials may be stored. At this level the table rarely needs utilities.

Storage (K–2)

Casework should include base cabinets with student-level counters along two walls for additional work and preparation space. Wall cabinets should be placed above base cabinets for safety reasons. Most counters will be 24 inches deep. Even though chemicals and cleaning supplies are to be stored in another room, teachers will want some lockable classroom cabinets, because even relatively innocuous materials such as glues and paints can tempt students and result in poisoning.

Poster drawers under 3-foot-deep counter

All countertops in classrooms, preparation rooms, and storerooms should have plastic laminate or other durable finishes resistant to water and chemicals. Countertops near a water source should have a backsplash with no seams. Give priority to selecting high-grade cabinets made of hardwood plywood with plastic laminate fronts. Avoid particleboard assembly, because this material reacts poorly to moisture. Flexible storage can be provided by a variety of cabinets with drawers and doors of different sizes. A larger map cabinet is useful for storing instructional posters, maps, etc. Leaving a 30- to 36-inch-wide knee space under a counter will allow students a place to sit at the counter. Drawers in some lower cabinets can provide convenient storage for both teachers and students.

One or two tall science storage cabinets, separate from the teacher's personal cabinet and bolted to the wall, will store items of various sizes, especially if it has vertical dividers that hold adjustable shelves. This cabinet should lock. Hinged doors are recommended for wall cabinets, because sliding doors waste about 3 inches of cabinet depth. Typical depths for wall cabinets are 12 and 16 inches, with tall cabinets being 16 or 22 inches deep.

Mounting heights for wall cabinets will depend on whether students are to have access to them: 42 inches from the floor for students, 54 inches for adults. All cabinets should have positive latches that can withstand seismic events without opening. Some cabinets also must meet the Americans with Disabilities Act Accessibility Guidelines (ADAAG). At least 18 linear feet of book shelving, 10 or more inches deep, some at student height and some at adult height, should be provided.

It is important to set aside a suitable area for hats and coats and cubicles (cubbies) for student backpacks so that they will not be in the way. If these "cubbies" are in a L-shaped alcove, make sure the area is visible to the teacher. Large storage bins with lids for recycling paper, cans, and bottles are also a good idea. Plant carts are very useful for growing various flora for instructional uses. Window shelves can also accommodate plants, terrariums, aquariums, and small animal cages, but should not be placed on west walls because of the tendency of overheating. Aquariums are often placed on perimeter countertops. Don't forget to plan for an adequate number of (and safe placement of) GFI outlets to accommodate the need for light and electricity to run equipment such as heaters and filters.

Display Space (K–2)

One wall should be kept largely free of cabinets to allow places to display student's artwork and instructional aids like maps, charts, and posters. Tack boards can be hung in any unused wall space, and tack strips can be installed above cabinets.

Dry-erase marker boards have become standard, because chalk dust can be harmful to both computers and people. However, there is also a concern about the toxicity and odor of the markers, and all manufacturers'

information and MSDSs should be studied. Water-based inks are preferable. Sliding, multiple-panel boards can be used to extend the marker board without increasing the amount of wall space used. If a marker board is to be used by students, it should be mounted with the bottom edge 24 inches above the floor. As this is an uncomfortable height for most adults, the board should be taller than standard height to accommodate adults.

Storage behind and beneath the marker board

The space behind and below a marker board can be used for storage or for book shelving by recessing shelves into the wall. The sliding panels of the marker board cover this storage until it is accessed. Drawers below the marker board can add significant highly useful storage capacity. Such storage requires thickening of the wall behind the board.

The instructional focus area must support a variety of instructional presentation formats, including video, DVD, slides, digital projection, projected microscope images, overhead projection, and dry lab activities. Controls, including light switches and dimmers, can be installed—often wall mounted—in the front of the room, easily accessible to the teacher. Electronic control systems, with hand-held remote controls, can be installed to allow the teacher to control lighting, sound and projection systems from anywhere in the room. Permanent mounting of equipment such as those used for projection and sound solve problems including theft and trip/fall hazards.

A projection screen should be mounted on a wall or the ceiling. The screen size should be at least 5 feet by 7 feet, but 6 feet by 8 feet is preferable for best visibility. If the screen is to be mounted on a high ceiling, include an additional "tail" of material at the top of the screen; the bottom of the screen will then be approximately 3 feet above the floor. Mounting a projection screen on a diagonal in a corner of the room can allow use of the marker board at the same time the screen is employed. Marker boards generally do not make good projection screens, because their surfaces do not reflect light well.

Because so many elementary students have temporary, frequency-dependent hearing challenges, it is recommended that every classroom have built-in speaker systems to accommodate field sound systems. These systems make audiovisuals more audible, and can easily be hooked to a lavaliere microphone to help teachers reach students more effectively.

A variety of interactive electronic marker board systems have been developed that allow the user to input data to a computer program using special markers that transmit their movements to a sensor in the system. These can be used in conjunction with a digital projection system to enhance instructional materials. Many of these systems consist of a screen, either mounted on the wall, or on a movable frame; others have sensing devices that mount on an ordinary marker board with suction cups. If use of one of these systems is envisioned, space should be provided for the screen.

Utilities (K–2)

Electrical power should be installed with ground-fault interrupters (GFI) on every circuit. Provide plenty of duplex electrical outlets and data outlets (at least one hard-wired data port equipped with a wireless network) around the perimeter of the room for the movable tables that are brought close to them when power is needed. Three duplex outlets are needed on the instructional wall for the teacher's administrative and instructional equipment. Overhead, pull-down electric cords, similar to those used in automotive shops, can supply power to the middle of the room, but must be used with extra caution. Power poles are inflexible and generally cannot stand much physical abuse and should be avoided.

Care should be taken to investigate the safety features of any alternative to wall outlets. Everyone, including custodial staff, should be informed of procedures for their safe use. The number of electrical circuits in a classroom should be adequate to power the equipment expected to be used. At least three 20-amp circuits should be provided.

Gas is not used at this level. Flat-top hot plates (not typical kitchen hot plates) that limit heat, a microwave oven and a refrigerator for teachers' use, are standard equipment. The microwave oven (not for student use) and hot plates are best located in the preparation room, for safety reasons.

Emergency shut-off controls for electrical service should be near the teacher's station, not far from the door, and not easily accessible to students.

A room exhaust fan will be needed when an investigation or demonstration creates smoke or an unpleasant odor. Exhaust fans are often installed on the roof or in place of a windowpane.

Lighting and Darkening Rooms (K–2)

Many researchers have documented that the best light for learning is natural light. A bright elementary classroom needs at least 50 foot-candles per square foot of floor surface and 75 to 100 foot-candles at the work surface. Lighting design must be handled carefully to avoid washing out projected images while providing enough light to enable students to see their tabletops. If computers are to be used in the room,

Bulletin boards that roll across the window

directional diffusers are recommended, and the down lighting on the work surface can be provided by three-tube parabolic fluorescent fixtures with switches that allow the room to be darkened in stages from front to back. Pendant, indirect fluorescent fixtures supplemented by compact, low-voltage downlights also work well in rooms with computers, but not as well with projectors.

Room darkening can be accomplished with blinds or shades. At this grade level, blinds are probably sufficient to darken the room for video projection. Some new schools are being constructed with bulletin boards that are rolled across the windows to darken the room. The

Blinds

Shades at a greenhouse door

Room Sizes: Classroom 33' × 32'9" (1,081 SF)
(10m × 10m = 100m^2)
Prep/Storage: 18' × 32' 9" (590 SF)
(5.5m × 10m = 55m^2)

NOTE: Separate dedicated science lab/classrooms for grades K–2 and 3–5 with shared prep/storage space that also serves as a "mud room" for outdoor activities.

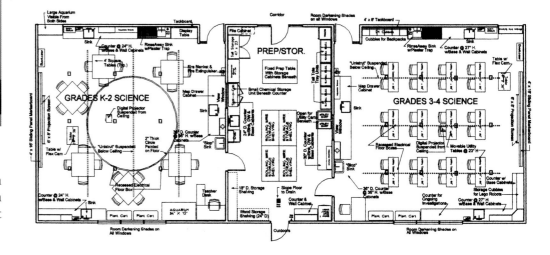

front row of lights in the instructional area can be wired so that they can be turned off when projection is needed, but students need light to take notes or see their paper.

Computers, charger, and wireless hub on wheels

Computers (K–2)

Today, connectivity is the norm. New schools are almost universally built with wireless networks. Students are learning to do research, electronically, from very early grades. They gain access from flexible banks of laptops or smaller word processing hardware. It is not recommended that classroom space be limited by many fixed computer stations, because that creates both space and safety problems. Laptops and smaller hand-held computers can be used virtually anywhere, but should be kept away from the faucets. Lockable laptop storage carts, which allow the units to be recharged when not in use, can include a printer and a wireless network hub. Provide floor space for the cart when planning the room layout.

Furnishings (3–5)

Classroom needs are somewhat different for grades 3–5 students, not only because the students are taller than younger students, but because their developmental needs are different and the curriculum is more de-

manding. In the upper elementary grades, it is even more important for science classes to be held daily.

The arrangement of the science room should be similar to that for the younger elementary students. However, at the fourth- and fifth-grade levels, students often attempt large and long-term projects and conduct independent investigations. Because these activities may involve building tall structures on the floor, ample floor space and storage space for use between classes should be provided.

For information and details on the following, consult the earlier section on furnishings.

Sinks (3–5)

Perimeter countertops at student height should have one sink for every four or five students. Provide one large (15 × 25 × 10 inch) sink and an adjacent 6- to 8-foot section of counter space, 36 inches high, for the teacher's use. Every sink should have hot and cold water. At least one must have wrist blade handles and be accessible to students with disabilities.

"Rinse away" sink

Standard, stainless steel, single- or double-bowl kitchen sinks (15 × 15 inches), with fairly deep bowls at least 8 inches deep, may be used by students. They should have tall, swiveling, aerated faucets, and one of them should have a dual, hands-free eyewash. Another possibility is the "rinse away" sink: a molded fiberglass sloping top with raised edges and curved corners that drains to an integral sink. These units are ideal for messy cleanups and may provide the best location for a hand-held body drench that can also

Plaster trap

be used as a sprayer to clean up the sink. A plaster trap to catch sand or gravel that may otherwise be washed down the drain is a good idea. However, some plaster traps may not fit under 27-inch-high cabinets.

Work Space (3–5)

For upper elementary students, 21- to 23-inch-high table heights and 27-inch-high countertop heights are appropriate. At this level, countertops are usually plastic laminate, but if the science curriculum is going to include dyes or caustic materials, the more expensive resin top may be worth the higher cost. Consider also the use of phenolic resin tops, which come in different colors, and are less costly than the epoxy resin. Varying the seating height will help accommodate all students. Since science laboratory casework manufacturers do not usually provide cabinets for 27-inch-high counters (29 inches is the standard), some custom casework may be necessary. Again, flat-topped tables that can be moved easily and rearranged into a number of configurations are recommended. A good size for two-student tables is 24 by 48 inches. If apparatus rods are to be used, sockets may be provided for them in the countertops or tables, because standard plastic laminate countertops are too thick (1 ½ inches) to accommodate most "C-clamp" apparatus rods.

Chairs or stools without backs will provide adequate seating.

Storage (3–5)

As teams plan storage for this level, it is important to establish the guidelines for what will be stored and how much. The general answer is: "As little as possible." Guidelines for limited inventories can be found in the NSTA series on safety.

Each type of chemical or piece of equipment requires its own type of storage. Alcohol, acids and bases, and

Library card catalog unit

chemicals that might be potentially toxic (including cleaning materials) each require their own specialized separate storage facilities. So most schools opt to use these chemicals only in a designated science lab or discovery center, and not to distribute them among general classrooms, which won't have the right type of cabinets or security. Flammables should be stored in an appropriately sized, UL-approved, locked flammables cabinet. Corrosives such as acids and bases should be stored in a separate locked corrosives cabinet.

Base cabinets should have several configurations of drawers and doors, and one or more adjustable shelves inside. A 30- to 36-inch-wide knee space should be provided below some lowered counters, for student workstations. Map drawer units are often useful, but the countertops above them will have to be deeper than normal, usually at least 30 inches to allow for the storage of reasonably sized posters or maps. Provide tall storage cabinets, wall cabinets with solid doors, and bookshelves similar to those used in the younger grades. The appropriate mounting height for wall cabinets in this space is 45 inches from the floor for students and 54 inches for adults.

Display Space (3–5)

Ceiling hooks, a 1-inch-diameter steel pipe or an industrial strut system suspended from suitable structures above the ceiling tiles will provide places to hang various items. Each hook should have at least a 50-pound capacity, and the pipe or strut should hold at least 200 pounds per foot.

Utilities, Lighting and Darkening Rooms (3–5)

In general, provide the same wiring, utilities, and lighting as the room for kindergarten through second grade, including a room exhaust fan and GFI protection on every electrical circuit.

Computers (3–5)

The upper elementary student will have more need for computers, and will use them for more purposes. But the previous recommendations, which include wireless connectivity, flexibility, and the ability to move them around as needed, still apply. More than a decade ago, schools were spending significant portions of their budget trying to channel all video, internet, and other computer use through supervised media sites. As computer use becomes more varied and pervasive, it is clear that this is not a job that can be handled by hardware alone. Software, teacher professional development and training, and well-enforced school policies are all parts of a comprehensive internet security policy, and it is probable that

any hardware investment that promises to provide internet security will be dated as soon as it is in place. (See Chapter 2.)

Teacher's Space

In addition to the table or cabinet for demonstrations, a desk with some shelves and a file cabinet in a room corner, or a desk in the preparation room, can serve as a "home space" for the science teacher. This area should be off-limits to the students. Make a telephone, electrical power, and a computer network port available at the desk. Many classrooms with networked computers keep a fast, powerful printer at the teacher's desk for use by the entire class. It is not recommended that printing jobs be sent out of the classroom.

Preparation and Storage Areas for K–5

Teachers need space to prepare activities at the beginning of the day for the different classes that will visit the science room. For kindergarten through second-grade classes, this area should contain base cabinets with counters at adult height, a sink, and space for several rolling utility carts used to move chemicals and equipment in and out of the classroom. A refrigerator and a microwave oven are desirable. If windows occupy much of the exterior wall of the science room, provide additional storage space in the preparation area. Tote-tray storage units and cabinets of various sizes, with adjustable shelves and some lower cabinets with drawers allow teachers to store the items related to a particular lesson in a single container that can be pulled out at the appropriate time. A recycled library card

catalog or an industrial bin unit can be useful for storing the many small items that may be used in an elementary program in labeled compartments.

For grades 3–5, a separate preparation room next to the science room is needed for an effective science program that provides students with the concrete learning experiences required to learn about the natural world. Many K–5 science programs utilize hands-on materials kits, which require special open storage areas. Storage for these special kits should be planned for in the regular classroom, in a special storage room, or placed in the science discovery room. A view window between the preparation room and science room facilitates supervision of students. The room should have base and wall cabinets of various sizes; one or two tall, compartmentalized storage cabinets; a desk with a telephone and electrical and network connections; and counter space with a large sink, and a spark-free refrigerator with an icemaker. The storage space needs open shelves, where the prepared materials for another class can be safely stored. In seismically active areas, installing lips on the shelves will help prevent breakage and accidents. Adequate ventilation and safety equipment are required. Storage rooms provide needed security and specialized storage for large, expensive, or sensitive equipment.

Hazardous materials should be very limited at this age level. But dilute acids for rock identification and alcohol are often included in inventories, so it is important to recognize that they need special, secure cabinets. A secure cabinet in the preparation area, 3 feet by 3 feet, for the lower grades and larger for the upper grades will suffice. If flammables, such as alcohol, are used, an appropriate storage cabinet should be available. In some cases, depending on the types and amounts of chemicals the curriculum calls for, a separate, secure, ventilated, chemical storeroom may be needed. However, a cabinet containing flammables should never be vented. Flammables, such as alcohol, must be stored in either a UL-approved flammable storage can or small cabinet. Corrosives should not be stored in a flammables cabinet, but in a specifically designed corrosives cabinet.

Preparation and storage space for grades K–2 and grades 3–5 can be shared successfully if the location is appropriate and sufficient space is provided for concurrent use.

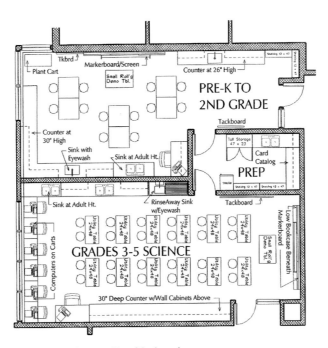

Elementary science suite with shared prep room

CHAPTER 5

Designing Facilities for the Middle School (6–8)

Key ideas in this chapter:

- Make science facilities the core that is accessible from each wing.
- Recommended space for the middle school laboratory/classroom is 60 square feet per student with a maximum of 24 students for any one class.
- Additional space is needed for multiple courses taught in same room, for technology, and for ADA requirements.
- Laboratory/classroom designs allow greater flexibility and encourage more concrete laboratory activities, which lead to greater depth of understanding.
- Planning for project-based learning and long-term student projects requires careful planning and designs that support both curriculum and instruction.

While most trends in middle school curricula emphasize integrating subjects, they also provide specialists who teach science. This means that students in the middle grades must change classes several times a day, even though research and best practice encourages small communities of learners. A high-quality middle school science program requires science classrooms with safe, well-designed laboratory space, and school designers must consider the distance students will have to travel to these classes. Trying to balance high quality science facilities with smaller, integrated subject subunits (sometimes called pods or houses) creates

challenges for facility planners and designers.

In traditional construction, science facilities were clustered in one wing of the school, bringing plumbing, gas, ventilation, and specialized fire protection together and reducing construction costs. In middle schools today, the "house" curriculum model is gaining popularity. In this model, the large student body is divided into smaller groups that share the same teachers for all of their basic subjects, and each group has its own classroom for most of these subjects.

Building a school to accommodate teaming can be much more expensive, because it requires that science rooms, storage rooms, and other science facilities be replicated in each cluster. Some of this expense can be avoided by making the science facilities part of the central core of the building, easily accessible from each wing of the school (see diagram on page 7). A building so designed can function in either curricular model, because the wings can be used to house the different teams or the different disciplines. If the science rooms must be decentralized and distributed among the houses, clustering rooms that need running water, such as science, fine arts, industrial arts, and consumer science rooms, with custodial closets and the cafeteria will help reduce costs. It is also important to plan ahead for storage facilities near the point of use; transporting

Technology in the laboratory

chemicals and other types of equipment can create dangerous situations.

Easy access to outside instructional sites is highly recommended. Field investigations and gardening activities provide concrete learning experiences about the natural world and should be integrated into the science curriculum.

Grouping Facilities for Integration

Whether the goal is to have separate departments, to team teach, or to be able to accommodate any model, planners will want to consider opportunities for integrating other subjects with science by grouping several facilities for science with related subjects such as math, applied sciences, and technology.

Applied science, such as engineering activities, can be integrated within a science program. Some schools require students to construct projects using scientific analysis and design to create a device, such as a miniature car, or robot using the resources of the career/technical area. Clean computer rooms with access to computer-aided drafting and design programs (CADD) are often located immediately adjacent to the technical education area. Locating these areas adjacent to the science core can enhance both programs.

Mathematics is the field most commonly integrated with science. When mathematics classrooms are located near the science area, interrelated projects that combine the two subjects can be developed and carried out in the science department's student project area. Mathematics and technology programs especially benefit, because of their increased emphasis on hands-on activities in recent years. Research provides evidence that integrating mathematics and science improves student performance in mathematics (Judson and Sawada 2000).

Media production facilities also provide excellent opportunities for integration with the sciences. Student teams can develop and produce media programs, using equipment and resources from the science area and technology from the media center. With imagination, almost any room in the school can be designed as a potential location from which to broadcast to the rest of the school. This topic is treated more in depth in Chapter 2.

Finally, if family and consumer science, formerly known as home economics, is located close to a science room, joint projects and investigations in life science can be conducted in either space.

Space Requirements

Class size is an important design factor, because it helps determine the amount of space and number of lab stations that will be needed. To accommodate current technology needs and teaching practices, a good middle school science room will generally require a minimum of 60 square feet per student for a combination laboratory/classroom, or 1440 square feet for a class of 24 students.

The 2006 NSTA position statement on laboratory science recommends a maximum class size of 24 students in the middle school. The 2000 NSTA position statement on Safety and School Science Instruction states the following:

The maximum number of occupants in a laboratory teaching space shall be based on the following:

1. the building and fire safety codes
2. occupancy and load limits
3. design of the laboratory teaching facility
4. appropriate supervision and the special needs of students

See Appendices G and H for NSTA Position Statements on Laboratory Science and Safe Science.

Additional space of at least 15 square feet is needed for each individual computer station or instructional equipment such as an interactive electronic marker board. An additional space of 20 square feet is needed to accommodate a lab station for a student with disabilities. At least 10 square feet per student is needed for teacher preparation space and storage space. Space is also needed for conducting and storing longer-term student projects.

A ceiling height of 10 feet is desirable for a science room. The rooms should have at least two exits and doorways that accommodate students with physical disabilities.

There are several reasons why the middle school science classroom requires more space than the elementary science classroom. To begin with, student lab stations in middle school are larger. Each middle school student needs about 30 inches of horizontal work surface to safely conduct science activities. Because activities are more prolonged and projects may extend over many class periods, space is needed where group and individual projects can be left in place for several days or weeks.

Depending on the size of the school, at least one science room per grade level and one for every 120 students will be needed.

The Combination Laboratory/Classroom

Science rooms at the middle school level may be generic, allowing an integrated science program to be taught in any room, or they may be specialized for single field science disciplines. The trend is toward designing for flexibility, which allows changes in space allocation as well as future curriculum and technology needs.

Two models for middle-level science classrooms have proven particularly practical. Both are combination laboratory/classrooms and both provide flexibility for various types of instruction if adequate space is provided.

1. *Movable Lab Stations Design*. This design allows furniture to be moved to accommodate either laboratory or classroom activities. Sinks and utilities are located along the perimeter of the room. This room arrangement allows for a variety of instructional strategies and techniques and configurations for laboratory and classroom work.
2. *Fixed Lab Stations Design*. This design has a room with fixed laboratory stations and a designated classroom area. This arrangement may require more floor space than a flexible room, because it has separate zones for each type of activity. This design does allow for more efficient use of the instructional time because no furniture needs to be moved as students move back and forth between lab and class activities.

The greatest advantage of these two arrangements is that they provide ongoing access to laboratory activities for each class. Research has shown that up to 50% more hands-on science is taught in combination laboratory/classrooms (West, Motz, and Biehle 2000).

An important design consideration in either case is the room's ability to accommodate each type of instruction well. During non-lab instruction in the classroom area, all students often need to face the instructor or the marker board. During laboratory activities, the teacher must have easy supervision of the students at their lab stations.

For any room layout, always allow unobstructed aisle space of at least 4 feet between a counter or table and the areas set aside for general seating. There should be 8 feet between the front wall of the classroom and the first tables. An overcrowded room is a serious safety hazard. See Chapter 3 for linkage between overcrowding and increased accident rates.

Movable Lab Stations Arrangement

In this design, sinks and utilities are located on the perimeter counters or in service islands in the middle of the lab area. Students can use the movable laboratory tables for both general classroom and laboratory work.

For example, two 60-inch long × 24-inch wide tables, each seating two students on a side, can form each lab station. The tables, which are flat-topped, can be grouped to form flat surfaces and rearranged to suit a variety of activities throughout the room. To avoid the necessity of moving the tables when changing from a discussion format to a laboratory format, separate 1 or 2 student, desk-height, flat-topped tables can be used for the "classroom" activities and taller laboratory tables used for the laboratory activities (see diagram).

Each group of four students has use of a sink; a source of heat, such as a hot plate; electric power for equipment and computers; and network connections.

Movable Lab Stations With Perimeter Utilities

This design provides the maximum flexibility and makes the most efficient use of space.

Two Science Lab/Classrooms With Shared Small Group Space

Room sizes: Lab/CR 29' × 28' + 22'6" × 36'6" (1,652 SF)
(9m × 8.5m + 6.9m × 11.1m = 153.6m²)
Small Group Space: 2 @ 16' × 12'3" (196 SF Each; 392 SF Total)
(2 @ 4.9m × 3.7m; 18.25m² Each; 36.5m² Total)

NOTE: These two generously sized middle school lab/classrooms are shown in two different possible furniture arrangements.

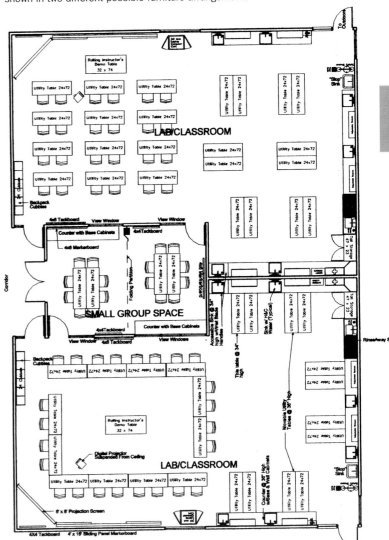

The 60-inch long tables are placed adjacent to the counter to form the lab stations. The sinks should be installed in such a way that when the tables are drawn up to the counters there will be enough space between the tables for students to access the sinks safely and easily. A surface-mounted "raceway" may be installed above the counter's backsplash to bring in electric outlets at regular intervals along the counter.

An advantage of the movable furniture with perimeter service lab/classroom arrangement is that the furniture can be arranged in a number of configurations to suit the needs of a particular lesson. All fixed casework is located at the perimeter; leaving a large, flexible, open space for a wide variety of science experiences. This movable furniture approach is, generally, less expensive to construct than other alternatives because fixed furniture is more expensive than movable furniture. One disadvantage of movable lab tables is that providing electrical power to table locations other than adjacent to the perimeter counters can be very challenging. Another disadvantage is the lost instructional time due to moving furniture to different configurations for either different types of activities during the same class, or if the next period's class is a difference course and requires different equipment or materials.

Movable Lab Tables With Fixed Freestanding Service Islands

This laboratory/classroom design provides access to power and utilities in the middle of the room. Laboratory tables are moved to the islands when lab activities are used. If the room is large enough, the islands may be installed

A flexible lab/classroom in the classroom mode

A flexible lab/classroom in laboratory mode

at one end of the room. This design allows the teacher to see all students during laboratory activities, but has less flexibility than the perimeter utilities design due to the fixed islands in the middle of the room. However, the classroom area provides a flexible area. Proper placement of the islands is critical to provide adequate space for not only the laboratory tables, but a safe 4-foot space between the tables and any other furniture.

Trifacial Service Islands

Trifacial (triple table hub) service islands with large, deep sinks are six-sided units that do not include built-in work surfaces. Instead, laboratory tables are drawn up to the three longer sides, creating work areas for groups of four students. Students share the central sink, which is accessed from the three narrow sides of the hub. Electrical outlets, and communications data wiring are provided along the three longer sides.

Each island can accommodate 12 students at either three large tables or six small ones.

Two islands thus provide laboratory workspace for 24 students. A disadvantage is that fixed furniture in the middle of the room decreases the instructional flexibility and the water source is close to electrical outlets. Selection of service islands that will remain stable for decades is important.

The movable tables may also be combined and arranged in other configurations. Tables with electrical "pigtails" and outlets can be plugged into the trifacial unit, providing power and data wiring at the far end of the table for computers and other electrical equipment.

Square Service Islands

Small square islands provide utilities and a sink. Lab tables are drawn up to each side of the island during lab activities. Eight students share a central sink. Electrical outlets and computer data wiring can be provided. Three service islands provide laboratory workspace for 24 students. If the room has the recommended space, then the service islands can be located at one end of the room with the classroom in another area.

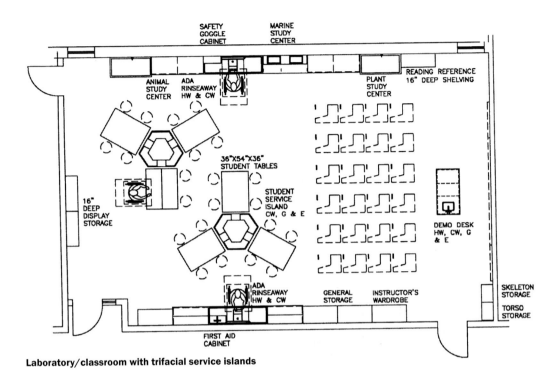

Laboratory/classroom with trifacial service islands

Trifacial service island

Fixed Lab Stations Arrangement

The two types of fixed lab stations are perimeter and freestanding. There are advantages and disadvantages with both types. Both require adequate space to be safe and instructionally effective. Designs with fixed freestanding lab stations in the middle of the room tend to require more space.

Fixed Perimeter Lab Stations

Fixed perimeter lab station designs include "fingers or piers" and "banjos" designs that extend into the classroom from the perimeter counters.

The "banjos" design generally does not provide at least 30 inches per student of horizontal work surface area needed for safe science activities. Another hazard with the "banjos" design is that it creates spatial traps where a student may be unable to readily escape in an emergency. Therefore, the "banjos" design should be avoided.

The fixed perimeter "pier" or "finger" design allows for a more efficient use of the instructional time as previously discussed because furniture does not need to be moved with changes of activities or classes. This lack of ability to rearrange work surfaces could be considered a disadvantage. However, the classroom area can provide such flexibility if adequate space is allocated. Some advantages of the fixed perimeter "finger" lab station design are easy supervision of all students and ready availability of all utilities.

A separate classroom area provides seating for the nonlab portion of the curriculum. Seating here can be flat tablet armchairs or tables in a classroom format for one or two students with chairs or stools.

A potentially dangerous trap (the "banjo" design)

Fixed Freestanding Lab Stations

There are variations of this design. The best version of this design provides ample workspace with the utilities located so that they don't interfere with the work area. Some fixed island lab stations have small sinks in the middle that are not large enough to wash glassware, are difficult to reach making them less safe, and should be avoided. Designs that use large fixed islands can provide sinks of adequate size on the perimeter counters. Other fixed island lab stations, typically round or octagonal, have inadequate horizontal work surface area for students to work safely and should be avoided. Some freestanding islands have only electricity with sinks located on perimeter counters. These will provide lab stations for six students.

Some advantages of the fixed lab station design are easy supervision of all students and ready availability of all utilities at the utility islands. Disadvantages include inflexibility (the islands will be fixed in their locations for the life of the facility, limiting the possible arrangements of furniture within the space), sinks that are too small or in the middle of a large island, and greater expense of construction.

Fixed Freestanding Long Lab Stations

This design provides long lab benches with multiple students on each side. The lab bench is usually a long rectangular bench or a series of connected octagons. A disadvantage of this design is that there can be a great distance between the teacher and a student who may have a safety problem and needs the teacher's immediate help. There is a sink either in the middle or end of the bench or the sinks can be located on the perimeter counter. Large fixed freestanding furniture requires more space and is the least flexible for laboratory activities. However, the adjacent classroom area can provide the flexibility for nonlab activities. Utility racks that often run along the tops of these long lab benches should be avoided because they obstruct the teacher's ability to supervise.

Electrical outlets for any lab station design should not be located on a surface where the electrical cords either interfere with the lab activities or on the facia where the cord hangs over the edge to get caught by someone's hand and pulling the equipment over the edge.

At least one lab station for a student with

Laboratory/classroom with trifacial work stations

disabilities should be provided in each laboratory/classroom; such lab stations should be integrated with the other lab stations in the space to ensure inclusion of all students in the laboratory activities. This lab station should be located for safe exit during an emergency.

Furnishings

The following describes the needs of a flexible laboratory/classroom with movable tables and perimeter counters, sinks, and utilities. With a few exceptions, the text also applies to laboratory/classrooms with fixed stations.

Sinks

Sinks for student investigations should be fairly wide and deep and equipped with swiveling gooseneck faucets, with vacuum breakers, that allow students to fill pails and large vessels under the faucet. The sink size should be at least $15 \times 15 \times 10$ inches. A good rule of thumb is to provide one sink for four students. Resin sinks are preferable, because they resist chemical degradation. However, if corrosive chemicals are seldom used, stainless steel sinks with deep bowls may be acceptable, but are usually more costly than epoxy resin types. Hot water is required at all sinks and student lab stations, for hygienic reasons.

Faucets should come equipped with aerators. Serrated nozzles adapted for the attachment of hoses are an option, but they cause an increase in water pressure and splatter water around the sink, and are not needed for middle school science activities. When aerators are not furnished, teachers often respond by attaching a length of rubber hose to the serrated nozzles to alleviate the splashing problem. However, contaminated water can be drawn up into the water system through the hose.

It is also an advantage to have a large, deep ($24 \times 24 \times 12$ inch) sink with hot and cold water and adjacent counter space for various purposes, such as cleaning extra-large containers.

Two types of sinks that are very handy in middle school laboratories:

- A "rinseaway" sink, which has a 6- or 10-foot-long molded fiberglass tray with raised edges that slopes down to a sink basin, facilitating the cleanup of plant and animal specimens and messy items. This tray accommodates investigations that need running water and a drain and require long-term storage. The sink may be equipped with a garbage disposal or a plaster trap to catch sand or gravel. A pullout face shower on a hose can be used for cleaning up at the sink, but cannot substitute for a dual hands-free eyewash. (See photo, p. 51.)

- A deep, porcelain-enameled, wall mounted janitor's slop sink, which is very useful for cleaning large containers and for filling deep vessels with water. Avoid the typical fixed faucet and opt for a swiveling, gooseneck one, because the fixed faucet reduces the open area of the bowl.

Slop sink

Glassware drying racks come in various sizes, and are often useful if installed above the perimeter sinks. Mount each rack so that it drains directly into the sink rather than down the wall. Request a high backsplash to protect the wall, so the drying rack can be mounted high enough above the sink to clear the faucet. The perimeter electrical raceway, if used, should not pass under the drying rack. Some teachers use a standard kitchen-counter drying rack, which can be removed and stored beneath the sink when not in use.

Work Space

For work space, counters 30 or 36 inches high from the floor and tables 30 or 36 inches high are convenient for most students. It may be advantageous to vary the counter height some-what, in order to accommodate all students.

Countertops should be made of epoxy resin or a similar chemical-resistant material. They should be caulked between the backsplash and the wall, and along any other joints, using clear silicone. Backsplashes 4 inches high are standard. Backsplashes should also run along the counter beside any tall cabinets and other surfaces that interrupt or are set into the counter space.

Movable laboratory tables should be at least 60 inches long—long enough to seat two students on one side—and 24 inches deep. These may be used with chairs or stools in the classroom area. The legs at each end of resin-topped tables subtract about 6.5 inches from the width of the knee space under the table. The knee space of a 48-inch table will usually be only 21 inches per student. For stand-up purposes, the height of the table should be 36 inches.

For durability, choose an oak- or steel-framed laboratory table with a resin top, available from most manufacturers. Sockets can be installed for laboratory apparatus. Check the connection between the leg and the table frame for durability, as the tables will be subject to abuse during their lifetime. Tables constructed with lag bolts may come apart when they are moved. A better design bolts the leg to a steel plate set into the frame. Stronger still is a design that bolts the leg to the plate using a bolt that passes completely through the leg and is held in place with a nut and washer. Any tables taller than 30 inches should be equipped with H-shaped stretchers that provide extra support for the legs.

The resin tops come in various colors. Col-ored resin is more expensive than the standard black, but helps to brighten up the space.

Teacher's Demo Table

Many teachers prefer to use a movable demonstration table, because science is no longer taught with only teacher demonstrations. Instead, students are actively engaged in learning science by "doing science." Teachers also feel that a fixed table at the front of the room separates them from the students and interferes with students' access to the board. A fixed demonstration table is expensive and also defines a space 8 feet deep across the front of the room that is perceived as unavailable for uses other than the teacher's demonstrations. In a 30-foot wide room, this might be as much as 17% of the total floor space. A mobile teacher's table can have base cabinets or drawers, knee space, its own water and gas, and an electric cord, enabling it to be used nearly anywhere in the room.

Storage

It is desirable to provide base cabinets and countertops along at least two walls for storage and additional workspace. All upper shelves and wall cabinets should have base cabinets beneath them, for safety reasons and as an ADA requirement. High quality cabinets, such as those made of hardwood plywood (wood millwork only), should be a priority. Avoid particleboard assembly for casework, because this material is affected by moisture and generally will not withstand the abuse of a middle school environment.

Stretcher-reinforced table frame

Movable teacher's demo table

Every room should have several types of base cabinets. Consider units with drawers of various sizes, drawer and door units with adjustable shelves, and tote-tray cabinets that allow the teacher to store all of the items for an activity in one bin. Tote-tray cabinets are also useful for storing student kits that can be brought out at laboratory time.

Wall cabinets with solid doors rather than glass-fronted doors are either 12 or 15 inches deep, and should be mounted about 18 inches above the countertop. Bookshelves should be at least 10 inches deep and should be adjustable to different heights. Shelves over 30 inches long should be made of one-inch thick hardwood plywood.

Cabinets of various heights and depths will be needed for specialized storage of items such as rock and mineral samples for Earth science, and microscopes and glassware for biology and life science, as well as stands for aquariums, terrariums, and plants. Physical science makes extensive use of materials and equipment of varying sizes, types, and weights.

Allow space in the classroom for use of equipment such as laboratory carts, laptop computer storage carts, a human skeleton on a stand with rollers and its special storage cabinet, an animal

Portable skeleton cabinet

A variety of useful drawer sizes

cage, and a stream table. Teachers may choose to integrate recycling into classroom activities by including large storage bins with lids. It is also important to provide storage for student's coats and book bags to keep these items out of the way during lab work.

No cabinet of any size should have doors with glass that are below five feet. The glass in this type of cabinet is typically broken within a short amount of time after installation and represents a significant hazard. Laminated safety glass is recommended to avoid serious accidents.

Display Space

Marker boards and tack boards are hung at roughly countertop height that is 32 to 36 inches for students and 36 inches for adults. Dry erase marker boards have taken the place of chalkboards, because chalk dust can be harmful to both computers and people. However, there is also concern about the toxicity of permanent markers, and manufacturers' information should be studied. Sliding, multiple-panel boards can be used to extend a marker board without requiring more wall space.

The space behind a marker board can be used for storage or for book shelving by recess-

ing shelves into the wall. The sliding panels of the marker board cover this storage until it is accessed. Drawers below the marker board can add significantly useful storage capacity. Such storage requires thickening of the wall behind the board.

Sliding panel marker board with storage

The instructional focus area may support a variety of presentation formats, including video, DVD, slides, projected microscope images, and overhead projection. Since a moving teacher's table is frequently used, controls, including light dimmers, may be installed in a wall panel that is easily accessible to the teacher. Electronic control systems, with handheld remote controls, can be installed to allow the teacher to control lighting, sound, and projection systems from anywhere in the room.

A projection screen should be mounted on a wall or the ceiling. The screen size should be 6 feet by 8 feet. If the screen is to be mounted on a high ceiling, include an additional "tail" of material at the top of the screen; the bottom of the screen will then be approximately

Vertical dividers for flat objects

3 feet above the floor. Mounting a projection screen on a diagonal in a corner of the room can allow use of the marker board at the same time the screen is employed.

Marker boards generally do not make good projection screens, because their surfaces do not reflect light well.

A variety of interactive electronic marker board systems have been developed recently that allow the user to input data to a computer program using special markers that transmit their movements to a sensor in the system. These can be used in conjunction with a digital projection system to enhance instructional materials. Many of these systems consist of a screen, either mounted on the wall, or on a movable frame; others have sensing devices that mount on an ordinary marker board with suction cups. If use of one of these systems is envisioned, space should be provided for the screen.

Ceiling hooks, a 1-inch diameter steel pipe or an industrial strut system suspended from suitable structures above the ceiling tiles will provide a place to hang demonstration and experimental apparatus. Each hook should have at least a 50-pound capacity, and the pipe or strut should hold at least 200 pounds per foot. It is advisable to over-design the suspension system.

Utilities

All circuits (20 amp) or electrical outlets in the lab/classroom should have ground-fault interrupter (GFI) protection, to protect occupants from shocks. In order to avoid overloading circuits and eliminate the need for extension cords, overlapping wires, and plug-in outlet

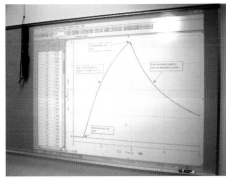
Interactive electronic scanning device mounted on a marker board

extenders, lab/classrooms and preparation areas should be equipped with plenty of duplex electrical outlets on several circuits. These should be available at frequent intervals along walls that have counters and cabinets. One duplex outlet for every two students at the laboratory stations is recommended. Three duplex outlets are desirable along the front or instructional area wall, and three on any wall that lacks cabinets. Outlets should not be placed beneath counters because electrical cords should not hang over the edge. At least one hard-wired network connection should be provided in each room.

DC power can be provided using small dry cells such as 9-volt batteries (never automotive storage batteries). The teacher may also use a portable DC converter that plugs into the AC outlet and is protected by a circuit breaker.

Providing outlets for electric power, cable television, and computer networking in an appropriate location will make it possible to connect a digital projector for viewing internet sites, videotapes, DVDs, or images from a microscope or flex-cam.

It is never safe to run wires or conduits across a classroom floor in an attempt to supply power for equipment that may be set up there. However, there are several ways to provide electric power to locations in the center of the room.

One example is pull-down, retractable electric cords, similar to those in automotive shops. These can be arranged as multiple outlets. The primary drawbacks of this system are the dangling overhead wires and the tendency of the retractors to pull the cords back quickly, damaging ceiling tiles. Recessed floor outlets can bring utilities to the center of the room. Floor boxes should comply with Underwriters Laboratories (UL) water exclusion requirements and should never be located close to water sources or areas where water is used.

Care should be taken to investigate the characteristics with respect to safety of any alternative to wall outlets.

Two-way communication between the classroom and the office is essential. Teachers need and want good phone communications from their laboratory/classroom to the school's main office. Phones should be provided in every science classroom, preparation room, and workroom/office.

Middle school programs should not require gas, and gas service is not recommended. There are specialized hot plates available that have controlled heat and use minimal power. Warming candles can also be used for heat. In the rare case that a higher level of heat is needed for a demonstration or special program, a butane stove or Bunsen burner can be used and then securely stored. If central gas is used, it should be located at the perimeter, near the sinks. The room should have a button-activated emergency shut-off valve. Place emergency shut-off controls for electrical service, and gas near the teacher's station, not far from the door, and not too easily accessible to students.

Other utilities, such as vacuum and deionized or distilled water are used so rarely at this level that the cost of installing a central system for any of them is usually prohibitive. Many classrooms can share portable vacuum pumps. Remember to provide storage space for these units in a preparation or storage room. Distilled water can be purchased in bulk, or a small still can be set up in a preparation room. Water demineralizers or deionizers are available for mounting on the wall above a sink. Water containers are filled using a hose connected to the faucet.

Lighting and Darkening Rooms

Research tells that students learn better in natural light. General light levels of at least 50 foot-candles per square foot of floor surface are required for general classroom and laboratory work, and 75 to 100 foot-candles at the work surface. Because glare from direct light sources interferes with images on projector screens and computer monitors, parabolic fluorescent fixtures with grids that direct the light straight down are often used in rooms that have computers.

Three-tube fixtures wired so that the middle tube is switched separately from the two outer tubes allow three levels of room lighting: three tubes lit, two tubes lit, and only one tube lit. Providing separate switches for each row of lights allows additional options for room darkening. For example, when images are being projected onto a screen at the front of the room, just the front row of lights might be off.

Indirect lighting has been used successfully in rooms that have computers. In this type of fixture, the light shines onto the ceiling, bounces back, and is diffused throughout the room, providing strong lighting levels at the work surface without producing a bright light that reflects off computer screens. These fixtures can also be three-tube fixtures that operate as described above.

The increased use of digital projectors, videocassette recorders, DVDs, and television images has complicated lighting design further. Projection screens tend to reflect all light, and a bright overall illumination produced by indirect fixtures may wash out the projected image.

Providing recessed, dimmable, compact fluorescent light fixtures as supplemental lighting throughout the room allows the teacher to turn off the more intense general lighting, and the down-lights provide the necessary desktop illumination for note taking. Lights mounted under wall cabinets can provide additional light that may be needed when students are conducting activities on side counters. If these wall cabinet lights are being considered for use during projector presentations, then care needs to be taken so that the lights do not shine directly into student's eyes in adjacent seats.

All of these lighting alternatives are more expensive than the traditional recessed, prismatic light troffer, but their use will become increasingly necessary over time.

A study of 100 fourth and fifth graders (Grocoff 1996) concluded that skylights provide

Rolling bulletin board darkens room

the most comfortable classroom lighting for students. The study tested fluorescent lights of various correlated color temperatures at two levels of illumination. The participants ranked a general illumination of 50 foot-candles more comfortable than that of 100 foot-candles and reported various physical and behavioral symptoms when light at the extreme color ranges was used.

5000K lamps with parabolic lenses may be used to provide a warm color that is closest to daylight, although 4100K lamps are acceptable substitutes.

The ability to darken the classroom includes the need to eliminate glare from sunlight, which, besides interfering with computer and projection use, hampers some investigations in physics, chemistry, and Earth science. For this purpose, one-inch miniblinds work well in general, but they are not sufficient for optics investigations that must be conducted in almost complete darkness. Rolling bulletin boards can be very effective for darkening rooms.

Room-darkening shades are available that block almost all the light from windows. They are made of a completely opaque material and have both edge and bottom tracks. Care should be taken in specifying room-darkening shades to avoid extremely wide units as the bottom rail of the shade may buckle and pull the material out of the sidetracks. Remember, too, that window-mounted exhaust fans let sunlight in around their edges, and windows into preparation rooms or in the classroom doors are yet another source of light. Room-darkening shades are fairly expensive and are needed only when near-total darkness is required. If necessary, only one science room could be so equipped, in order to keep costs down.

Computers

Counters on which desktop computers are to be permanently installed should be at table height and not higher than 32" and there should be knee space beneath them. Space and GFI-protected electric power will be needed to accommodate computers. Each desktop computer station takes up about 15 square feet,

Laptops with a wireless network can go anywhere

and a 20-amp GFI-protected electric circuit can service three computers. Surge protectors are also needed. Most new schools are being built with wireless computer networks, providing one

or two hard-wired data ports in every classroom. More commonly available, laptop computers can be used virtually anywhere, but should be kept away from the faucets and chemicals. Lockable laptop storage carts, which allow the units to be recharged when not

Computers, charger, printer, and wireless hub on wheels

in use, can include a printer and a wireless network hub. Provide floor space for the cart when planning the room layout.

When power outlets are beneath the counter or when tower units are used, leave a 2-inch-diameter hole with a rubber grommet in the countertop for the wire connections. There are two reasons for not installing computers on countertops near sinks, the more obvious being that computers can be damaged by water. The other is that standard countertops are too high for comfortable computer use.

Some schools have equipped their science classes with handheld computing devices or PDAs. Probe-ware manufacturers have adapted their units to connect to these

Technology keeps shrinking

units allowing great flexibility both within the lab/classroom and in remote locations. Newer handheld units can connect directly to a wireless network.

Workstations for Students With Disabilities

An appropriate work area for students with physical disabilities includes a sink accessible to a person in a wheelchair. The *ADA Accessibility Guidelines for Buildings and Facilities* (ADAAG) specifies a number of requirements, including maximum counter heights, reach ranges, adequate space for feet, and grasping and twisting limitations. These specifications are for adults, but ADAAG recommendations are available for younger students. See Appendix B.

For an adult, the top of the sink must not be mounted higher than 34 inches above the floor. Knee space of at least 27 inches high and a minimum of 30 inches wide are required; by necessity, the

An accessible workstation integrated with other workstations

sink depth will be no more than 6 ½ inches. Controls for the faucet must also comply with the ADA guidelines, which require lever or wrist-blade handles. The intent of the Americans with Disabilities Act (ADA) and the Individuals with Disabilities Education Act (IDEA) is to include students with disabilities with their peers, rather than segregating them at workstations remote from the class. At least one furniture manufacturer of utility islands produces a unit that meets ADAAG specifications.

Some schools use a mobile ADA workstation. It can have a gas bottle and includes a water supply operated by an electric pump, and an electric power cord that is plugged into an outlet, and a holding tank for wastewater that must be emptied regularly. It can be stationed anywhere and can be moved from room to room as needed. In order to make every room accessible, each room must have sufficient wall space, as well as cabinets and electrical outlets suitable for use with these mobile units.

Teacher's Space

Teachers need their own space for preparing lessons, making telephone calls, keeping essential papers and texts, and meeting with students. Some successful arrangements are:

- a teacher's desk in an alcove in a laboratory/classroom
- an individual office in a preparation room but not where chemicals are stored, as described below
- a space between two laboratory/classrooms
- an assigned space in a departmental office that has movable office partitions and a central meeting space for groups.

When teaching is done in teams, using integrated curricula, the group office arrangement may work best. In this type of arrangement, provide distinct spaces for each teacher, a meeting area where the team can plan as a group with one or two students, and a storage area for shared equipment.

At a minimum, each teacher should have a desk area with an electrical outlet, computer network connection, telephone, file cabinet, and storage cabinet, all arranged to indicate that it is private and off-limits to students. The teacher's space should not be located in a classroom that is shared with other teachers.

Some schools have located "slump spaces" where students and teachers can sit in comfortable chairs and relax near the teachers' office

A "slump space"

spaces. These allow "serendipitous interactions" among students and teachers that create learning opportunities outside the classroom.

Preparation and Storage Rooms

A preparation/equipment storeroom (10 sq ft per student) is essential at the middle school level, and it is most convenient if it is next to, and accessible from, the laboratory/classroom. All doors to the room should lock. Use the minimum space guidelines at the beginning of this chapter to size this space. A larger room located between two laboratory/classrooms can serve two teachers successfully. There are two types of storerooms: equipment/materials and chemical.

Whether separate or combined preparation and equipment storage rooms will be needed depends on the science program. A separate, secure chemical storage room may open off the preparation room.

The preparation/ equipment and materials storeroom should have base and wall cabinets, tall storage units, shelves that are no higher than eye level, and counter space. Floor space for laboratory carts is also needed; these can be stored in recesses beneath the counter. There

Utility cart stored beneath counter

should be a large sink with hot and cold water with a swivel faucet and aerator nozzle, and a glassware drying rack is often required. This is also a good place for a refrigerator with an icemaker, a microwave oven, and a dishwasher. Gas may be needed, depending on the curriculum. For some middle school programs, a fume hood is needed in the preparation room. A hood with glass sash on two sides can be shared between the prep room and the adjacent lab/classroom. A two-sided hood used this way should be able to be locked from the preparation room side to ensure security of chemicals and equipment.

A teacher's desk may be built into the counter space by installing a table-height 6-foot

Fume hood shared between prep room and lab/classroom

length of counter with knee space, adjacent file drawers and a 2-inch-diameter hole at the back of the counter for the computer wiring (unless power and data are in a raceway above the counter). Provide GFI-protected electrical circuits, at least one computer network hookup, and a telephone.

Locating the room so that it gives teachers access without going through a classroom is desirable, because it allows teachers who share the room to work without disrupting classes in the adjacent space. A view window into the adjacent laboratory/classrooms enables teachers to observe any activity in those rooms and lets students know when the teachers are in their office.

Equipment storage rooms provide needed security and specialized storage for large, expensive, or sensitive equipment. Programs and enrollments change more often in middle schools than at other levels, so it is prudent to preserve as much flexibility as possible by installing tall cabinets, wall cabinets, a variety of base cabinets with different sized drawers,

and open shelving. If the school curriculum integrates the sciences or offers alternating modules, centralized or movable storage units may be useful.

Hinged doors are preferable on the cabinets, because sliding doors waste about 3 inches of interior cabinet depth and can knock over bottles. Cabinets should have positive latches that can withstand seismic events without opening. Storage shelving of several depths is needed: 10 inches for books, 12 to 15 inches for multiple uses, and 18 to 24 inches for bulky items. A rule of thumb for shelving depths is: 12 inches for chemistry, 16 inches for biology/life science, and 22 inches for physics/physical science. Shelving is best mounted on standards that allow adjustment to different heights. Some standards can lock in place for use in seismic areas.

Shallow drawers for storing poster board are very popular with middle school teachers. Flat-stock drawer units will require a cabinet with at least a 36-inch-deep countertop. Cabinets that fit under 24- and 30-inch-deep counters have drawers that are only 21 and 27 inches deep, respectively. A cabinet with vertical dividers beneath a counter can store panels and other large, flat objects.

Rolling compact shelving units that require only one aisle for several banks of shelves are useful when space is at a premium and for schools where Earth, life, and physical sciences are integrated. These units tend to be expensive and add a significant structural load to the floor system.

Chemicals should be stored in either a separate, lockable/secure storeroom or in the preparation room in a locked cabinet that is

vented to the outside of the building, above the roofline, and away from air intakes. Chemicals should be stored safely. The flammables should be stored in a UL-approved flammables cabinet whether the cabinet is in a separate storeroom or not. Chemicals should be stored by category: acids stored separately from bases, with nitric acid stored separately from other acids, and so on. Corrosives should be stored in a locked corrosion-resistant cabinet vented to the outside of the building. Cabinets with metal shelves, metal shelf support clips or metal hinges are not appropriate.

In general, one can never have sufficient storage. A critical inventory of all existing items can determine whether some items are no longer used and might be discarded. In case of a fire or accident, a complete list of what is stored, together with material safety data sheets (MSDS), will be needed.

Student Project Areas

With science curricula becoming more inquiry-oriented and more directed toward individual and small-group work, there is an increasing need for space for long-term student projects. This space should be as close to the laboratory/classroom as possible. It is important to have a window between the two rooms or between the corridor and the student project room to facilitate supervision. A door from the corridor will allow students and teachers to use the project space without disrupting nearby classes.

Student project space has always been at

View windows between prep room and lab/classroom

Storage space for plant stands needs to be considered

a premium. One practical layout is to place base cabinets with countertops around the perimeter. A central-island work area made up of movable tables or additional base cabinets arranged back-to-back and covered with a resin countertop would make the space much more useful. Electric power with GFI-protected circuits and computer network connections should be installed along the perimeter and at the center island. Allow sufficient space between the perimeter counter and the center island so that students can access both areas. A minimum aisle should be 4

Student project space

to 5 feet wide. Surface area on which to store projects that require more than one class period to complete will be needed in the student project room; adjustable shelving of various depths is also useful. Ideally a room about

Student project space in a science magnet school

the size of a laboratory/classroom is needed to allow projects from multiple classes to be carried out and/or stored simultaneously.

References

Grocoff, P. N. 1996. *Effects of correlated color temperature on perceived visual comfort.* Doctoral dissertation, University of Michigan, College of Architecture and Urban Planning. (Available from University Microfilms, 1-800-521-3042.)

Judson, E., and D. Sawada. 2000. Examining the effects of a reformed junior high school science class on students' math achievement. *School Science and Mathematics* 100 (8): 419–425.

West, S., L. Motz, and J. Biehle. 2000. *Building state of the art science facilities.* NSTA National Conference, Saint Louis, Missouri.

CHAPTER 6

Designing Facilities for the High School (9–12)

Key ideas in this chapter:

- Making science facilities the core of a design allows more flexibility and choices.
- Integration provides other disciplines usage of the science resources.
- Combination laboratory/classroom designs allow greater flexibility and encourage more concrete laboratory activities, which lead to greater depth of understanding.
- Recommended space for the laboratory/classroom is 60 square feet per student with a maximum of 24 students for any one class.
- Combined laboratory/classrooms should be the basic, preferred model for designing high school science facilities.
- Direct planning for technology needs to be part of the initial design phase for facilities.

Computers in the lab/classroom

When we participate in a school building program, we create learning environments that will last for many decades. So a major principle of good science facilities planning is to avoid building for a single curricular model. Since continued change in educational trends is inevitable, any plans for science space should allow as much flexibility as possible in order to avoid the expense and considerable inconvenience of having to reconfigure the space at a later date.

Traditionally, the high school program, served by a fully equipped wing of science rooms, has emphasized divisions between departments. In part because construction costs are reduced when water, gas, and special ventilation systems are concentrated in a single area, the departmentalized model for high schools has remained the norm.

However, as schools have grown in recent years, educators have found that large schools are barriers to educational goals. Based on sound research about "smaller communities of learners," many high school programs have divided their large student bodies into smaller "houses" of 500 students or less. These operate as schools-within-schools, with faculty teams teaching only the students in their own houses. Each house has its own classrooms for social studies, English, mathematics, and other subjects, and students move less frequently through the larger school structure. But equipping each house with its own science area presents a considerable challenge to cost-conscious planning teams, since this normally requires that gas, water, ventilation systems and equipment be replicated in several areas in the school.

The dual goals of smaller communities of learners and efficient construction are not irreconcilable. One way schools have preserved the ability to use either departmentalized or "house" models, while keeping costs down and not sacrificing quality, is by placing their science facilities at the center of a "spoke" or pod configuration. This arrangement makes it possible to locate either the houses or separate departments in each wing, with the science department clustered at the center. The cost savings in equipment that is shared rather than duplicated can be as much as $100,000. It also allows future staff to reorganize space in ways that continue to serve the needs of the student body.

Easy access to outside instructional sites is highly recommended. Field investigations and school site ecological activities provide concrete learning experiences about the natural world and should be integrated into the science curriculum.

9–12

Grouping Facilities for Integration

Another important design consideration is clustering related facilities. Grouping science facilities together benefits from both teaching and the sharing of equipment and resources. The trend toward integration with other subjects brings the additional leverage of coordinating related programs with portions of the science

Student project space with power tools

curriculum and energizing subjects such as mathematics and the applied sciences.

Increasingly, high school science and technology curriculums are becoming integrated in the areas of engineering. Technology and design education classrooms are being placed near physics classrooms to allow students to plan and design engineering projects, then construct and carry them out using the facilities of the technical education labs.

Locating a mathematics classroom close to the science area allows students to reap the benefits from conversations and coplanning between science and mathematics teachers. Such collaboration is an advantage to the mathematics program because student performance increases when mathematics and science are integrated (Judson and Sawada 2000). It is also an advantage to the science program because mathematics is used throughout science. In addition, the mathematics program again benefits, because newer models for teaching mathematics emphasize inquiry and discovery applications, and space in the traditional mathematics classroom is often insufficient for those experiences. Projects that combine the two disciplines can be housed in the science department's student project area.

Finally, if family and consumer science (formerly known as home economics) is adjacent to the science area, some joint projects and investigations in the life sciences can be carried out in either space. Since cooking or use of foods in science lab/classrooms is strongly discouraged due to safety concerns, the teaming of these courses can maximize both.

Types of Science Rooms

In high school, science rooms are almost always specially designed with separate teaching spaces. As in the middle school, the increasing integration of science curricula makes it even more important to ensure that the school's facilities do not limit the types of subjects and strategies that can be used. Given sufficient

space, flexible furniture arrangements, and appropriate equipment, almost any type of science instruction can be possible in most spaces.

Some schools have designed generic laboratories that, with few exceptions, have everything necessary for any science course. This creates maximum curricular flexibility, since tomorrow's biology will have much more chemistry, and newer physics or physical science courses often integrate Earth science or chemistry elements. This approach has the advantage of allowing curricular changes and future enrollment growth that may require changes in the allocation of space. Placing extra conduits for utilities in the floors and walls during construction is an easy way to provide additional flexibility for expansion and future improvements.

The two most commonly used models for science rooms are

- separate laboratory and classroom space, and
- combination laboratory/classrooms.

Recent trends in science education strongly indicate that the combined lab/classroom should be the basic, preferred model. Significantly more "hands-on," exploratory and inquiry-based science teaching occurs in a combination space, since the students can move from discussion to hands-on activities and back again several times during the same class period (West, Motz, and Biehle 2000). Further, overcrowding in some schools has caused separate laboratory spaces to be used for nonscience classes when not being used for science, a practice that is both unsafe and greatly limits the science faculty's ability to set up and take down equipment between classes. Non-science faculties are not trained to supervise students in science lab/classrooms with all of the science equipment, materials, and utilities that are typically present in science rooms.

While an effective science room today is generally expected to accommodate work in all science disciplines, additional laboratories or lab/classrooms may be desired for specialized or advanced courses that require special equipment, fixtures, ventilation, dust collection system, or other resources.

Space Requirements

Class size is a critical design factor, because it helps determine the amount of space and number of workstations that will be needed. To safely accommodate current technology needs and teaching practices, a good high school science room will generally require a minimum of 60 square feet per student for a combination laboratory/classroom, 1,440 square feet for a class of 24 students.

The 2007 NSTA position statement on laboratory science recommends a maximum class size of 24 students in high school.

A built-in computer in a physics table

The 2000 NSTA position statement on Safety and School Science instruction states the following:

The maximum number of occupants in a laboratory teaching space shall be based on the following:

- the building and fire safety codes
- occupancy load limits
- design of the laboratory teaching facility
- appropriate supervision and the special needs of students

Plan additional space for the use and storage of various types of technology used in science instruction. If you plan to use a bank of laptops, an additional space of 15 square feet is needed for a laptop computer storage cart, and 20 square feet for a workstation to accommodate a student with disabilities. If you use instructional equipment, such as a movable interactive electronic marker board, an additional 15 square is needed. At least 10 square feet per student is needed for teacher preparation space, equipment storage and chemical storage space. In a hands-on, inquiry-based science program, spaces are also needed for small group student planning sessions that may take place during or after class, as well as for conducting and storing long-term student projects. Additional space should be considered when multiple different courses are taught in the same lab/classroom.

A ceiling height of 10 feet is desirable for a science room. This is particularly important for classes in physics, where some investigations may require a high ceiling, and in chemistry, where an investigation may produce clouds of

smoke. Using the recommended projection screen that is 6 × 8 feet won't work well in a room with a ceiling less than 9 feet high, because tables and chairs will block the lower portions of the screen. Under no circumstances should a classroom ceiling be lower than 8 feet.

For safety and flexibility, a rectangular room at least 30 feet wide is recommended. The room should have at least two exits and doorways that accommodate students with physical disabilities. If the lab/classroom is larger than 1000 square feet, then two exits are required (NFPA Life Safety Code 101).

The least flexible design, and therefore not recommended, is one where the laboratory workstation doubles as both the lab work station and the student's classroom seat. This design leaves little room for varying instructional strategies and little flexibility for future changes in curriculum and instructional practices.

Small group meeting space

No More Separate Laboratories and Classrooms

Science curricula require both laboratory and classroom space. As mentioned previously, student-centered inquiry-based science programs need both classroom and laboratory facilities in the same space. The greatest advantage of a lab/classroom design is that it provides for ongoing access to laboratory activities for each class. Up to 50% more hands-on science is taught in combination laboratory/classroom spaces (West Motz, and Biehle 2000). The combination laboratory/classroom has several other advantages over a stand-alone laboratory, including providing for maximum instructional options and the most flexible use of space needed for various types of instruction, as well as allowing more student-centered, concrete learning opportunities. For the reasons given, NSTA does not recommend providing separate science classrooms and laboratories. A separate classroom area provides movable seating for the nonlaboratory portion of the curriculum. This allows flexibility in the classroom area for a variety of instructional strategies and techniques and student groupings.

The Combination Laboratory/Classroom

When designing any kind of science room three principles of room layout should be observed:

- All students should be able to face the teacher when they are in the classroom mode.
- Sufficient space should be allotted to the students so they can work safely.
- During laboratory activities, the teacher should be able to supervise the students easily and movement around the room should be unimpeded. Paths for egress are a vital safety factor and must be kept clear at all times.

A combination lab and classroom workstation

In all room arrangements, there should be a minimum of 4 feet between the perimeter counters and the areas for general and group seating, and at least 4 feet around each grouping of tables. In a classroom format, provide a minimum of 8 feet from the front wall of the classroom to the first table. The teacher will then be able to move around easily, and have use of a table and equipment such as a projector or a movable demonstration table. Rooms that are more square rather than long and narrow are recommended.

Science teachers, supervisor, facility planner, architect and other stakeholders must review the amount of work surface area to ensure that individual student workstations provide adequate horizontal work surface per student (30 inches × 30 inches). Students should also have safe and easy access to utilities and to sinks that are of adequate size.

In lab/classroom design, the separate classroom area provides movable seating for the nonlaboratory portion of the curriculum. This allows flexibility in the classroom area for a variety of instructional strategies, techniques

and student groupings.

There are two types of lab/classrooms: ones with fixed lab stations and ones with movable lab tables. Any design that provides both lab and classroom furniture in the two separate areas provides instructional flexibility.

Fixed Lab Stations

Fixed lab station design has fixed lab furniture in a designated lab area and a separate classroom area. This design allows for efficient use of the instructional time because no lab furniture needs to be moved as students move back and forth between lab and class activities. An additional advantage occurs when more than one type of course is taught in the same room and labs can be left set up when a different class is using the room, thus more efficiently using instructional time. This design, like others that have separate sets of lab and classroom furniture, has the potential to be safer because of less pressure on the teacher to set up and take down labs as classes change. Lastly, this design offers a variety of instructional options.

Both the fixed perimeter workstation design and the utility service islands are described below and both usually provide open space in the middle of the lab area, whereas the utility service islands have open space around them. Each of the designs has positive and negative attributes that stakeholders must weigh to maximize student learning.

Fixed Perimeter Pier Design

Fixed perimeter lab station designs include "fingers" and "banjos" designs that extend into the classroom from the perimeter counters.

Sinks should be placed at either the end of the aisle or at the end of the pier or "finger," but never in the middle of a lab bench. The fixed "fingers" do not allow for the rearrangement of work surfaces and may limit flexibility in lab scenarios, thus requiring the separate classroom area to provide for instructional flexibility.

"Banjos" Design

The "banjos" design generally does not provide adequate student workstation space. 30 inches per student horizontal work surface area is needed for safe science activities. Another hazard with the "banjos" design is that it creates spatial traps where a student may be unable to readily escape in an emergency. Therefore, the "banjos" design should be avoided.

"Pier," "Finger," or "Peninsula" Design

The fixed perimeter "pier" design allows a more efficient use of the instructional time than designs with only one set of movable tables that must serve both the lab and classroom areas, because the tables need to be moved

A fixed pier with end sink and cover

with changes of activities or classes. The pier design's lack of ability to rearrange work surfaces could be considered a disadvantage. However, the classroom area can provide this flexibility if adequate space is allocated. Some advantages of the fixed perimeter "pier" lab station design are easy supervision

A potentially dangerous trap

of all students and ready availability of all utilities. Lastly, labs do not have to be dismantled with a new class arriving each period or a change of activities during the same period.

Fixed Island With Work Surfaces

This design uses various shapes of utility islands with built-in work surfaces for student workstations.

Fixed Octagonal Islands

The fixed octagonal workstations have troughs and water supplies at each end. Covers for the troughs create a longer, flat surface. However, sinks must be added to the perimeter counters since the troughs are not functional as sinks and the length may not be adequate for some physics activities.

Fixed Rectangular Islands

Fixed rectangular islands have workstations and central sinks that can be modified to provide a 6-foot-long work surface, but these sinks are usually too small, too difficult to reach and can be harder to cover, because the faucets are

Fixed octagonal islands

often in the center of the table. However, this design can be modified so that the sinks are attached to one side for safer and easier access.

Both designs can be equipped with sockets for apparatus rods, if desired, and outlets for computer network connections.

Movable Lab Tables

This design allows one or two sets of tables to be moved to accommodate either laboratory and/or classroom instruction. This room arrangement allows for a variety of configurations for laboratory and classroom work, thus providing a very flexible design. However, if only one set of tables is provided, it requires moving of furniture as the instruction shifts back and forth between lab and nonlab activities or between different classes, thus losing instructional time. Also, the tables must be of good design to withstand constant moving.

There are several types of movable lab tables designs:

Movable Lab Tables at Perimeter Design

In this design the lab tables are moved to the perimeter where sinks and utilities are

Movable lab tables

located. If a room that is being renovated is smaller than the recommended safe size, then this design is useful. This design allows the most flexibility for various instructional strategies.

Two laboratory tables, each serving two students on a side, form a lab station when placed together against a counter, with the longer table sides perpendicular to the counter with the sinks at the end of the aisles. Each group of four students has use of a sink, a source of heat, such as gas or hot plate, electric power for equipment and computers, and, often network connections. The sinks should be installed in such a way that when tables are drawn up to the counters, and there will be enough space between the tables for students to access the sinks safely and easily. Gas jets, if used, are between the sinks at the head of the tables and as are the electrical outlets so that the wires or tubing more safely lie along the length of the tables and do not hang over the edge.

A surface-mounted "raceway" may be installed above the counter's backsplash to bring in electric power and data outlets at regular intervals along the counter.

Movable Lab Tables at Utility Islands Design

Lab tables are moved to freestanding fixed utility islands in the middle of the room. This design requires a little more space that the perimeter utilities design.

Trifacial Service Island

One design for fixed utility islands is the trifacial service island (triple table hub). Movable tables are drawn up to the three longer sides of these six-sided islands, creating work areas for students who share large, deep sinks that they access from the three narrower sides. Gas, electrical outlets and computer data wiring can be installed at the three longer sides, adjacent to the tables. Each trifacial island can accommodate three large tables (48 × 60 or 72 inches) or six small tables (21 or 24 × 60 or 72 inches), and thus provide laboratory workspace for 12 students at each hub. Careful attention must be paid to having adequate space and to the layout of trifacial arrangements to ensure that sufficient clearance is provided between the radiating tables of adjacent hubs and to allow for sufficient space for additional activities in the room.

The tables may be combined and rearranged as necessary to permit activities required in the various disciplines. Tables are available with electrical "pigtails" and outlets that plug into the hub units, providing power and data wiring to the far end of the table for computers and other electrical equipment. This allows the electrical wires to lay lengthwise down the middle of the table, thus avoiding the hazard of wires hanging over the edge of a table.

Fixed Lab Stations Without a Separate Classroom Area

This design uses large fixed lab stations with

Trifacial service island

built-in utilities. It offers the least flexibility in instruction and seating arrangements. Versions of this design have adjustable height work surfaces and built-in sinks and can be arranged so that four students sit on one side of the curved or angular work surface, facing the teacher. In classroom mode, the work surface can be lowered to desk height (say 30 inches) and in laboratory mode it can be raised to standing counter height (36 inches). Utilities are located at the sink that protrudes from the opposite side of the unit and remains at a fixed height when the work surface is raised or lowered. Care must be taken to ensure that each student has 30 inches of horizontal linear work surface on this type of unit. The lips on these units aid in preventing items from falling off the unit or spills from reaching the floor. Note taking sometimes is uncomfortable due to the lip.

There are advantages and disadvantages of the fixed lab stations in a modern science curriculum. With fixed lab stations, all utilities, including water, gas, electricity can easily be provided at the workstation. On the other

9–12

hand, fixed lab stations are, by definition, not movable, and this design does not have a separate classroom area, thereby greatly limiting the flexibility of the space. As most science spaces are expected to serve for 30–40 years, reconfiguration of a lab space with fixed stations can be expensive and time-consuming. However, if the lab/classroom is designed with 60 square feet per student net, then there is adequate classroom space for flexibility in most cases.

Long lab stations, either freestanding or attached should be avoided. They impede supervision and safe egress during emergencies. Freestanding stations should not have tall reagent racks that can block visibility throughout the room and unsafely allow chemicals to be stored above eye level.

Avoid tall reagent racks that screen students from view.

Classroom Area

The classroom portion of the room should be as flexible as possible and provide various arrangements for student seating. At least 800 square feet should be allotted for the classroom area only to accommodate 24 students. Otherwise, desks or tables end up having to be placed in the lab area that is neither safe nor a good instructional decision. One- or two-student, flat-topped tables with separate, stackable chairs may be used. Flat-topped tables with stackable chairs can be combined to create larger work surfaces and provide a better workstation than desks for any science activities. Movable tables can also be moved to the perimeter to create more open space as necessary. The table should be sized to accommodate books and electronic equipment such as a laptop computer for each student. Desk and chair combinations and tablet armchairs are not recommended. However, if desk and chair combinations or table arm chairs are chosen, perhaps for better classroom management, they must be flat-topped so they can be used for various science activities.

Flat-topped tables used as student workstations allow multiple arrangements and combinations for laboratory work and small-group activities that would not be possible with desks with sloping tops.

Furnishings

The following describes the needs of a flexible laboratory/classroom with either fixed or movable lab stations and perimeter counters, sinks, and utilities.

Sinks

Sinks for student investigations should be fairly wide (15 × 18 inches) and deep (8 inches) and have swiveling, gooseneck faucets that allow students to fill and clean large containers. Provide

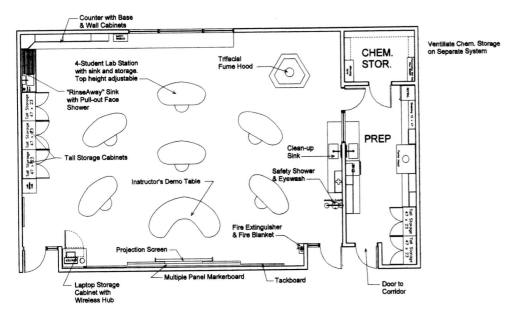

A multi-sciences lab/classroom with fixed lab stations

Physics lab/classroom floor plan

Room size. 30' 0"× 50' 0" (1500 SF)
(9.1m × 15.24m = 139.5m2

NOTE: As all furniture is movable, the arrangement shown is one of many possible within this space.

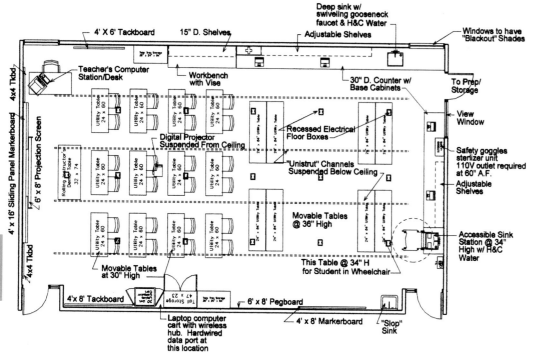

A deep perimeter sink with pull-out face shower

one sink for each four students. Resin sinks are recommended, because they resist corrosion; however, stainless-steel sinks may be an acceptable money-saving alternative in a room that is used only for programs such as physics, where the use of corrosive chemicals is minimal. Small cup sinks, troughs or sinks smaller than 15 inches wide are virtually useless for a high school science program and should be avoided. Cup sinks are usually only in fume hoods. Several sinks should be equipped with dual hands-free eye-washes.

All sinks should have hot and cold water. This minimizes the need for separate heating facilities in many investigations and improves student hygiene. Schools need to be mindful of the maximum temperature of the hot water and keep it safely below the scalding point. Check state and local regulations for hazardous materials to see what chemicals, if any, can be poured down the drain, and if special installations will be needed. If the program calls for corrosive

chemicals, supply the teacher's sink with an acid neutralization tank. This tank is filled with limestone chips that neutralize the acid before it enters the regular waste-piping system. A more effective, but also more expensive method of dealing with large volumes of corrosive wastes is with an acid-resistant piping system and central acid neutralization tank.

Sinks with plaster traps or acid neutralization tanks need periodic maintenance to clear out the accumulated debris or to replace the limestone chips. Such maintenance should be regularly scheduled at least twice a year. If inadequate amounts of corrosives flow through the limestone chips they will foul, creating bad odors.

Faucets should be equipped with vacuum breakers and aerators. Serrated nozzles adapted for the attachment of hoses are an option, but they increase the pressure of the water, causing splattering. If serrated nozzles are needed, these should be ordered separately, in addition to the aerators, and installed and removed on an as needed basis. When aerators are not furnished, teachers often respond by attaching a length of rubber hose to the serrated nozzles to alleviate the splashing problem. This can lead to contamination of the water supply when contaminated water is drawn up the hose.

It is also an advantage to have a large, deep sink with hot and cold water and adjacent counter space for various purposes, such as cleaning large containers. Two very convenient specialty sinks to consider for the laboratory are:

- a "rinseaway" sink, which has a 6- to 10-foot-long molded fiberglass tray with raised edges that slopes down to a sink basin, facilitating the cleanup of plant and animal specimens and messy items. This tray accommodates investigations that need running water and a drain, and require long-term storage. The sink may be equipped with a garbage disposal or a plaster trap to catch sand or gravel. A pullout body drench on a hose is useful both for safety and cleaning up at the sink, but it cannot substitute for a dual, hands-free eyewash. (See photo p. 51)

Slop sink

- a deep, porcelain enameled, wall-mounted janitor's slop sink, which is very useful for cleaning large containers and filling deep vessels with water. Avoid the typical fixed faucet and opt for a swiveling, gooseneck one, because the fixed faucet reduces the open area of the bowl.

Glassware drying racks come in various sizes, and are often useful if installed above some or all of the perimeter sinks. Mount each rack so that it drains directly into the sink rather than down the wall. Request a high backsplash, because the drying rack must be mounted high enough to clear the faucet. The perimeter electrical raceway, if used, should not pass under the drying rack. Some teachers prefer a standard kitchen-counter drying rack, which can be removed and stored beneath the sink when not in use.

Work Space

For work space, counters and tables 36 inches high are convenient and safer for most high school students. Countertops should be at least 24 inches deep. A counter depth of 30 inches will provide increased work space. Chairs or stools should not be used for seating during lab activities, for safety reasons. It is recommended that students stand for laboratory activities.

Countertops should be made of resin or a similar chemical-resistant material. They need to be caulked between the backsplash and the wall, and along any other joints, using clear silicone. Backsplashes 4 inches high are standard. They should also run along the counter beside any tall cabinets, all fume hoods, and other surfaces that interrupt or are set into the countertop. Always use one-piece countertops with backsplashes and no seams.

Flat-topped, movable tables, 24 × 60 inches or 24 × 72 inches, and 30 or 36 inches high can be used for both classroom and laboratory work and may be pushed together to form larger surfaces. The tables should be large enough so two students can work on one side with each student having 30 inches of linear horizontal work surface area. Allow at least 12 inches between the bottom of the table and the chair seat. Each student needs a knee space 24 inches wide, or as close to it as possible. Forty-eight-inch-long tables should not be used because they lack the 30 inches per student workstation needed. Additionally, most 48-inch-long resin-topped utility tables have knee space only 36 inches wide—not wide enough for two—because the legs at each end reduce the amount of space under the table.

These tables should have tops made of resin, or similar material, and may be equipped with sockets for apparatus rods.

For durability, the best choice is an oak- or steel-framed utility table with a resin top. Laminate tops should never be considered for a science laboratory table or countertop. Cheaper materials for laboratory furniture do not withstand the use of water and chemicals and ultimately have to be continually replaced. The connection between the leg and table frame is critical for the durability of these otherwise sturdy tables. Many manufacturers lag-bolt the legs to the frame, which often causes failures when the tables are moved around, because the leg acts as a lever and pulls the bolt out. A better design bolts the leg to a steel plate set into the frame. In the strongest design, a bolt passing through the plate and leg is held in place with a nut and a washer. Any tables taller than 30 inches should be equipped with H-shaped stretchers that provide extra support for the legs. Since these tables will be subject to a lot of abuse during their lifetime, the strongest table is worth the extra expense.

A steel-framed table with resin top

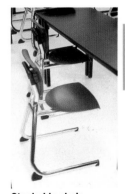
Stackable chair

The resin tops come in several colors, but these tend to be about 20% more expensive than the standard black. Phenolic and epoxy resin are available in colors but phenolic resin is less expensive than epoxy resin. The lighter colors may brighten a dark room, but they may be subject to discoloration by some of the dyes used in secondary courses.

Casework manufacturers have introduced

9-12

tops made of marblelike products similar to those used for kitchen countertops and vanities. These materials are expensive and may be stained by lab chemicals or excess heat; they do not have the history of proven chemical resistance that resin has. Natural stone is expensive and often has seams that are inherent weaknesses in the product and will generally not withstand the use demanded by most high school science programs.

Many teachers prefer to use a movable demonstration table, because science is no longer taught with just teacher demonstrations. Instead, students are actively engaged in learning science by "doing science." Teachers also feel that a fixed table at the front of the room separates them from the students and interferes with students' vision of the board. A fixed demonstration table is expensive and also defines a space 8 feet deep across the front of the room that is perceived as unavailable for uses other than the teacher's demonstrations. In a 30-foot-wide room, this might be as much as 17% the total floor

Rolling physics table

space. A mobile teacher's table can have base cabinets, drawers, knee space, and its own water, gas and electrical service, enabling it to be used nearly anywhere in the room.

For safety reasons, workstations for many courses where chemistry-type activities occur should be at standing height and no stools

and chairs should be used in the laboratory area. Biology classes may desire seating for microscope work; however microscopes on 30-inch-high tables or 36-inch-high counters are not easily used in a seated position so they are often used with tall stools or no seating.

Physics students need a clear work surface at least 2 meters long for equipment such as air tracks. Many standard designs for science casework are shorter than 6 feet, so non-standard casework should be specified as needed. However, this length can be obtained with both fixed perimeter piers and moveable 36-inch high tables that are moved to the perimeter counters.

Physics teachers also like long, flat tables with apparatus rods clamped to the edges or fitted into sockets recessed into the top. "C-clamp" apparatus rods have limited clamp depth and should be used with tabletops that are no more than 1 1/4 inch thick. Some physics rooms have installed 1 3/4 inch tabletops made of maple (similar to butcher block). Fixed rod sockets should be specified only in cases where they are essential, because they limit flexibility and interrupt the smooth surface of the tabletop, making it difficult for some lab activities and note taking.

Laboratory/classrooms specific to physics may require less perimeter casework as work surface area and storage if provided elsewhere. Fewer sinks are required for physics than comparable rooms for biology or chemistry; one sink may suffice for the class. Large, movable tables serve well for classroom work and investigations in physics rooms, provided that sufficient space is available for their use in various configurations.

Many physics activities use large pieces of equipment that require adequate space to operate and store.

Lab/classrooms that are closer to square than long and narrow tend to work well for physics. Some open wall space without counters, cabinets or boards allows for the mounting of various apparatus such as Atwood machines, etc.

Storage

It is desirable to provide base cabinets and countertops along at least two walls for storage and additional work space. A third wall without upper cabinets provides space for teaching resources such as large maps, periodic table, etc.

Flat tray storage

High-quality cabinets, such as those made with hardwood plywood with wood veneer or plastic laminate fronts, should be a priority. Avoid particleboard assembly for casework, because this material is affected by moisture and generally will not withstand the use of a high school environment.

Every room needs several types of base cabinets. Consider units with drawers of various sizes, drawer and door units with adjustable

A variety of useful drawer sizes

shelves, and tote-tray cabinets that allow the teacher to store all of the items for a class or activity in one bin. Tote-tray cabinets are also useful for storing student laboratory kits that can be brought out at laboratory time and for setting aside make-up work. Map drawer cabinets are useful for storing USGS maps and posters. Wall cabinets are typically either 12 or 15 inches deep, and should be mounted about 18 inches above the countertop. Bookshelves should be at least 10 inches deep and adjustable to different heights.

Cabinets of various heights and depths will be needed for specialized storage of items such as rock and mineral samples, sets of globes or universe models, weather data collectors for Earth science, skeleton storage, microscopes and glassware for biology and life science, and stands for aquariums, terrariums, and plants for biology, aquatic and environmental science. Physical science makes extensive use of materials and equipment of varying sizes, types, and weights. A variety of storage sizes and shapes are more useful than uniform storage designs.

Allow floor space in the lab/classroom for use of equipment such as laboratory carts, laptop computer storage carts, an animal cage, a planting area, a telescope and a stream table. It is also important to provide storage for students' coats and book bags to keep these items out of the way during lab work.

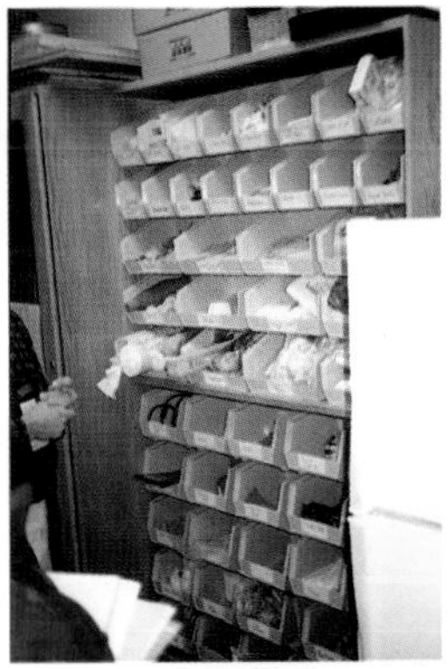

Small bins for small items

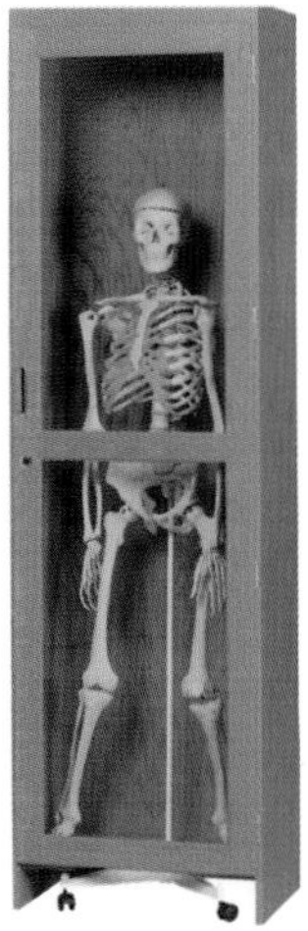

Portable skeleton cabinet

A torso storage cabinet

Instructional Walls and Space

Marker boards and tack boards are hung at roughly counter height. Dry-erase marker boards have taken the place of chalkboards because chalk dust can be harmful to both computers and people. However, there is also concern about the toxicity of the permanent markers, and manufacturers' information and MSDSs should be studied. Sliding, multiple-panel boards can be used to extend a marker board without requiring more wall space.

The space behind and below a marker board can be uniquely used for storage or for book shelving by recessing drawers or shelves into the wall. The sliding panels of the marker board cover this storage until it is accessed. Drawers below the marker board can add significantly useful storage capacity. Such storage requires thickening of the wall behind the board.

Tote trays are useful for storage and active use

The instructional focus area may support a variety of presentation formats, including video, DVD, slides, projected microscope images, and overhead projection. The permanent mounting of equipment such as digital projectors to the ceiling discourages theft and reduces fire and tripping hazards from multiple electrical wires. Since a movable teacher's demonstration table is frequently used, controls, including light dimmers, may be installed in a wall panel that is easily accessible to the teacher. Electronic control systems, with handheld remote controls, can be installed to allow the teacher to control lighting, sound, and projection systems from anywhere in the room.

Storage behind and beneath sliding marker board

A projection screen should be mounted on a wall or the ceiling. The screen size should be 6 feet by 8 feet. If the screen is to be mounted on a high ceiling, include an additional "tail" of material at the top of the screen; the bottom of the screen will be approximately 3 feet above the floor. Mounting a projection screen on a diagonal in a corner of the room can allow use of the marker board at the same time the screen is employed. Marker boards generally do not make good projection screens because their surfaces do not reflect light well.

A variety of interactive electronic marker board systems have been developed recently that allow the user to input data to a computer program using special markers that transmit their movements to a sensor in the system. These can be used in conjunction with a digital projection system to enhance instructional materials. Many of these systems consist of a screen, either mounted on the wall, or on a movable frame; others have sensing devices that mount on an ordinary marker board with suction cups. If use of one of these systems is envisioned, space should be provided for the screen.

Projection screen

Provisions should be made for suspending objects from the ceiling. Tracks with sliding hooks, similar to a hospital curtain track, can provide a variety of places for hanging various teaching aids and models. The hooks should have at least a 300-pound capacity. It is advisable to over-design the suspension system. Another option is to suspend a heavy-duty, industrial strut system below the ceiling with a variety of hooks and clamps that can be relocated as needed; such a system should be

Unistrut system for suspending items below ceiling

designed to support at least 300 pounds per linear foot.

Utilities

Laboratory/classrooms will need plenty of duplex electrical outlets carrying standard household current on separate circuits to avoid overload, all with ground-fault circuit interrupters (GFI) for safety. Using voltage greater than 120v is unsafe and should be avoided. Analyze the equipment that will be used in order to determine if any higher voltages are needed. In order to avoid overloading circuits and eliminate the need for extension cords, overlapping wires, and plug-in outlet extenders, lab/classrooms and preparation areas should be equipped with plenty of duplex electrical outlets on several circuits. These should be available at frequent intervals along walls that have counters and cabinets. One duplex outlet for every two students at the laboratory stations is recommended; provide several 20-amp circuits in each lab/classroom.

Four duplex outlets are desirable along the front or instructional area wall, and three on any wall that lacks cabinets. Several 20-amp circuits should be installed for adequate electrical capacity. At least one hard-wired network connection should be provided in each room. DC power can be provided by small dry cells, not automotive storage batteries, or by portable units that plug into AC outlets and are protected by circuit breakers.

Science rooms need power at each student workstation. It is never safe to run wires or conduits across a classroom floor to provide power to workstations or equipment in the center of the room. However, there are several ways to provide electric power to these locations. These include:

- Pull-down electric cords, similar to those in automotive shops. These can be arranged with multiple outlets and equipped with computer network outlets. The primary drawbacks to this system are the dangling overhead wires for things to get tangled in and the tendency of the retractors to pull the cords back quickly, damaging ceiling tiles.
- Power poles (like those that are popular in open offices). These provide a more permanent arrangement. Again, both electric and

computer network wiring can be delivered anywhere in the space, fed from the ceiling. The primary drawbacks of this system are a lack of flexibility because the poles cannot be moved easily and the relatively fragile nature of the pole systems, which are not designed for the type of abuse possible in a classroom. Power poles are not recommended for science classroom use.

- Recessed floor boxes have lids with rotating "wire-management blocks" that open to allow wires to pass through and close when not in use. These boxes can contain several power outlets as well as data and video access ports. The electrical outlets in the boxes should be raised above the bottom of the floor box to provide additional protection from any spills in that area of the floor. A model is available that holds the outlets vertically, away from the opening of the floor box. Floor boxes should comply with Underwriters Laboratories water exclusion requirements and should never be located close to water sources or areas where water is used.

Do not use the old "tombstone"-type floor outlets that are fixed and stick up above the floor, because these are tripping hazards and greatly reduce the flexibility of the room. Also avoid floor outlets that have hinged brass or plastic cover plates that may break off easily, exposing the outlet to dirt and spills.

Extra care should be taken to investigate the pros and cons with respect to safety of each alternative, especially the floor boxes, and to ensure that everyone, including the custodial staff, is informed of procedures for the safe use of the floor boxes.

"Tombstone" floor outlet (not recommended)

To ensure future flexibility for the science program, all lab/classrooms built today should have wireless data connections. As described in Chapter 2, this access may be provided within the department, the school, or may be part

"Flap-type" outlet

of a wider area system. Two-way communication between every classroom and the school office is essential as well, and should not rely on an individual teacher's cell phone. Phones should be installed in each science room.

Today, gas is used less often than in the past because it is expensive and requires particular caution and diligence. It is primarily used in chemistry, physical science, and AP biology. If the science program requires its use, gas should be installed at the perimeter, near the sinks but at the head of the lab stations so that the gas hose runs the length of the lab stations out of the

way and not hanging over the edge of a counter. On the other hand, the sink should be placed at the head of the aisle for easy safe access. Sinks should not be placed in the middle of the lab bench. This placement is awkward to use, takes up valuable work space, and thus is unsafe. When gas is provided by a central system, an emergency shut-off valve, activated by pushing a highly visible button, will be needed. A central control valve can enable the teacher to shut off the gas in the room when not in use. Emergency shut-off controls for electrical service and gas should be near the teacher's station, not far from the door, and not easily accessible to students.

Distilled water is used almost daily in high school science, and some schools build in their own still system. Because distilled water can readily be purchased in bulk, and because central still systems are expensive and can be maintenance headaches, they are not generally recommended for high schools. However, lab counter space needs to be provided for the large containers. Water demineralizers or deionizers can be mounted on the wall above a sink, so that containers can be filled through a flexible hose connected to the faucet. Some high school classes need vacuums, and portable vacuum pumps may be the best option for this. Whether it is built in or not, this equipment requires specialized storage. Compressed air is rarely needed and, if required, should be achieved using a portable air compressor. Compressed air can be extremely dangerous and should be rigidly controlled, if not avoided completely.

Because curricula change rapidly, it is necessary to consider fume hoods in every high school science laboratory/classroom. Chemical fume hoods are used in certain physical science, chemistry, and life science classes, and are required in laboratories where hazardous and vaporous chemicals are used. If a fume hood is provided in a lab/classroom, one must be made accessible to students with disabilities. Some well-designed portable (ductless) fume hoods have been developed that allow the hood to be moved from place to place or from room to room. Air filtration is accomplished through a set of replaceable filter packs that can be selected for the particular application. The advantage of a portable system is that one hood may serve several lab/classrooms; on the other hand, the filter packs are expensive and must be replaced periodically and disposed of as a hazardous waste. The ductless chemical fume hood does not require installation of ductwork and has lower energy consumption (see p. 104).

Specialized hoods, such as laminar flow hoods or biological safety cabinets, may be required for advanced biology courses.

Lighting and Darkening Rooms

While natural lighting is best for learning, it is not possible to achieve enough natural light and at the same time ensure a way to shade the room for projection. Classroom lighting has become a more difficult design problem because of the rapid increase in the use of computers, cable TV, and digital projectors. Light levels of at least 50 foot-candles for the general classroom and 75 to 100 foot-candles at the work surface are required for general classroom and laboratory work, but computer screens and projection screens do not perform well in the glare from direct light sources. Parabolic fluorescent fixtures with grids that direct light straight down have become standard in rooms

that have computers. Three-tube fixtures with the middle tube switched separately from the outer tubes allow four levels of lighting: all three tubes, two tubes, one tube, or no tubes lit. Separate switches for each row of lights

A lab/classroom with indirect lighting

provide flexibility in room darkening. For example, when images are being projected onto a screen at the front of the room, the front row of lights can be turned off, the middle of the room may have only one tube lit, and the rear may have two tubes lit.

Indirect lighting has also been used successfully in rooms with computers. With this type of fixture, the light bounces off the ceiling and is diffused around the room, providing strong lighting levels at the work surface without producing a bright visible light source that would reflect off computer screens. These fixtures are also available as three-tube fixtures and can be operated as described above.

The increased use of videotapes, DVDs, television, and images projected onto large screens from digital projectors has complicated

lighting design still further. Projection screens tend to reflect all of the light that shines onto them, and bright, overall illumination will "wash out" the desired image. These projection systems frequently encounter sound problems as well, since they may be mounted against ceiling materials that are not ideal from an acoustic standpoint. (See Chapter 2)

Providing recessed, dimmable, compact fluorescent light fixtures as supplemental lighting throughout the room allows the teacher to turn off the more intense general lighting. The down lights provide the necessary desktop illumination for note taking without washing out the image in the projection screen.

All of these lighting solutions are more expensive than the traditional recessed, prismatic light troffers. However, they should be considered when designing the laboratory/classroom of the future.

The ability to darken the classroom is very important, because daylight coming through the windows creates glare on computer screens, washes out images on the projection screen and hampers certain investigations in physics, chemistry, life science, and Earth science. One-inch mini blinds work well in most rooms, but they are not sufficient for optics investigations that need almost complete darkness. They are also easily damaged, collect dust, and are difficult to clean. Room-darkening shades that slide into side and bottom tracks, and are made from totally opaque material, block out most of the light from windows. Care should be taken in specifying room-darkening shades to avoid extremely wide units as the bottom rail of the shade may buckle and pull the material out of the sidetracks. These shades are fairly expensive, and they should be considered only when almost complete darkness is needed. Several new schools have used sliding bulletin boards to darken windows and provide extra display space at the same time.

Remember that when exhaust fans replace windowpanes, they let light in around their edges and through the dampers. Windows in preparation rooms and windows in doors also admit light into the classroom. A means of darkening these problem areas needs to be found.

Laptops can go anywhere

Computers

Computing devices are a fixture of the high school science lab/classroom; however, the exact physical format of such devices is difficult to predict. Counters on which desktop computers are to be permanently installed should be at table height, not higher than 32", and there should be knee

Computers, charger, printer, and wireless hub on wheels

space beneath them. Most schools are now moving to laptop computers in a wireless networking environment; however, some

schools have passed beyond laptops to handheld devices such as PDAs. Access to the Internet for at least the wireless hub and a desktop computer for the teacher should be provided in each lab/classroom. A desktop computer station, including room for a person sitting at

PDA connected to probeware

the computer, or a piece of equipment such as an electric portable interactive marker board, occupies about 15 square feet of floor space.

Lockable laptop storage carts, which allow the units to be recharged when not in use, can include a printer and a wireless network hub. Provide floor space for the cart when planning the lab/classroom and equipment room layout. The room would also benefit from having a high-speed printer for producing student reports using the laptops and the school's file server.

Tomorrow's science investigations will involve more and more computer-interfaced instruments and measurement devices, as well as links to data sources around the world like satellites and geologic sensors. To take advantage of these devices, classrooms need special facilities for both use and storage. A permanent site for reception and recording such data might be appropriate in a classroom. Since the instruments are often small and delicate, specialized secure storage is also recommended. For more details on such possibilities, see Chapter 2.

Stations for Students With Disabilities

A work area for students with physical disabilities includes a sink and utilities accessible to a person in a wheelchair. The Americans with Disabilities Act (ADA) requires that at least one sink in each laboratory area be in compliance with its guidelines. Controls for the faucet usually have lever, or "wrist blade," handles. The regulations prescribe a maximum sink height and minimum clearance below the sink for the seated student. It is difficult to meet these requirements with a resin sink attached to the bottom of a resin countertop, because the cross-supports beneath the sink reduce the space available for the sink assembly.

An accessible workstation integrated within main lab space

Some schools use a mobile workstation and fume hood for a student with disabilities. The workstation can have a gas bottle and includes a water supply operated by an electric pump, and an electric power cord that is plugged into an outlet, and a holding tank for wastewater that must be emptied regularly. It can be stationed anywhere and can be moved from room to room as needed. In order to make every room accessible, each room must have sufficient wall space, as well as cabinets and electrical outlets suitable for use with these mobile units. The intent of the Americans with Disabilities Act (ADA) and the Individuals with Disabilities Education Act (IDEA) is to include students with disabilities with their peers, rather than segregating them at workstations remote from the class. Most casework manufacturers have developed accessible workstations that can be located among the standard workstations in a lab/classroom.

The ADA workstation needs to be located for safe egress during emergencies. Do not build every student workstation to meet ADA requirements because those standards are not designed for the safe use by people without disabilities and can create potentially hazardous conditions.

Teacher's Space

Teachers need their own space for preparing their lessons, making telephone calls, keeping essential papers and texts, and meeting with students. This must be separate from a storage space for both security and the teachers' health. There are a number of successful arrangements:

Science department faculty office

- a teacher's desk in an alcove in a laboratory/classroom
- an individual office in a preparation room (not where chemicals are stored), as described below
- a space be-

"Slump space" within the science area

tween two lab/classrooms
- an assigned space in a departmental office that has movable office partitions and a central meeting space for groups.

At a minimum, teachers should have their own desk areas, each with a computer, telephone, file cabinet, and storage cabinet, arranged to indicate that it is private and off-limits to students. The teacher's space should not be located in a classroom that is shared with other teachers and should never be in a chemical storage room.

A group or departmental office space can create additional collegiality among the science faculty. Some schools have located "slump spaces" with internet connections where students and teachers can sit in comfortable chairs and relax near the teachers' office spaces. These allow "serendipitous interactions" among students and teachers that create learning opportunities outside the classroom.

Preparation and Storage Rooms

Adequate, proper, and safe and secure space must be provided for:

1. preparation of lab materials
2. storage of lab and field equipment and materials
3. storage of chemicals

Chemicals should be locked, with access to only certified/authorized employees, in a properly designed chemical storeroom

Large view windows between prep room and lab/classroom

and never stored in a lab/classroom or prep and/or equipment storerooms. Stolen chemicals can be deadly. Chemical vapors are damaging to the health of humans and corrosive to equipment.

The preparation/ equipment storage

Glassware storage shelves with lips

room should be next to, and accessible from, the laboratory/classroom. All doors to the room should have locks. Access to the corridor is desirable, as it will allow the teacher to use the preparation room without disturbing a class in the next room. A view window into the laboratory/classroom facilitates supervision of students and lets students know when the teacher is in the prep/equipment storeroom. Storage in a combined preparation/equipment storage room should be for equipment and materials and must be supplemented by a separate, locked chemical storeroom, which may open off the preparation room.

The preparation/equipment storeroom should be sized using the minimum space guidelines at the beginning of this chapter. A larger room located between two laboratory classrooms can successfully serve two teachers.

The room should have base and wall cabinets, tall storage units, 12-inch adjustable shelves, and counter space. Allow floor space for laboratory carts and space for desired equipment, such as a distillation unit or an autoclave. A sink with hot and cold water is needed and, frequently, a glassware drying rack. A teacher's desk may be built into the counter space by installing a 6-foot length of counter at table height, with knee space, adjacent file drawers, and a 2-inch-diameter hole at the back of the counter for the computer wiring. This desk should not be near the sink. The preparation room is also a good place for a dishwasher, a microwave oven, and a laboratory refrigerator with an icemaker labeled "Lab Materials Only." Provide separate electric circuits with GFI-protected outlets and a telephone. Gas may be needed, depending on the curriculum. A fume hood is also needed for most programs. This hood may be shared with the adjacent lab/classroom by specifying a hood with a sash on both sides. However, some means of locking the prep/equipment storeroom must be used to avoid unauthorized access. It is important that this space have good communication with the school office and other security personnel, since teachers might be working in these spaces when the building is not occupied.

Storage rooms provide needed security and specialized storage for large, expensive, or sensitive equipment. When planning a storage

Fume hood shared by prep room and lab/classroom

room, provide base cabinets of various types, wall cabinets, tall cabinets, and flexible, open shelving. Consider a variety of base cabinets with drawers of different sizes, drawer and door units, and adjustable shelves. Drawers in lower cabinets provide easier access than door units to stored items. Tote-tray cabinets are frequently included. If the school curriculum integrates the sciences or offers alternating modules, centralized or movable storage units may be useful.

Hinged doors on wall cabinets are recommended, because sliding doors waste about 3 inches of interior cabinet depth, and the slides tend to become corroded when the cabinets store chemicals. Tall cabinets can accommodate models and other large lightweight objects.

Large paper items, such as maps or poster board, can be stored in shallow drawers. These flat-stock drawers require a base cabinet with a countertop at least 36 inches deep, because cabinets that fit under 24- and 36-inch-deep counters have drawers that are only 21 and 27 inches deep, respectively. Drawers with a

width of 35 to 36 inches will accommodate most posters. Vertical dividers beneath a counter can store panels and other large, flat objects.

The storage system should have provision for labels on the outside of the cabinets. Many teachers prefer glass doors on cabinets that are used for equipment, in spite of their expense and fragility because it is easier to find materials in them or dust does not accumulate on the stored items as quickly. However, glass doors can also make the cabinets a housekeeping and security problem and are not recommended, particularly in the lab/classroom areas. Glass is never recommended on doors in lab/classroom cabinets below 60 inches because of the frequency of breakage when students fall or are pushed into them. Laminated safety glass is recommended for storage cabinets for safety purposes.

Cabinet with broken glass

A well-designed prep/equipment storage room

Storage shelving comes in several depths: 10 inches for books, 12 to 15 inches for multiple uses, and 18 to 24 inches for storing bulky items. It is best mounted on standards

9-12

Rolling compact shelving used for science

that allow adjustment to different heights. Shelving for chemical storage should always be constructed of wood or other materials that resist corrosion and joined by plastic or plastic-coated connectors and shelf fittings. Corrosion by stored chemicals of metal shelves, shelf supports or attachments cause chemical spills and injuries. Prefabricated particleboard shelving units with plastic laminate or melamine surfaces generally are not constructed to support the types of loads typical of a school science program. All shelving over 30 inches long should be at least 1 inch thick. Lips on the edges of shelves or other similar modifications increase safety for chemical storage and are mandatory in seismically active areas. Lips increase the ability to contain the spilled chemicals.

When space is at a premium, high-density track shelving, the rolling compact shelf units often found in libraries, may be used. These shelving units are lined up closely in rows until they are needed, at which time they are accessed by making use of the one aisle that serves the units. The track shelving should have an anti-tip mechanism, adjustable shelves made of hardwood plywood with lips, and tracks that are ADA compliant. If these are to be used, a professional analysis of the loading capacity of the floor structure will be needed, because the units concentrate much higher loads than fixed storage shelving. These units must be kept clamped to their rails at all times, except when they are being moved. If they should break loose and roll freely, they will

damage most any object they hit.

Today's trend toward micro-scale chemistry brings with it a reduction in the quantity of chemicals used. This increases safety and reduces the storage needs of the chemicals. Teachers should always use stock bottles and prepare solutions outside the student area. Chemicals should never be stored in the preparation/equipment storeroom or lab/classroom.

Separate ventilation, with vents at the floor level and at the ceiling, should be provided

Storage cabinets in a lab/classroom

BIOLOGY STUDENT PROJECT SPACE

Room size. 25' 0" x 33' 0" (825 SF)
(7.62m × 10m = 76.7m²)

NOTE: Space for long-term student projects serving five nearby Biology lab/classrooms.

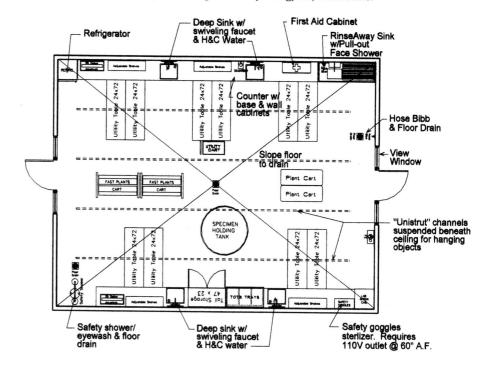

for all rooms or closets in which chemicals are stored. This ventilation should be available all the time, and not become part of an energy-saving timer system. All chemicals should be kept in dedicated, lockable cabinets or separate chemical storerooms. Chemicals must be divided into their compatible families, and incompatible chemicals are stored separately, with sufficient distance from each other. Secure, compact storage units for acids, flammables, and corrosives are available. Consult sources such as commercial catalogs for guidelines on storing chemicals, cleaning products, and flammables. In case of a fire or accident, a complete list of what is stored, together with material safety data sheets (MSDS) will be needed, in some cases, required. A good practice is to have three sets of MSDS: one in the administrative offices, one in the nurse's office, one in a notebook in a clear plastic holder attached to the door of the chemical storage room. Check with local fire marshal to see if an MSDS notebook is desired.

It is a truism that there is never sufficient storage space in science facilities. It is important to take inventory of all items that are being stored, not only to make better use of space and meet good housekeeping practices. Old and forgotten chemicals are a serious safety concern because they can become hazardous, with resulting fires or explosions. Items that are no longer useful should be discarded safely or sent to authorized disposal facilities.

Student Project Areas

The increasing emphasis on inquiry and individual and small-group work, as well as the

A long-term student project space

guidelines suggested by the National Science Education Standards to increase students' capacities for conducting long-term investigations and competition projects has resulted in a greater need for space for conducting and storing student projects. This space should be as close to the laboratory/classroom as possible. It is important to have a window between the two rooms or between the corridor and the student project room, to facilitate supervision. A door from the corridor will allow students and teachers to use the project space without disrupting nearby classes during class time.

One practical layout is to place base cabinets with countertops, wall cabinets, and at least two sinks with hot and cold water around the perimeter. A central-island work area can be made from movable tables or additional base cabinets arranged back-to-back and covered with an epoxy resin countertop. Electric power with GFI-protected circuits should be installed along the perimeter and at the center island. If gas is used, the jets should be at the perimeter, and an emergency gas shut-off button will be necessary. Depending upon the types of projects conducted, a shower/dual eye/face wash

and fume hood should be included.

Surface area in which to store projects that require more than one class period to complete will be needed in the student project room; adjustable shelving of various depths is also useful. Ideally a room about the size of a laboratory/classroom is needed to allow projects from multiple classes to be carried out and/or stored simultaneously.

To allow for student projects of various types and durations, the floor finish should probably be sealed concrete. Water sources and floor drains should be provided. If possible, a large pair of doors or a roll-up industrial door should be provided for direct access to the outdoors. The ability to suspend objects from a high ceiling should also be provided.

A small group meeting area

Small Group Spaces

In a project-based environment, small spaces in which students can meet during and/or after class to plan and discuss their projects should be provided. In some schools these are essentially small conference rooms with one or more tables, chairs, a marker board, and access to the Internet. Such spaces may be located between adjacent lab/classrooms to be shared by both classes, or may be alcoves in corridors near the science spaces. Enclosed rooms should have glass walls to allow for supervision.

A student work area adjacent to the science lab/classrooms

Vivarium

Other Spaces

Other spaces may also be required to provide for a complete high school science program. These might include a space for an electron microscope that may have been donated by a neighboring industry, a genetics lab, an optics lab, a shop space containing hand and/or power tools for fabricating engineering projects, a vivarium or animal room, a greenhouse, or a larger plant window. Each of these should be individually planned for the specific use required.

A genetics lab

References

Judson, E., and D. Sawada. 2000. Examining the effects of a reformed junior high school science class on students' math achievement. *School Science and Mathematics* 100 (8): 419–425.

West, S., L. Motz, and J. Biehle. 2000. *Building state of the art science facilities,* NSTA National Convention, Saint Louis, Missouri.

9–12

CHAPTER 7

Green Schools

Key ideas in this chapter:

- Learning environments can extend to the entire school site and beyond.
- Faculty needs to plan how to use greenhouses within the prescribed curriculum.
- Proper design is critical so the plan must be well researched.
- Access to natural settings is an important resource for the science program.
- Wherever possible, outdoor areas surrounding the school should help shape the facility design plan.
- Natural areas such as ponds, waterways, and rain gardens can be provide invaluable learning resources.
- Planned courtyards can be designed to be unique and effective learning areas for such creations as sundials, weather stations, fossils, and planetary models.

Schools aren't just made of brick and mortar; they are special places where children grow. That means that science facility planners cannot just stop at the edge of the foundation.

Learning environments can extend to the entire school site and beyond. Landscaping and environmental engineering can greatly expand a school's potential to nourish its students.

"Thinking green" includes not only making room for plants and other greenery. As a school's staff models environment consciousness, it teaches lessons in citizenship that last a lifetime.

While everyone in a school community should share responsibility for the "greening" of a school, it is often the science teachers who make the best use of these facilities, basing their lessons on the components of a green school that have been built around them. This chapter talks about many ways in which you can prove to your students that "it *is* easy being green."

Start Inside

Growing plants in a controlled environment, such as a greenhouse, can be a wonderful enhancement to any science program. In an inquiry-based, project-oriented curriculum, a greenhouse can be a necessity. Thoughtful planning, proper design and faculty advocates who support the greenhouse as an important asset to their curriculums are necessary for a school greenhouse to be successful. The greenhouse concept can be as simple as an alcove with water and grow lights, or a large space with specially designed ventilation and irrigation. But large or small, a greenhouse takes both maintenance and advocacy. Unless these facilities are properly designed and have at least one very strong faculty advocate for the greenhouse, the result can be an expensive eyesore, often at the heart of the school's science department.

The most important resource a school greenhouse must have to succeed is at least one member of the science faculty who will advocate for it. Better still, the greenhouse with its use and maintenance should be built into the curriculum, with specific uses and lessons at every grade. Greenhouses are expensive and can be wonderful amenities, but if no one on the science faculty uses the greenhouse as part of his or her curriculum, the space will become abandoned and used for storage.

As with all science facilities, during the early planning stages of a project, before the budget is set and before the architect has located and designed the greenhouse, the science faculty needs to identify how the greenhouse will be used in the science curriculum. Some typical questions to be answered are:

Interior of a greenhouse

An abandoned greenhouse

- Will large groups of students (say an entire class of 24) be conducting activities in the greenhouse at one time?

Freestanding greenhouse

A small freestanding greenhouse

Plant window cantilevered from a building

- Will the greenhouse be available to students or the community at times other than normally scheduled class periods?
- Will individual or small group projects be carried out in the greenhouse in addition to activities involving the entire class?
- What type of climate should the greenhouse maintain? (At the Missouri Botanical Garden, for example, there are several greenhouse structures: one maintaining the climate of a tropical rain forest, another of a desert, another of the Mediterranean coast.)
- What types of plants will students grow and what will happen to them during summer vacations?
- Will other faculty members, student groups, and/or staff have access to and use of the greenhouse?

A greenhouse facility can be a large, freestanding facility in which students experiment with manipulating crop mutations and cross-pollination, or it may be a more modest space, an integral part of the science department, surrounded by lab/classrooms, or it may be simply an enlarged plant window, extended out from the wall of a single lab/classroom to provide an area for living plants on a relatively small scale. It could also be a climatarium or several plant carts. Whatever the scale and location, design of the space is essential.

Important design considerations include:

- orientation
- ventilation
- cooling and heating
- water supply and drainage
- lighting
- materials of construction and furnishings
- location

Orientation

Research the proper orientation and equipping of the greenhouse. In the northern hemisphere, the best orientation is due south; however, southeast and southwest orientations can also be acceptable. Greenhouses are usually constructed of glass or translucent extruded cellular polycarbonate and, therefore, allow lots of daylight inside. This may be fine for some uses, but may be too much light for others, leading to the need to provide some form of shading. Plants can die because several days of intense, direct sun causes them to dry out too quickly. Commercial greenhouses provide shading by means of aluminum slats or mesh or ultraviolet-resistant saran fabric, which roll up and down on the outside of the structure like ordinary window shades. More elaborate and expensive options include motorized shades that can respond automatically to the amount of sunlight on a given day.

Ventilation

Proper ventilation is crucial, for without it the greenhouse can rapidly become unacceptably hot. Most greenhouses have vent panels in the roof and near the ground that can be manually opened and closed to allow fresh air in to mitigate heat buildup; the primary drawback to a manual operation is the chance that the person responsible will forget to close the vents at night or on a cold day, or forget to open them the next morning (plants have died because someone forgot to close the vent). For a price, the vents can be automated

Well-ventilated greenhouse with both a fan system and operable wall panels

and thermostatically controlled to open and close depending on the inside temperature of the greenhouse. An automatic ventilating fan system should also be considered with the fan at one end and an automated louver at the other, both controlled by a thermostat to bring in fresh air as needed.

Cooling and Heating

Evaporative cooling—the mechanical equivalent of the old cartoon of a person setting up a fan to blow across a block of ice—is a relatively inexpensive way of cooling a greenhouse while at the same time increasing the humidity level. Such a "swamp cooler" should be controlled by a thermostat.

An evaporative cooler wall

In most climates in the northern hemisphere, heating the greenhouse is also a necessity. While the space can rapidly heat up during a sunny day, it can quickly become cold enough to allow plants to freeze at night, or even during the day, when the weather outside is frosty. Small gas furnaces can serve the greenhouse space itself, or the building heating system can be extended into the greenhouse. In a St. Louis–area school renovation, a small lean-to greenhouse was installed on the roof of a heated space, and the school's steam heating line was extended up through the floor to a small radiator with a thermostatically controlled steam valve that kept the greenhouse warm on the coldest of days. Consider also using solar heat reradiated from a *Trombe wall*—a massive wall facing the sun that absorbs the sun's heat during the day and reradiates it at night—as an energy-saving source that can be supplemented by a more traditional heat source. A trombe wall can be an amenity, but it must also be carefully considered and designed because, once the wall has absorbed the sun's heat, it will reradiate it and controlling this heat is tricky. A trombe wall has no on/off switch.

Water Supply and Drainage

Another occasionally overlooked necessity is a water supply. Plants do, after all, generally need to be watered, either manually, or by an automated system. A small greenhouse might include a laundry sink with both hot and cold water and a threaded faucet to which a hose and watering wand may be attached. Larger greenhouses should probably have one or two hose bibbs centrally located to allow the connection of a hydroponic watering system or simply a hose. Also, the overflow from watering plants needs someplace to go, so one or more floor drains are needed. The floor of the greenhouse should be constructed to slope toward these drains. The water supply should have an in-line vacuum breaker in the event a hose is inadvertently left in a tank of dirty water.

Lighting

Lighting should also be provided. Waterproof fixtures should be chosen, probably with fluorescent lamps; how the greenhouse will be used should determine how it is lit. Are "grow lights" needed to supplement the daylight? If the greenhouse is also an architectural amenity, should it be lit at night? Also consider the need for electrical receptacles within the greenhouse. Both the lights and the receptacles should be on ground-fault protected (GFI) circuits.

Example of good lighting

Materials of Construction and Furnishings

The floor in a greenhouse should probably be bare, sealed concrete. Rubber mats can be placed in walkways between plant benches, allowing water to flow along the floor while minimizing the chance for a person to slip and fall. Plant benches should be either aluminum or of a structural plastic that is resistant to ultraviolet radiation. Freestanding plant benches will allow flexibility in arrangement as well as in periodic cleanup. Provide a table or counter as a potting bench and tall cabinets for storage of materials and supplies. Such casework should not be made of wood or plastic-laminate covered particleboard, as these will rapidly deteriorate in a moist environment. A door directly to the outdoors can often be

Example of appropriate plant benches

helpful, particularly if the greenhouse is adjacent to an outdoor garden space.

Location

Finally, make sure that the resulting greenhouse design works as a greenhouse—it is used and cared for, and not just a visual, remote addition to the school grounds. Location is important. If the greenhouse is remote from the science lab/classrooms that it is supposed to support, it may be ignored (out of sight, out of mind). A large midwestern university plant science building was designed with greenhouses on the roof as architectural elements that, from the outside, looked like diamonds studded into the top of the tower. Unfortunately, these greenhouses were on a separate floor from the teaching spaces they supported and, after a time, were seldom used, becoming unsightly storage spaces.

Architects have a tendency to use greenhouses as an architectural amenity, providing both the wonder and delight of living plants inside the space and an attractive, glass enclosed building feature on the exterior. Both are admirable goals, from the point of view of science education, but if the plants in the greenhouse don't live, the greenhouse will not do much to enhance science education. One high school greenhouse was designed to provide a two-and-one-half-story jungle at the end of the cafeteria. Unfortunately, the tall space experienced temperature layering with some portions getting too much heat and others not getting enough. Expensive modifications to alleviate these problems were required after construction was completed and the problem was discovered.

When properly planned and designed, a good working greenhouse or plant window can be an excellent science teaching resource.

A greenhouse as an architectural amenity

A tall greenhouse that didn't work well

Outdoor Facilities

Access to natural settings is an important resource for a science program, even in urban environments, and especially at the elementary level. Wherever possible, the outdoor areas surrounding the school should be included in the facilities design plan. Providing nature trails, prairie grass areas, garden plots with various crops and herbs, and outdoor areas for weather balloon use and other investigations requires few physical facilities other than occasional tables, which may also be used for picnics.

In the few urban areas of the country where allowing students to leave the building is not safe, there are still many ways to bring the outside in—bird and animal feeding areas (even in the middle of cities!), beehives (carefully designed to keep the bees away from the students), roof gardens, and even two-way video for observing animals and various exotic plants at distant sites.

One idea used successfully for a recent urban elementary and middle-level school was to arrange the shared building in a "doughnut" configuration, with a central courtyard providing space that is used by both schools for outdoor activities.

Native Plantings

Careful planning during construction can help minimize disruption to existing plantings and any adverse impact on the natural communities. If a school has been built with little regard for the existing environment, native plantings can be established to restore some of the natural vegetation while providing windbreaks, shade, or other amenities. Planning, planting, and maintaining the school grounds can be a science project for all grades. A high school in Mesa, Arizona, was constructed as a bridge across a natural arroyo; the arroyo was left undisturbed and can be observed from the outdoor plaza adjacent to the cafeteria.

Schools built adjacent to forests or wetlands can take advantage of these natural amenities to enhance teaching programs. A middle school in Illinois was constructed adjacent to a wetland and the planning documents specified that this area be protected and incorporated into the landscape of the

A natural arroyo

campus as a natural area. The same school reintroduced native plants and shrubs as landscape features in the site plan.

Ponds and Waterways and Rain Gardens

Small ponds can be incorporated into courtyards to provide both a visual amenity to those looking out and an educational resource. A school in Indianapolis has several courtyards and alcoves, which bring live animals, birds, and fish right up to the building to be observed by all students. A science magnet school in St. Louis has a replica of a

A wetland

Missouri Ozark stream running through its courtyard, ending in a pond complete with fish and amphibians. Creative thinking on the part of the architect of a school in Boulder, Colorado, turned a drainage ditch into a boulder-strewn mountain stream complete with Rocky Mountain wildflowers.

Missouri Ozark Stream

A mountain stream with wildflowers

Rain gardens, in which the need for storm drainage is combined with the natural tendency of plants to divert and filter water, can be visual and educational amenities for a schoolyard. More information and photographs of rain gardens may be found on the internet. One useful site is *www.raingardens.org*.

Courtyards and Outdoor Classrooms

Courtyards can also be used as gathering spaces and as areas for outdoor demonstrations. Several schools have incorporated a sundial or a compass in the paving and construction of courtyards. Another included a narrow strip of colored concrete with round plaques spaced to demonstrate the relative distances between the planets of the solar system.

One school has a walkway leading from the edge of a pond to the cafeteria door; footprints of various amphibians, birds and animals and fossils of similar creatures line the edge of this path, ranging from a small frog at water's edge to a human footprint at the door. A weather station and a windmill help connect what's happening in the atmosphere with science education.

The space immediately outside a standard classroom can be incorporated as a teaching space and outdoor classroom. An elementary school in the San Diego area used low walls to define outdoor classroom spaces adjacent to pairs of classrooms; teachers bring students out to work on projects of all types. Stepped concrete benches and a latticed overhang create a shaded outdoor classroom at a community college in Mesa, Arizona. A deck protruding into the woods outside a freestanding elementary school science pavilion in Baltimore

An interior science courtyard

A combined compass and sundial

Courtyard weather station

Solar system model

extends their glass-enclosed classroom among the tall trees, providing a delightful place to observe nature and work on projects. The same school has a climbing apparatus in the shape of a strand DNA in an adjacent playground.

Many of these outdoor amenities were inexpensive to build because they were conceived during the early planning stages of their school by a planning team that considered the surroundings of a school building important resources for learning.

Beyond Photosynthesis

Thinking green involves more than just plants. It involves building maximum energy efficiency into buildings, as well

School courtyard windmill

as facilities for maximum recycling and minimal waste. These are all ways to embed lessons into the walls.

Energy conservation has been mentioned in many of the previous chapters. The judicious use of skylights, good insulating materials, and energy-conserving ventilation controls are both cost-effective and educational.

Solar and wind electrical generators may not provide all the power a school needs, but they are powerful lessons for both students and the community. When such generators are erected on a schoolyard, it is great to bring the data

Conducting green roof research (temperature control)

on how much power is being generated right into the science classroom.

Another way to teach conservation is to allow students to participate in efforts to conserve water. Bring the data on how much water is being used up front (in a hall or classroom display) and help students develop their own plans to reduce usage.

Finally, don't hide the trash. Feature the school's recycling facilities as part of the curriculum. Build a compost pile close to the cafeteria. Record the nonrecyclable trash, and enlist student assistance in reducing the flow.

Conducting green roof research (water run-off)

Outdoor classroom

Building Conservation In

In some schools, it is appropriate to use recycled materials in construction. When that happens, "say it loud." A great track can be built from recycled tires. Enlarge a photo of the tiny tire bits that are visible in the track and feature it in a student display. Other types of furnishings can be purchased that are made from recycled plastics or lumber.

Another concept gaining favor is formaldehyde-free wood. Formaldehyde is a chemical used as a binder in many pressed wood products such as cabinets. Since formaldehyde causes cancer in laboratory animals and the World Health Organization recommends that exposure should not exceed 0.05 parts per million, choosing alternative materials for wood cabinets and drawer fronts in laboratory classrooms is worth considering. Columbia Forest Products (*www.specifycolumbia.com*) manufactures all of their plywood with a formaldehyde-free bonding agent called "PureBond." The company's materials qualify toward the U.S. Green Building Council's LEED green building program requirements. Another company,

Sierra Pine, produces a material called Medex, a wood-based panel product made with formaldehyde-free synthetic resins. The company received independent certification from Scientific Certification Systems verifying that Medex is manufactured from 100% recovered and recycled wood fiber content and contains no added formaldehyde.

For more information on the LEED Green Building Rating System, go to *www.usgbc.org*. For more information about Scientific Certification Systems, visit *www.scscertified.com*.

CHAPTER 8

Buildings That Teach

Music hallway Slinky

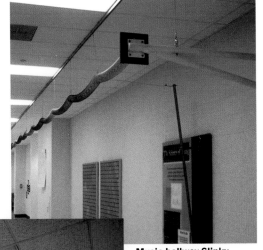

Periodic table on the ceiling

A periodic table on the ceiling of a chemistry lab/classroom, footprints and fossils of amphibians and animals in a courtyard sidewalk, a 60-foot slinky suspended from the ceiling, and a tessellation pattern in the floor tile extend science learning beyond the classroom door.

These are all ways in which school buildings can teach. And, surprisingly, many of the innovative facilities are inexpensive and practical. This chapter has a number of ideas to spark creativity of your own team.

If They Look at the Ceilings During Class

Many components of the science classroom can be easily modified to add an educational component. Some of these ideas have been described in previous chapters:

- Sliding shades that double as bulletin boards
- Two-way windows that enable students to share their projects with the hallway
- Patterns in the walls or floors that students can decipher

Often the educational potential of classroom space is only limited by a teacher's creativity. Can the chairs be color-coded and placed in a problem-solving pattern? Can the materials for some furnishings illustrate their age, origin, or original (recycled) use?

For all these ideas, it is wise to plan with the architect at the start rather than try to add them later.

Imaginative Planning Just Beyond the Classroom Door

Science learning doesn't have to stop at the classroom door. A well-designed project takes as many opportunities as possible to give students additional scientific stimulation. The four examples at the beginning of this chapter are only a small sample of good ideas, many suggested by members of the science faculty, that enhance schools around the country. The best part of these ideas is that they are inexpensive or free, if incorporated into building planning in the early stages. Here are just a few ideas.

In a Denver school for the gifted, the architect included a fractal pattern in the resilient floor tile, generated by a mathematical program developed by a colleague. When the contractor had finished the floor, the architect found two incorrectly installed tiles. The first was a mistake by the flooring contractor and was corrected; the second was the architect's error in translating the results of the computer program. This one was left in place and the architect added a sign on the wall of the space describing fractal patterns, indicating that one tile in the pattern was incorrect, and offering a cash reward to the first student who could determine which tile was incorrect and explain why. This clever enhancement added nothing to the construction cost of the building.

During a renovation of a 1930s-era school in St. Louis, the science teachers requested

A fractal pattern in the resilient floor tile

that a model of the solar system be included. A local model builder fabricated the planetary models and a local artist painted the Sun in a corner of the new science room. The planets were to one scale and their separation was at a different scale; the architect added a sign on the wall explaining the concept of scale and why two different scales were required for the solar system model. The total cost of this unique enhancement was $1,500.

Fabricated planetary models

An independent school in Massachusetts replaced several of the standard ceiling tiles with pieces of clear acrylic and added lighting above the ceiling so that students could see the various pipes, ducts and wiring of building support systems normally hidden from view. The added cost was for several pieces of acrylic and two inexpensive light fixtures. The same school had the contractor install a clear acrylic tube in the stair tower. The tube was ruled and filled with water to act as a barometer.

New school science facilities around the country include dozens of similar ideas rang-

Clear acrylic ceiling tile

ing from a simple sundial created with a flag in a stair tower to a whale skeleton hanging in an entry atrium. At the same time one can observe an equal number of opportunities missed where no one suggested to the design architect that a simple enhancement of the basic design could create additional science learning opportunities for students. Another creative example is utilizing the floor of the science lab/classroom. One school painted and sealed the lab's concrete floor with a large example of a DNA strand.

A prime example of creative thinking is the main entry tower at the Kent Denver School's new science center: a teacher observed the

A simple sundial

DNA strand stained in concrete floor

Astrometric time lapse

round tower in the architect's schematic design and suggested adding a glass lens to the top of the conical roof. The result was an astrometrics lab in an otherwise utilitarian space.

No space in a school should be left uneducated! Label that drinking fountain H_2O; classify the cornerstone, or cut the wood for a beam in such a way that students can count the growth rings. These ideas may not be developed naturally by your architect, but once the thought process begins, it's infectious.

When planning new or renovated science facilities, science teachers should think beyond the box, imagining "cool" ideas that could be incorporated in the design for little or no additional cost. This thinking must take place early in the planning process, at a time when the architect has not yet really finalized his or her design, or at a time when a little "tweak" could add significantly to learning opportunities without adding much, if any, cost. Not every idea will work. There are certainly guidelines from fire and building codes that would eliminate some.

Saving energy and conserving resources are key ingredients in good school design today and they can illustrate graphically the benefits of these concepts. Some of these ideas were described in Chapter 7, "Green Schools."

Day-lit science classroom

Day lighting provides physical and psychological benefits to both students and teachers while, at the same time, reducing electrical energy consumption in the building. Orienting the long side of a building to the south and incorporating light shelves that, on the one hand, shield the occupants from the harsh glare of the sun in late spring and early fall and, on the other hand, bounce daylight off the ceiling far inside the classroom provides quite adequate lighting that can be supplemented as needed by electric lights on light sensors. A sky-lit atrium can bring daylight into interior spaces that can participate in this amenity by the use of glass walls.

Sky-lit corridor

Alternative energy sources ranging from windmills to solar panels to ground source heat pumps can provide electric power and heating and cooling to buildings in ways that can greatly reduce a building's dependence on the municipal power grid and pay for themselves in saved operations costs

Light shelves

Courtyard with permeable paving

within a few years. Incorporating these systems in such a way that students can observe the amount of power generated by each source adds educational value to a practical design concept.

Rainwater can be captured and stored for use within a building and to irrigate lawns and plantings, while natural purification cycles can be used to clean wastewater enough to be used in toilets or for additional irrigation. Permeable paving can absorb rainwater, allowing it to soak into the ground, while providing an attractive walking surface. Green roofs, with plants growing on the top, reduce the heat gain and lower heating requirements while increasing the amount of carbon dioxide removed from the atmosphere.

For a more complete discussion of green buildings and sustainable design, go to

the website of the U.S. Green Building Council (*www.usgbc. org*).

Finishing Materials for Science Rooms

In selecting finishing materials, planners should consider that floors, walls, and ceilings in science rooms must be functional, durable, reasonably easy to maintain, and cost-effective.

Floors

Flooring materials should be chosen for easy maintenance and resistance to the chemicals that will be used in the room. Terrazzo (marble chips in a ground and polished concrete matrix) is still the most durable flooring available for public buildings, but the cost is usually prohibitive. While carpet has attractive sound absorbing and room-softening qualities, it is not a good choice for science classrooms or laboratories, particularly those where furniture will be moved around frequently. Chemical spills can damage or stain a carpet and make repairs a major problem. Dander from classroom animals and molds resulting from leaks remain embedded in carpets, causing health hazards.

Terrazzo floor

Vinyl composition tile is a very good choice, because it resists wear and damaged areas can be replaced in small sections. Damaged tiles can be replaced easily in sections 12 inches (30.5 cm) square, from an overstock provided by the flooring contractor at the time of installation. Tiles, 1/8-inch (32 mm) thick, are the most widely used flooring materials in school science laboratories. They come in several formulations that vary in their ability to resist chemicals. The floor will have a lot of joints, but these are not visible once the floor has been installed and finished correctly.

The 12" × 12" (30.5 cm × 30.5 cm) tiles provide the opportunity for some creative, science-elated designs. The corridors of a school in Denver have the floor tiles set in a fractal pattern; those in a science lab/classroom in St. Louis are in a tessellation pattern. An elementary science pavilion in Baltimore has a tile pattern in a *Fibonacci* spiral, while at a middle school in Wildwood, Missouri, the tile joints are aligned due north-south and accent tiles indicate the major points of a compass.

Seamless or welded-seam resilient floors, particularly of the types developed for hospitals, perform well in science facilities, but they are much more expensive than vinyl composition tile and more difficult to repair, so they are normally considered only for high school laboratories. This type of flooring is nearly twice as expensive as the 1/8-inch vinyl composition tiles. The main advantage of these floors is that they resist staining and deterioration caused by most chemicals used in a school setting. The material comes in rolls, and the joints are heat-welded with matching strips. The resilient flooring may be rolled up the walls to form an integral base.

Fluid-applied composition flooring has also been proposed for science laboratories and classrooms. However, it is more expensive and harder than resilient flooring. This makes it difficult to patch, and it may crack if the underlying surface should move.

Ceilings

Ceilings may be made of suspended acoustic materials, to create the desired classroom environment and provide easy access to mechanical and electrical systems. If there is insufficient space to allow a suspended ceiling, interlocking square tiles, 12 inches (30.5 cm) on a side, may be glued directly to the deck above or to gypsum wallboard panels. Attention should be paid to the surface texture and plastic coating of the tile, particularly in

Bowling Ball Pendulum Suspended From Ceiling

Before the bowling ball is released for this enegy conservation demonstration, what preparation was needed?

A 3/8" eyebolt is mounted to the ceiling bar joist. Tensile strength of bolt is over 1,000 pounds. The braided nylon rope has a tensile strength over 400 pounds.

Attach the ball securely to the braided rope with a U-bolt.

(Photos from Dale Freeland Portage Central High School, Portage, MI)

rooms in which chemistry or biology will be taught. A tile surface that is deeply fissured is likely to become dirty from absorbed smoke. Plastic-coated acoustical tile that can be wiped down and resists some chemicals is available. However, attention needs to be given to creating an environment where the noise does not impede instruction or harm hearing.

The science room's ceiling should be 10 feet (3 m) high and can be used as a teaching tool. For example, one chemistry class recently stenciled the periodic table onto the ceiling tiles of their classroom. Other schools have used their ceiling suspension systems to display models of animals, fish, and birds. Suspending a steel strut system, as described in Chapters 4, 5, and 6, below the ceiling can provide support for items of various weights to be suspended from above.

Walls

Wall finishes in science rooms should be washable, durable, and easy to repair. School walls have long been built of very durable materials such as concrete block or plaster. These materials resist the damages of youthful exuberance, but provide no flexibility for running electrical and communications wiring and piping or for changing the space to meet new needs. Gypsum wallboard installed on metal studs offers this flexibility, but maintenance is needed whenever the surface is dented. Although wallboard repair is a simple and inexpensive process, other needs often take precedence, and the dented wallboard is not repaired.

Fiber-reinforced gypsum wallboard with an extremely durable surface is available and may be substituted for the standard gypsum board. This material costs about 80% more than standard wallboard. Installation costs are slightly higher, and may add 5% for a large job and up to 15% for a small one.

Heavy-duty, textured vinyl wallpaper over gypsum wallboard provides a durable surface that allows student work to be attached to it.

Some architects recommend using a thin coat of plaster on top of gypsum board lath, with a washable finished surface. Standard paint, with an eggshell or semi-gloss finish, works well and is easy to patch. Vinyl wall coverings also provide good surfaces, but are more difficult to patch than the paint. Hard surface finishes, such as epoxy paints, are difficult to patch, and probably not worth the extra expense for a school science room. Some recently formulated multicolor, spray-on, decorative finishes are easy to clean, but quite difficult to patch. Ground-faced concrete block is not recommended for science classroom walls, because it does not provide much flexibility and is difficult to clean.

CHAPTER 9

Science for All

Key ideas in this chapter:

- It is challenging to design facilities that maximize opportunities for diverse student populations.
- The American Disabilities Act of 1990 (ADA) defines standards for physical access to facilities for all persons.
- ADA requirements must be part of the budget and planning process for new or renovated science facilities.
- Schools are becoming more of a 24-7 community of learners, so safe, secure learning facilities need to be the norm.

We say it often, and the phrase appears in the National Science Education Standards and many state and local documents as well. "All students should have opportunities in science." But that vision is harder to achieve in practice. It is especially challenging to design facilities that maximize opportunities for the diverse student populations that will enjoy them now and in the future. But since we know that the facilities we build today will serve many more—and more diverse—students in the future, it is important to look at them through the eyes of students with individual needs.

In previous chapters of this guide, there have been many notes on the requirements of the Americans with Disabilities Act for spaces and furnishings for physically challenged students. Those requirements are again summarized here.

ADA Guidelines

Since good science experiences are important for students, they must be available to all students. Restricting persons with disabilities to different facilities is illegal. The obligation to accommodate persons with disabilities increases when renovations are planned.

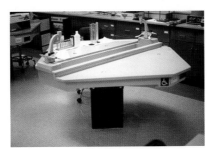

Wheelchair-accessible chem-table

The Americans with Disabilities Act of 1990 (ADA) defines standards for physical access to facilities for all persons, including students and teachers who use public buildings. For purposes of the act, a disability is defined as a "determinable physical or mental characteristic of an individual which may result from disease, injury, congenital condition of birth, or functional disorder which is unrelated to

the individual's qualifications for employment or promotion."

The 1997 Individuals with Disabilities Education Act (IDEA) defines the rights of students with special needs in U.S. schools. IDEA mandates the inclusion of students with disabilities in school programming more clearly than ever before. All science laboratory/classrooms should be built to accommodate every student who chooses to study in them. Providing wheelchair access, communication devices for hearing-impaired students, and Braille assistance for blind students in regular science laboratory/classrooms are factors that must be considered when we build today's facilities. Co-teaching by special educators in the regular classroom is becoming more common and is being incorporated into best practice, since it is difficult to prove that studying a laboratory science in a special education classroom provides equal opportunity to learn.

Guidelines for applying the ADA are found in the *Americans with Disabilities Act Accessibility Guidelines for Buildings and Facilities* (ADAAG). They are enforced by the Department of Justice. Because the ADAAG regulations are not specific to science facilities, some interpretation is required. The recommendations in this book include regulations and adaptations of related guidelines.

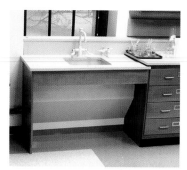

Wheelchair-accessible sink

Generally, architects are familiar with the basic requirements of accessibility. Many schools built before 1990 are not accessible to persons with disabilities. While these schools may remain compliant by making reasonable progress toward expanded access, they have an obligation to provide complete accessibility when they start a renovation. Typical deficiencies found in older buildings include steps, narrow doors and aisles, a lack of elevators, workstations that cannot be used by a student in a wheelchair, and controls that require movements that are not possible for some people with disabilities.

The ADA requires that existing deficiencies be corrected as each area in the building is renovated. A percentage of the renovation costs must be spent on upgrading the rest of the building along the path of travel from the entrance to the renovated space. Doors and aisles must be wide enough for wheelchairs—32 inches for doorways and 36 inches for aisles—toilet facilities must be wheelchair-accessible, and emergency facilities must be built at appropriate heights in all new construction.

Every area of the school used by any student or teacher must have access for persons with disabilities built in during new construction. A person in a wheelchair should be able to move without assistance from the parking lot to every essential area of the school.

In science laboratories, this often means adjusting the height of some laboratory facilities and sinks, widening aisles, and relocating equipment.

ADA Guidelines for High School Laboratory/ Classrooms

The dimensions given in the following are the adult requirements, which apply to high schools. The Architectural and Transportation Barriers Compliance board has published draft *ADA Accessibility Guidelines for Building Elements Designed for Children's Use* in the Federal Register (January 13, 1998) intended to apply to building elements used by children ages 12 and younger. As of this writing, these guidelines have not been incorporated into the Department of Justice accessibility standards but they do suggest recommended design guidelines for elementary and middle school facilities.

Laboratory Workstations

Many equipment manufacturers have developed workstations with lowered decks and lever, push-button, or electronic controls that can be used in place of regular laboratory stations to accommodate persons with disabilities. These stations may be equipped with water, gas, electrical power, and sockets for

Ductless fume hood accessible to student in wheelchair

apparatus rods. Controls should not require tight grasping, pinching, twisting of the wrist, or exerting more than five pounds of force to operate. If mobile workstations and portable equipment are used, space to accommodate the workstation should be provided in every laboratory. Since it is the intent of IDEA to include all students in a class activity, workstations for students with disabilities should be located so that the student with the disability is not isolated from the rest of the class.

It is important to note that the lowered decks are too low for many persons without disabilities to safely conduct science activities. Some planners make a mistake by adjusting all of the countertop heights or fume hoods to the 34-inch level, thus making them unsafe for the 99% of the users who do not have such a disability.

Laboratory Sinks

Laboratory sinks are a special challenge, because the ADAAG specifies a sink depth of no more than 6½ inches, so that a wheelchair can fit under the sink without having the sink be too high; the sink's rim must be at a maximum height of 34 inches for adult-sized students. This leaves little space for a heavy sink assembly and a 6½" deep sink does not allow sufficient space to safely wash most items. Some planners make the mistake of selecting an accessible sink as the only sink in the prep room that actually needs an oversized one to accommodate safe cleanup of lab materials and equipment, particularly glassware. A minimum vertical knee space of 27 inches and knee-space width of 30 inches are prescribed; the knee space must be protected from hot pipes. The sinks must have lever-controlled faucets or a similar alternative.

Fume hoods

Fume hood manufacturers have lagged behind; they have lowered decks to the necessary 34-inch maximum, but many have not

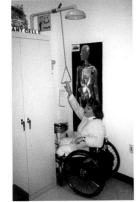

Wheelchair accessible eyewash and shower

yet developed the necessary controls such as electronic controls or paddle handles. Knee space requirements for seating at a fume hood are the same as for sinks. Again, it is important to note that the 34-inch deck is too low for persons without disabilities to use and should not be substituted for a standard hood for use by the general population.

Eyewashes and Safety Showers

The standard emergency eyewash/shower unit has the eyewash bowl mounted 38 inches above the floor, and the pull handle for the shower at about 68 inches above the floor. These can be modified to approximately 32 to 34 inches and 54 inches, respectively, to accommodate students and teachers with disabilities as well as the general population. Unlike the 34-inch fume hood deck problem discussed above, the ADA eyewash and shower can be used by both the general population and the persons with disabilities. The objective is to have the eyewash spout height at a maximum of 36 inches above the floor, the standard for a drinking fountain. If there is a second shower or eyewash in the room, these may be at standard heights.

Other Adaptations

Wall cabinet locations are a potential hazard for students and teachers with disabilities, particularly to those who are visually impaired. Sharp or unexpected corners should be avoided, and all upper cabinets should have base cabinets beneath them. Eye protection goggles need a sanitizing storage cabinet. It is always advisable to build in wiring for

communication equipment for hearing impaired students, so that electronic aids can be installed easily. A proposal to set standards for classroom acoustics has been submitted to the Access Board, which references a draft ANSI S12.60, *Acoustical Performance Criteria, Design Requirements and Guidelines for Schools.* As of this writing, this standard has not yet become law, but it is available for reference on good practices.

Some of the guidelines for children 12 years old or younger include:

- *Eyewashes.* The spout height maximum is 30 inches above the floor, as for the water fountain standard. The eyewash bowl might be mounted 24 to 26 inches above the floor.
- *Sinks.* The maximum height of the sink rim is 31 inches. Knee clearance is 24 inches, minimum.
- *Tables and counters.* Table and counter height should be 26 to 30 inches above the floor.

Creating a barrier-free learning environment benefits every learner in the school community. For planning teams, the key factor to remember is that accessibility for students with disabilities is mandatory. When installing multiple science lab/classrooms, always consider one lab station to be ADA compliant.

ADA Checklist for Designing Science Facilities

ADA Requirements:

❏ Five percent of student stations must be ADA compliant.

❏ Doors must have a minimum of 32" of clear open space.

❏ Aisles must be a minimum of 36" wide.

❏ Clear areas must be provided for wheelchair access and to be able to turn around; area must be either a 60" diameter circular space or a T-shaped arrangement of 60" overall in dimension.

❏ Work heights must not be less than 28" high or not higher than 34".

❏ Knee spaces beneath counters for adults must be at least 27" high, 30" wide and 19" deep. If knee space is below a sink, the deepest sink allowed is 6½" in a 34" high counter. Knee spaces beneath sinks must protect the user from HOT pipes.

❏ Controls for faucets, electricity, gas, etc., cannot require twisting of the wrist or tight grasping to operate.

❏ Signage should have the Braille equivalent accompanying the printed text and should be mounted so that the center of the sign is 60" above the floor.

❏ The science spaces must be reachable by an accessible path.

❏ Electrical and data receptacles should be mounted not less than 15" above the floor.

Logical Recommendations:

❏ Accessible lab work surfaces for adults should be 34" above the floor.

❏ Accessible equipment and supplies on shelves should not be higher than 54" above the floor.

❏ At least one fume hood should be accessible with a 34" high deck, wrist blade handles on faucets and gas jets, controls within reach of someone in a wheelchair.

❏ Safety showers and eyewashes should be adapted for those in wheelchairs. Shower handles not higher than 54" above the floor, spray heads for dual eyewash not higher than 36" above the floor, and center of bowl 20–24" from wall.

❏ Wall cabinets should be mounted so that there is always something beneath them to protect a visually impaired person from hitting the cabinet with his or her head.

❏ Accessible workstations should be located so as to be integrated with the regular workstations in the laboratory/classroom.

❏ Counter height and other dimensions should be adjusted for the age group of the users (See ADA Accessibility Guidelines for Building Elements Designed for Children's Use).

❏ Classroom acoustics should be designed to enable all students to be able to clearly hear presentations and avoid extraneous noises that might detract from the experience of a hearing-impaired individual.

Information Sources

Title II of the ADA requires public schools to comply with either the ADAAG or the Uniform Federal Accessibility Guidelines (UFAS).

Independent schools must follow ADAAG requirements.

For help in applying ADAAG regulations to specific design issues, contact the Justice Department's technical assistance hotline at 1-800-514-0301. The Justice Department has established a network of Disability Business Technical assistance centers at 1-800-949-4232. The website is *www.adata.org*. Also consult the state ADA accessibility office to determine state requirements that may be more rigorous.

Information is also available from the Office of Technical and Information Services, Architectural and Transportation Barriers Compliance Board (also known as the Access Board), 1331 F Street, NW, Suite 1000, Washington, DC 20004-1111, Telephone: 1-800-872-2253 or 202-272-5434. Documents can be accessed at *www.access-board.gov*.

Publications are available, such as:

• A publications listing at *www.access-board. gov/po1.cfm*

• The Uniform Federal Accessibility Standards (UFAS) (Document S-04) *www.access-board.gov/ufas/ufas-html/ufas. htm*

• Title III of the ADA, with the latest requirements from the Justice Department on the ADAAG (28 CFR 36, Appendix A; Document S-14)

• An updated reprint of the *Americans with Disabilities Act Accessibility Guidelines for Buildings and Facilities* (ADAAG), with new guidelines for building elements designed for children's use (36 CFR 1191, Appendix A; Document S-08; Document S-30 for children's guidelines only), *www.*

access-board.gov/adaag/kids/final.htm. As of this writing, these new guidelines are not enforceable, because they have not yet been adopted by the Justice Department. See Appendix B for consolidated guidelines.

But wider doors, lower sinks and broader aisles are just the beginning of a process. When planning teams get together to create new learning environments, it is often wise to envision in them the most diverse student population imaginable. Here are just a few of the ways that science-learning spaces can accommodate all students.

24-7 Schools

We have been used to thinking of schools that work six or seven hours a day (except, of course, the athletic facilities). But tomorrow's schools will serve more students, of a wider range of ages and ambitions, over far more time. That is just economics! Communities cannot afford to duplicate labs in several sites for several different uses. Here are just a few of the implications of that trend:

Alternative schools: Many communities have established alternative schools for students who do not fit in the normal parameters of a traditional school program. Sometimes they attend for disciplinary reasons, sometimes because they don't attend regularly if school begins early. An alternative school can be housed in a regular high school, on an afternoon-evening schedule. But that has implications for design. If two sets of faculty will use the same facilities, they should have separate secured storage, and

securable places to set up materials for the next day. It is never a good idea to allow students access to materials with which they are not familiar. Neither should any teacher walk into a storeroom and wonder where a certain chemical or piece of equipment has gone.

Adult education: Adults often attend school in the evenings, too. But their needs are different. They need more support for learning, and are more likely to need assistive technologies. (See below.) But the same guidelines for additional, safe and secure, storage for their materials apply.

Distance learning courses: Colleges, and even some high schools, are now offering a wide variety of courses online or through video hookups. These courses occasionally meet face to face.

The moral? Do not design your science facilities under the assumption that your own faculty will be the only ones to use them. Do not think that if you don't have those separate storage and preparation areas, the administration will leave your facilities vacant when you are not around. Make sure there are options.

Signs of the Times

In American schools, our goal is often to help all of our students learn and communicate effectively in English. But that's not always the reality—at least not at the outset. Students should not have to wait to safely explore in science until their English is good enough. So in many school science facilities, multilingual

signage is recommended. You would never want an accident to occur because a new student misunderstood a direction or the nature of equipment or chemicals.

Depending on the school population, signage in Braille is required. It's not practical to wait until the day that a visually impaired student walks in the door of the science room to think about that need. Someone from the science department should participate in Individual Educational Planning (IEP) meetings and let the support team know that this is a priority. Even better, build the signage with Braille from the start. It's a good lesson for all students.

When designing or remodeling, don't forget to think about the size and height of the signage you'll need. Just because most middle school students are five feet tall doesn't mean that next year you won't have an enthusiastic three-foot-tall student. Make sure that the room is organized, well labeled, and clear to every student that enters. Even though a sign is mounted lower in height, it must also be repeated at 60" above the floor to be legal.

Taking the realities presented above (In "24-7 Schools") to heart, more signage is always better than less. It may seem obvious to mark one cabinet "chemical glassware," and another "life science glassware," or to put special labels on the materials that should only be used by the advanced placement students, but that may be just the "ticket" to avoid an accident during an off hour. Custodians need signage too—especially substitutes. Can we assume they know that the red trashcan is the biohazard disposal? Make sure that the room is organized, well labeled, and clear to every person that enters. The universal icons used by fire departments are recommended.

Can You Hear Me Now?

If a student with a documented hearing impairment is assigned to your room, you will probably know it immediately. The steps that you will need to take are probably listed in the Individual Educational Plan (IEP) and funded by the special education department. But most hearing impairments in school children are temporary or "sub clinical." They come and go, making verbal directions seem like so much buzz on certain days to students with allergies or chronic infections. So modifications to the design of classrooms that make sounds both louder and clearer are good for all students, all the time and should not wait until an Individual Educational Plan demands them. These modifications might include acoustic field systems (special speakers and microphone hookups), as well as professional placement of media equipment for maximum efficiency. It is also possible to put individual earphone hookups at some desks (preferably wireless) in order to accommodate students with greater degrees of hearing impairment.

In some rooms—chiefly physics and technology—the problem may be too much sound. If a room will house regular use of tools or machines, it may be wise to design sound-absorbing acoustic panels on the walls and ceilings. (These are very common in band rooms, as well.) But that sort of sound-absorbing engineering makes it more difficult for the teacher to be heard. So some technology rooms have two areas, one for direct instruction and an area where sounds are more easily muffled.

In recent years, some special-needs families have requested carpeting in their children's classrooms to provide less background noise and make it easier for speech to be discerned. Carpeting is never recommended or safe in a science room. Alternatives (like the field systems described above) should always be used.

Can I Sit in the Front?

In the years before contact lenses and laser eye surgery, it was more common to have students ask to sit in the front of the room so that they could see the marker board. Today, almost all students can be helped to a sufficient degree of visual acuity to see the instructional materials IF the room is structured in such a way that each seat has a good sight view of the instructional area.

But that isn't always the case. We've seen many schools where learning spaces that were extremely long and narrow have been remodeled. Because windows often line one of the long sides of the room, the potential for projection and board work is limited. If the teacher station is on one of the long walls, there can be many seats where students cannot comfortably see the board.

It is important that the architect consider the lines of sight in a classroom early in the planning process. While you cannot totally change the shape of some rooms, there are still steps that can be taken. One solution for renovating such a room is to look hard at the casework. Moving the lab sinks or the storage areas to the ends can cluster the desks more directly near the instructional station. Another type of solution involves using multiple projection screens. With today's technology, there is no reason to limit yourself to just one. Duplicating the digital projector costs just a fraction of what it would cost to move a wall. The architect may also examine the possibility of creating more storage or project rooms to enhance the main learning spaces.

Always on the Move

More and more students today display some characteristics of hyperactivity disorders—even more when they are not specifically certified as special needs. They are constantly moving and easily distracted. It is wise to think about the behaviors of young "Tiggers" as you plan science spaces.

When a planning team gets enthusiastic, it's often hard to know when to stop. Some rooms are so cluttered with museum specimens, display boards, and equipment that they are really distracting to hyperactive students. It's often valuable to consider the overall appearance of a room before the casework is ordered, to determine whether you'll have enough to look at or too much.

Older classrooms often have ceiling to floor windowed casework—often filled with jars and skeletons, rocks and other collections. These glass doors are not only distracting but they can be safety hazards. They can break when bouncy students bump against them, and they are not normally appropriate to store anything containing chemicals. It's better to order appropriate, closed cabinets and to create temporary displays that can be controlled and changed as the curriculum and class permits.

Research also shows that some forms (chiefly older types) of fluorescent lighting can exacerbate hyperactivity and other sorts of behavioral problems. Natural light that can be modified for projection is always the best choice.

Making Best Use of Our Gifts

While planning teams often consider special-needs students, it's also important to consider gifted students as well. To that end, many of the chapters in this book have included mention of special project rooms for independent research, distance learning, or advanced multimedia and game activities. Project rooms should always be visible to and directly supervised by the classroom teacher. That might imply an "L" arrangement or a glassed area off the main classroom.

Distance learning is also an option to broaden the curriculum for gifted students. There is a special section devoted to that in Chapter 2. In some schools, an area off the library or media center serves for these activities since a certified media specialist can supervise. Whatever the plan, it's important to realize that these kinds of specialized uses will become much more common in the future.

It Takes a Whole Community

Remember that schools belong to communities, and that classrooms must (by best practice and law) be accessible to all those who might want or need to visit. So designing your facilities "for all" should also include TDD services for hearing-impaired community members, ramps and wider doors into spaces that teachers use, and specialized parking—lots of it—for when the senior citizens come to call. Visitors may need extra seating or standing spaces. Some schools provide video equipment so that student presentations can be shared in other rooms for such visitors. Planning special display cases for visitors is a great PR move, and the "special events" rooms described in Chapter 8 are ideal for student programs.

Plan for the Worst to Achieve the Best

Finally, take a look at your emergency plan with special-needs students and adults in mind. Does an automatic fire door block access to a ramp that a wheelchair student might need? Is there clutter blocking a wider aisle to a shower or eyewash? Does your fire alarm system include both light and sound, for students with visual or hearing impairments? All of these considerations make it possible to say with confidence that a facility supports science explorations for all students.

APPENDIX A

Solar Energy for School Facilities

As demand for energy continues to grow, facilities planners should be aware of the possible applications of solar technology. Global warming seems to be accelerating due to human activity, and more use of solar energy could help to minimize the impact of a new school facility. Not only do solar energy systems help offset rising energy costs, but a well-designed facility may improve student performance and even add to the curriculum. Schools may go solar to solve a number of energy needs, from "daylighting" classrooms to reduce consumption of fossil fuels to cooling a classroom or heating water. In combination with other efficient energy resources, such as well-insulated walls and roofs and energy-efficient lighting, solar energy can provide significant savings over the long run.

Solar technology takes different forms, depending on institutional goals, site characteristics, budget, and other factors. Daylighting is a design-based strategy for bringing natural light into the interior of a building. A facility is constructed with most windows facing south to maximize daylight and may include skylights and "light shelves" that reflect window light into interior spaces. Not only does daylighting decrease the amount of electricity used for lighting, but it can also lower air conditioning needs, because the light fixtures produce less heat. Because of the amount of glass used, the main concerns associated with daylighting are heat gain during summer months and heat loss during the winter, which can be substantial in some regions. Such design strategies as overhangs above windows and shading systems over skylights help prevent the summer sun from entering the interior. Special window coatings and interior shades minimize heat loss through windows or skylights during the heating season.

In addition to lowering energy costs, daylighting provides a more comfortable light than fluorescent lighting. There is strong evidence that students perform better under natural light, as reflected in both attendance and test scores.

Passive solar technology uses the Sun for lighting and heating without the aid of mechanical or electrical devices. Heat is collected by thermal mass materials, such as masonry walls or roof ponds, and then released gradually during periods when the sun isn't shining.

The construction cost of a passive solar facility can run as much as or more than conventional building costs. Decreasing the size of heating and cooling systems saves in construction costs, however, and more savings are realized in the reduction in total energy use over time. Tests conducted by the National Energy Laboratory show that buildings with passive solar design use 47% to 60% less energy than those without.

Solar thermal systems use air or water heated by the sun as an energy source. In schools, solar-heated water can be used as is or can be run through other systems to heat or air-condition part of a building. Ferry Pass Middle School in Pensacola, Florida, supplies conditioned air to an 8,000-square-foot science wing using solar thermal panels as a source of energy. Initial costs of such thermal systems are usually high, but operating costs are very low.

Solar photovoltaic (PV) systems rely on cells, usually made of silicon, to convert sunlight directly into electricity. These are commonly used to power calculators and wristwatches. More complex systems, consisting of arrays of cells anchored in panels, can generate electricity to pump water, power communications equipment, or heat a classroom, often at less cost than conventional electricity. PV panels, fixed or adjustable, can be mounted on the roof or on the ground. The number of panels needed depends on the wattage required. Generally, PV power is not practical for large electrical loads.

The primary obstacle to the use of solar panels is the high cost of the initial installation. However, recent cooperative ventures among utility companies, manufacturers, and state governments are making solar power more accessible to school systems around the country.

When schools use solar energy, they also provide students with learning opportunities. Solar energy systems can be incorporated in the curriculum to teach students the specifics of alternative forms of energy production, as well as data collection and measurement techniques.

There are many resources available both online and in print regarding solar energy and technology. A good place to start is with *Schools Going Solar,* a booklet produced collaboratively by the Interstate Renewable Energy Council (IREC), the Utility PhotoVoltaic Group (UPVG), and the American Solar Energy Society (ASES) (available online at *www. eren.doe.gov/irec/programs/solarschools*).

Reference

Gibson, B., J. Mayotte, J. Cochran, and S. Kalish. 1998. *Schools going solar*. Washington, DC: Utility Photovoltaic Group.

Building for Safety in Secondary School Science Facilities: An Audit

Sandra S. West

School _____ Room No. _____ Classroom Teacher _____

Department Chair _____ Content Area _____

Please place a check mark in the appropriate column. "No" answers indicate a problem.

	YES	NO
I. Floor Space and Class Size		
Floor space is defined as "within the walls," excludes furniture, entry, alcoves, etc.		
A. 24 students or fewer per class (NSTA and NSELA recommendation) for safe supervision		
B. 60 sq ft/high school student laboratory/classroom space (within the walls, do not exclude furniture), minimum (NSTA recommendation)		
C. 55 sq ft/middle school student laboratory/classroom space		
D. 45 sq ft/elementary school student laboratory/classroom space		
E. 1 lab/workstation for each student		
F. 6 sq ft/lab workstation/student (36" wide × 24" deep horizontal work surface)		
G. 1 lab/classroom for each science teacher		
H. 6 ft. linear horizontal work surface/student (includes lab/workstations, countertops, lab tables not desks)		
I. Preparation and equipment/materials storage space		
1. 10 sq ft/student, minimum, preparation/equipment (preparation, equipment and materials) storage space (240 sq ft for each 24 student lab/classroom)		
2. 1 sq ft/student, minimum, for chemical storage		
J. Additional space		
1. ADA requirements (approx. 20 sq ft) for lab/workstation		
2. Technology equipment (lab/field and instructional) 50 sq ft		
3. Multiple different courses taught in same lab/classroom		
K. Lab/classroom width 30 ft, minimum for continuous instructional wall		
L. Aisles 4 ft wide, minimum (to allow students and teachers to move and egress safely)		
M. Doorways 36" wide, minimum		
N. Separate room/space for small group or individual or long-term research projects		
II. Communication System		
A. Telephone in every room		
B. "Hotline" to office in every room (emergency telephone or intercom button)		

	YES	NO
III. Shut-Off Controls		
A. Emergency shut-off controls are labeled, accessible to teachers, preferably near the teacher's station, but not too easily accessible to students (not at door entry or hallway)		
1. Gas		
2. Electricity		
B. Master shut-off controls are labeled (if separate from emergency shutoffs) accessible to teacher, but not easily accessible to students		
C. All shut-off controls (emergency and master) clearly labeled:		
1. Gas		
2. Electricity		
3. Water (source that does not shut off eyewash or shower)		
IV. Utilities		
A. Vandal-resistant:		
1. Water faucets		
2. Gas jets		
B. Electricity:		
1. Sufficient number of electrical circuits provided in lab/classroom to meet curriculum, including computer and other technical equipment (3–20 amp minimum)		
2. No DC lines (substitute small, dry cells for students or portable DC units for teachers, protected by circuit breakers or fuses)		
3. All outlets in lab/classroom, preparation/equipment room, storage room and project room protected by ground-fault interrupters (GFI)		
4. All outlets grounded and requiring 3-pronged plugs (OSHA requirement)		
5. No outlets within 3 ft of faucets or other water sources		
6. Sufficient number of outlets provided to eliminate need for extension cords, overlapping wires, or plug-in outlet extenders (e.g., 2 duplex outlets/student lab/workstation)		
7. Laboratory refrigerators, spark-free		
C. Water faucets		
1. Capped with an aerator, not a serrated hose connection		
2. Swivel and high-arched faucets		
V. Fire Control and Security		
A. ABC dry chemical fire extinguisher, or type required by local ordinance:		
1. Present in every lab/classroom, preparation/equipment room and storage room		
2. Present in every chemical storage room unless attached to preparation/equipment storage room (may require more than one type of fire extinguisher to avoid chemical reactions)		
3. In easily visible, unobstructed locations		
4. Located near escape routes (second extinguisher may be in interior of room)		

	YES	NO
5. Correct size (5 lb. minimum, 16 lb. maximum, charge weight)		
B. Access to fire exits (via doors and ground-floor windows):		
1. 2 exits in every lab/classroom if over 1,000 square feet with main door opening outward		
2. 2 exits in every preparation/equipment storage room		
3. Fireproof doors that open outward for all chemical storage rooms		
4. All exits labeled, unobstructed, and unlocked from inside		
C. General alarm system for entire building		
D. Smoke alarm present in every preparation/equipment storage room		
E. 2 smoke alarms in preparation/equipment storage room if 200 sq ft or larger		
F. Smoke and heat alarm present in chemical storage room		
G. Automatic sprinkler system (may be required under local or state fire codes):		
1. Present in lab/classroom, preparation/equipment storage room		
2. Recommended in chemical storage room (special head may be needed to protect against oxidizers; water reactive chemicals require protected storage)		
3. No obstructions within 18" of ceiling		
H. Lockable doors for all lab/classrooms, preparation/equipment storage rooms, and science storage rooms.		
I. Chemical storage room with unique key for science teachers and administrators (not available to others such as custodians, nonscience teachers, etc.)		
J. Safe ADA accessible entrance to roof, if roof-mounted weather station is to be used		
VI. Ventilation		
A. All lab/classrooms, prep/equipment, and chemical storage rooms air vented to outside of building, not recirculated in building's ventilation system		
B. All exhaust air vented to outside of building, at sufficient distance from air intakes to prevent re-circulation		
C. Lab/classroom ventilation at a rate of 4 air changes/hr, minimum (occupied ANSI Z9.5 & ASHRAE Standard 62, or later)		
D. Preparation/equipment storage room ventilation at rate of 1ft^3/minute/ 1ft^2 floor space, minimum		
E. Chemical storage room ventilation:		
1. Continuous, with exhaust vented to outside of building away from intake vent		
2. 6 air changes/hr, minimum (OSHA requirement) (minimum of 1 cfm/sq ft but not less than 150 cfm NFPA 30)		
3. Climate-controlled storage so that chemicals are not exposed to excessive hot or cold temperatures or humidity		
4. Exhaust vents at floor and ceiling		
F. Exhaust fan/purge system for supplemental ventilation		
1. Present in every lab/classroom, preparation/equipment storage room, for quick removal of excessive fumes		

	YES	NO
2. Provided with manual control		
3. Exhaust vented to outside of building		
4. Equipped with fan guards, if wall-mounted		
G. Fume hood:		
1. Present in every lab/classroom where hazardous or vaporous chemicals are used		
2. Present in every preparation/equipment storage room (may be single unit available to lab/classroom and preparation/equipment storage room, mounted on common wall)		
3. 2 or more fume hoods present in AP or advanced chemistry lab/classroom		
4. Exhaust vented to outside of building on roof or outside wall		
5. Deck height 36"		
6. Provides 80 to 120 linear ft, minimum, of air movement at hood face, for working with chemicals of low to moderate toxicity (ANSI Z9.5.7)		
7. Located at least 10 ft from main exit (ANSI Z9.5.4)		
8. Not located on a main traffic aisle (ANSI Z9.5.4)		
9. Located away from heavy traffic areas, doors, windows, and intake ducts so that fume hood airflow is not disrupted.		
10. If shared by two or more fume hoods, ventilation system adequately engineered for purpose		
11. Sash level marked for 100 ft/min of air movement and with date of measurement		
12. Meets ASHRAE 110 testing standard (at least 4.0 AU 0.10)		
13. Not used as storage area		
H. Lab/classroom ventilation meets ANSI Z9.5 standard		
VII. Lighting		
A. 50 fc/sq ft, minimum, general lighting level in lab/classroom, preparation/equipment room, and chemical storage rooms		
B. 75 fc/sq ft, minimum, on counter surfaces underneath wall cabinets		
C. Battery-operated emergency light:		
1. Present in every lab/classroom, storage room, and preparation/equipment storage room that has insufficient natural light or used at night		
2. Located next to doorway in lab/classroom and preparation/equipment storeroom		
D. Directed and diffused to avoid glare		
E. Controlled lighting with separate switches for rows of lights and room-darkening capability (shades, etc.)		
VIII. Work Areas		
A. All work surfaces made of chemical-resistant materials		
B. In lab/classroom:		
1. 6 linear ft work space/student (including lab/work stations and counters, not desks)		
2. 6 linear ft counter space adjacent to a large sink 24" × 36" × 11" minimum		

	YES	NO
3. Lab/work stations that allow a minimum of 3.6 sq ft/student lab station		
4. 1 sink/4 students, sinks 18" × 15" × 8" minimum, sinks with flexible, chemical-resistant mats (such as neoprene)		
5. Hot water available		
6. Heat source available		
7. Electricity with GFI-protection provided		
8. 10 ft ceilings		
C. Preparation/equipment storage room:		
1. 4 linear ft minimum, counter space adjacent to a large sink, 24" × 36" × 11" minimum		
2. 12 linear ft, minimum, counter space, does not have to be above floor cabinets		
3. Hot water available (120° F maximum)		
4. Heat source(s) available		
5. Electricity with GFI-protection provided		
D. Clear floor space for laboratory carts, technology, human skeleton, etc.		
E. Area(s) for safety equipment in every lab/classroom and prep/equipment storeroom:		
1. Space near fire extinguisher for safety equipment such as sand container and fire blanket		
2. Space for safety equipment such as first-aid kit and poster, chemical waste container, broken glass container, and spill kit		
3. Space for hanging aprons for 24 students in lab/classroom at entry to lab area		
IX. Equipment for Personal Protection		
A. Eyewash:		
1. Provided in every lab/classroom, access within 10 seconds of all lab/workstations (ANSI Z 58.1, 1998 or newer)		
2. Unobstructed		
3. Eyewash (dual eyewash, which treats both eyes simultaneously with equal flow pressure) located near safety shower (squeeze bottle and single eye drench not sufficient)		
4. Dual eyewash in every chemistry and physical science lab/classroom and every lab/classroom and prep/equipment storeroom where hazardous chemicals are used		
5. Dual eyewash provides instant, gentle, tempered flow of aerated water for 15 minutes, and can stay in open position, leaving user's hands free		
B. Safety shower:		
1. Available in every chemistry and physical science lab/classroom, within 10 sec. Access to all lab/workstations (ANSI Z 58.1)		
2. Unobstructed shower and valve handle		
3. Fixed valve pull handle (no chains unless provided with large ring)		
4. Sufficient water pressure (20 psi, minimum, for 68 gal/minimum)		
5. Floor drain with trap present or outlet placed so that it can be tested monthly		

	YES	NO
C. Eyewashes and safety showers meet ANSI Z358.1 standard		
D. At least one eyewash and safety shower accessible to students with disabilities (see below)		
E. Safety features for equipment (such as belt guards on belt-driven machinery) provided		
X. Storage		
A. Chemicals:		
1. Storage in secure, regulated areas, with entry only for authorized personnel (no students, custodians, etc.)		
2. No storage in classroom or areas to which students have access		
3. No storage of hazardous chemicals in preparation/equipment storage room, or rooms with sensitive equipment or electrical outlets		
4. Sufficient space for safe, specialized storage:		
a. Space for storing chemicals with sufficient distance between incompatible chemicals, preferably with impermeable partitions		
b. Vented, corrosion-resistant (nonmetal or coated metal) cabinet for storing acids, corrosion-resistant shelves, and supports		
c. Separate cabinet for nitric acid, away from other acids and readily oxidized substances		
d. Dedicated, grounded, and UL=approved cabinet or safety cans for storing flammables separately		
e. Lockable cabinet for poisons		
5. Protected location for water-sensitive chemicals, especially to shield from water sprinklers		
6. All shelves equipped with lip edge or rod to prevent bottle roll-off or drip from spills onto people standing in front of the shelf		
7. Shelves made of wood with plastic supports, or other corrosion-resistant materials		
8. Shelves for chemical containers 12" deep (maximum), so containers will not be stored more than 2 containers deep		
9. Sufficient shelf space available so chemicals can be reached easily and won't be knocked over		
10. Laboratory refrigerator in preparation/equipment room, spark-free to protect against ignition of flammables		
11. Chemical-resistant countertops only		
B. Gas cylinder: (Compressed gases are not normally used in secondary school science. Numerous safeguards are necessary, including the following. See American Chemical Society 1995, pp. 14–15.)		
1. Chained to prevent from falling over (with chain securely fastened to a stud or other wall support) and becoming a missile if it develops a leak		
2. Can be clamped tightly into place after being positioned for use		
3. Stored away from heat or ignition source		
4. Safety cap on when not in use		

	YES	NO
C. Cabinets in lab/classroom, preparation/equipment and other storage rooms:		
1. Wood (not fiberboard) cabinets and drawers in lab/classroom and preparation/equipment and other storage rooms		
2. Ample for storage needs, including at least one tall cabinet		
3. Secured to floor and/or wall with sufficient attachments to keep from falling		
4. Some lockable cabinets provided, to prevent theft of equipment		
5. Solid doors (no glass fronts) in lab/classroom		
6. Flat stock drawers for storing posters		
7. Specialized storage such as a cabinet for a skeleton on wheels		
8. Drawers of different sizes and shapes in many lower cabinets		
9. Allow sufficient lab/classroom countertop space for equipment such as large distilled water containers, plant growth trays		
D. Open shelves in preparation/equipment and other storage rooms:		
1. Ample for storage needs, in a variety of depths (12", 24", and 36") and lengths for the varied and odd shaped equipment science uses such as stream trays, plant growth carts, bicycle wheels, aquariums, etc.		
2. Equipped with lip edge or rod in earthquake-prone areas		
3. Hanging shelves secured to wall or ceiling with sufficient attachments to keep from falling		
4. Hanging shelves solid enough to support a substantial amount of weight		
E. Space in preparation/equipment or other storage rooms for:		
1. Protective clothing (teacher safety goggles, aprons, etc.)		
2. Carriers for transporting chemicals, such as acids		
3. Large items and equipment, such as supply carts, safety goggles sanitizer, and microscopes		

XI. Lab/Classroom Wall Space

	YES	NO
A. Leave an equivalent of one side wall clear of cabinets with space for maps, etc.		
B. Use front instructional wall for storage behind a movable marker board with drawers below		
C. Apron and goggle storage at entrance to lab area		
D. Analog clock with second hand mounted in the lab area (not on front wall)		

XII. Adaptations for Students With Disabilities

	YES	NO
A. Permanent laboratory station or space for portable laboratory station (with gas, if used, electricity, water, sink, and sockets for rods) that meets ADA guidelines		
B. Accessible controls (e.g., levers or electronic controls) for gas, electricity, and water		
C. Adapted seating at counter, table, or desk:		
1. Counter/table/desk height 34" maximum (26–30" maximum, recommended for students under 12 years old)		

	YES	NO
2. Vertical knee clearance 27" minimum (24" minimum, recommended for students under 12 years old)		
D. Adapted sink:		
1. Counter height and sink rim 34" above floor, maximum (30" maximum recommended counter height, and 31" maximum recommended sink rim height, for students under 12 years old)		
2. Sink depth 6½" maximum		
3. Vertical knee clearance 27" minimum (24" minimum, recommended for students under 12 years old), with protection from hot water pipes		
4. Accessible controls		
E. Accessible eyewash and safety shower:		
1. Distance from wall to center of eyewash bowl 20–24"		
2. Eyewash spout 36" above floor, maximum (30" maximum, recommended for students under 12 years old)		
3. Shower pull handle 48" maximum above floor if accessible from front only		
4. Shower pull handle 54" maximum above floor if accessible from the side		
F. Adapted portable or fixed fume hood when using chemicals, with 34" deck height, maximum (see previous seating, controls, knee space requirements)		
G. Aisles 36" minimum, and doorways 32" clear width minimum, for wheelchair clearance		
H. 5'-diameter turning space for wheelchair in all rooms		
I. Wiring for electronic aids, such as field monitors for hearing-impaired students		
J. No protruding upper cabinets or sharp corners on cabinets, for the vision-impaired		

Annual Inspection using this instrument (circle one)　　Yes　　No

XIII. Overall how safe is your lab? (circle one)

(low)　1　2　3　4　5　(high)

Recommendations:

_____

_____

Teacher Signature _____ Date _____

Administrator Signature _____ Date _____

Acronyms
ADA: Americans With Disabilities Act
ANSI: American National Standards Institute
ASHRAE: American Society of Heating, Refrigerating, and Air-Conditioning Engineers
NFPA: National Fire Protection Association
NSELA: National Science Education Leadership Association
NSTA: National Science Teachers Association
OSHA: Occupational Safety and Health Administration

References

American Chemical Society. 1995. *Safety in academic chemistry laboratories.* 6th ed. Washington, DC: Author.

American National Standards Institute. 2003. *Laboratory ventilation* (ANSI Standard Z9.5-2003). New York: Author.

American National Standards Institute. 2004. *Emergency eyewash and shower equipment* (ANSI Standard Z358. 1-2004). New York: Author.

American Society of Heating, Refrigerating, and Air-Conditioning Engineers. 1995. *Method of testing performance of laboratory fume hoods* (ANSI/ASHRAE Standard 110-1995). Atlanta, GA: Author.

Architectural and Transportation Barriers Compliance Board. 1998. *Americans with disabilities act accessibility guidelines for buildings and facilities.* Washington, DC: U.S. Access Board.

National Fire Prevention Association. 2006. *Life safety code* (NFPA Standard 101). Quincy, MA: Author.

National Science Education Leadership Association. 1998. *NSELA handbook.* Marblehead, MA: Author.

National Science Teachers Association. 1998. *NSTA handbook: 2006–07.* Arlington, VA: Author.

Occupational Safety and Health Administration. 2005. *Flammable and combustible liquids* (General Industry Standard 29 CFR 1910.106 OSHA 2206).

Developed by Dr. Sandra S. West © 1-1-07, version 4/2/07
Please do not copy without credit being given to the author.

Table of Critical Dimensions

ITEM	GRADES K–2	GRADES 3–5	MIDDLE SCHOOL	HIGH SCHOOL	REMARKS
TABLES					
Dimensions of Tabletop	30" × 30"	24" × 48"	24" × 60"	24" × 72"	Flat-topped tables recommended
Seating Height	18" to 20"	21" to 23"	25" to 30"	30"	29" preferable for h.s. biology
COUNTERS					
Depth	24", min.	24", min.	24", min.	24", min.	30" min. for map drawers
Height	24"	27"	32" to 36"	36"	ADA height 34", max.*
Knee Space (Horizontal)	24", min.	24", min.	24" to 30"	30"	ADA 30", min.*
Knee Space (Vertical)	18", min.	20", min.	22" to 26"	26"	ADA 27", min.*
SINKS					
Depth	8", min.	8", min.	8", min.	8", min.	ADA sink depth 6.5", max.*
Height	24"	27"	32" to 36"	36"	ADA height 34", max.*
Length and Width	15" × 15"	15" × 15"	15" × 15"	15" × 15"	One large sink, 15" × 24" needed
"Rinseaway" Sink Length	70 ½"	70 ½"	70 ½" to 114"	70 ½" to 114"	
BASE CABINETS					
Height	22 ½"	25 ½"	30 ½" to 34 ½"	34 ½"	Under 1 ½"-thick counter
Depth	21 ½"	21 ½"	21 ½"	21 ½"	Under 24"-deep counter
					27" min. depth for map drawers
WALL CABINETS					
Depth	12" to 15"	12" to 15"	12" to 15"	12" to 15"	
Mounting Height:	18" above counter	18" above counter	18" above counter	18" above counter	
Students	42"	45"	52" to 54"	54"	ADA height 48", max.*
Adults	54"	54"	54"	54"	ADA height 48", max.*
COMPUTERS (LAPTOP)					
Surface Area	10" × 12"	10" × 12"	10" × 12"	10" × 12"	Reserved counter space not required
Storage Cabinet for Laptops	15" D × 30" W × 30" H	15" D × 30" W × 30" H	15" D × 30" W × 30" H	15" D × 30" W × 30" H	Cabinet 15" deep holds 20 laptops
PREPARATION ROOM					
Minimum Size	8' × 12'	8' × 12'	8' × 16'	10' × 20'	10' × 20' desirable for m.s. and h.s.
Size of Teacher's Desktop	72" W x 29" to 30" H	72" W x 29" to 30" H	72" W x 29" to 30" H	72" W x 29" to 30" H	

*ADA requirement for adults.

ITEM	GRADES K–2	GRADES 3–5	MIDDLE SCHOOL	HIGH SCHOOL	REMARKS
SHELVING DEPTHS					
For Books	10", min.	10", min.	10", min.	10", min.	
For Equipment Storage	12" to 24", mixed	12" to 24", mixed	12" to 24", mixed	12" to 24", mixed	12" max. for chemicals, some at 30" for physics
AISLE SPACE					ADA 36" min. for continuous aisle
Between Tables	24" to 36"	24" to 36"	24" to 36"	24" to 36"	36" is preferable for safety
Between Tables and Counters	48"	48"	48"	48"	48" min. around perimeter of room
Between Tables and Marker Board	8'	8'	8'	8'	10' pref. for projector use
PROJECTION SCREEN					
Minimum Size	5' H x 7' W	5' H x 7' W	5' H x 7' W	5' H x 7' W	
SHOWER/EYEWASH					
Eyewash Bowls (Height)	24"	25" to 26"	32"	38"	Accessible eyewash spout height 36", max.
Shower Handles (Height)	N/A	N/A	54"	68"	Accessible height 54", max., if side access
FUME HOODS					
Deck Height	N/A	N/A	32" to 36"	36"	ADA height 34", max.*
LIGHTING					
General	50 fc, min.	50 fc, min.	50 fc, min.	50 fc, min.	Glare-free lighting recommended
At Work Surface	75 fc	75 fc	75 fc	75 fc	Glare-free lighting recommended
MARKER BOARD					
Minimum Width	12'	12'	16'	16'	Multiple sliding panels recommended
Mounting Height:					
Students	24"	27"	32" to 36"	36"	
Adults	36"	36"	36"	36"	
BULLETIN BOARD					
Minimum Width	6'	6'	6'	6'	
Mounting Height:					
Students	24"	27"	32" to 36"	36"	
Adults	36"	36"	36"	36"	

*ADA requirement for adults.

ITEM	GRADES K–2	GRADES 3–5	MIDDLE SCHOOL	HIGH SCHOOL	REMARKS
FLOOR SPACE					
Minimum per Student:					
Multiple-Use Classroom	45 sq ft	45 sq ft	N/A	N/A	
Laboratory/Classroom	N/A	N/A	60 sq ft	60 sq ft	
STORAGE SPACE					
Minimum per Student:					
For Chemicals	1 sq ft	1 sq ft	1 sq ft	1 sq ft	Included in 10 sq ft prep. and storage
For Preparation and Storage	10 sq ft	10 sq ft	10 sq ft	10 sq ft	
CEILING HEIGHT	10'	10'	10'	10'	
DOORWAY WIDTH	36", min.	36", min.	36", min.	36", min.	ADA 32" min. clear width for wheelchair clearance*

*ADA requirement for adults.

Equipment

Projection Systems and Screens

Projection screens should be mounted on walls or suspended from ceilings. Their dimensions should be at least 5 × 7 feet, but 6 × 8 feet is preferable. Remember to specify additional sections, or "tails," at the top of screens that are to be attached to high ceilings. The bottom of the screen will then be approximately 4 feet above the floor. Using marker boards as projection screens is not advisable, because their surfaces do not reflect light well. Interactive white board systems are quite popular and can replace the projection screen. As of this writing, the largest available screen is about 6 feet wide.

A digital projector may be mounted on a rolling cart together with a videocassette recorder and DVD player. Outlets centered about 12 to 16 feet from the projection screen can supply electricity, cable TV wiring, and computer input to the projector. The size of the projected image will be 6 × 8 feet. Images from a video camera connected to a microscope eyepiece can also be projected through the digital projector.

The emergence of digital projectors has made TV monitors less popular. Large-screen televisions are expensive, not as flexible as the digital projectors, and they produce lower resolution images than computer monitors or digital projectors.

There are several systems for projecting images onto a screen:

- an interactive whiteboard coupled with a digital projector
- a VCR or DVD player and television screen
- a video camera connected to a microscope and digital projector or television screen
- a digital projector connected to a VCR or computer
- an overhead projector

Approximate Cost of Equipment, in 2006 $US

Screen (6' × 8')	$400–$1,500
Large, flat-screen television	$1,200–$3,000
Interactive white board	$2,000–$6,000
Video camera with microscope adapter	$600
Microscope	$100 to $900
Digital projector	$900 to $2,000
Videocassette recorder	$200 to $600
Overhead projector	$400
Microprojector	$700

Planning for Equipment Purchases

It is almost impossible to plan the ordering of loose equipment for science programs during the construction process. However, in order to be ready for move-in day, some orders must be prepared ahead of time.

When ordering start-up supplies, outline the 10 or 20 most crucial laboratory experiences for a class and document everything you will need in order to offer those experiences. Remember the supplies that are often taken for granted, such as pencil sharpeners, paper towel dispensers, brooms, and dustpans. A new facility will have nothing!

The following lists are for discussion purposes. Costs are rounded to the nearest dollar. They are representative, and not specific product sale prices. The sample lists are based on a class of 24 students, with laboratory setups for each group of four students. Although the number of students in a class should not exceed 24, equipment for 28 is ordered, to cover breakage and loss. These lists may be useful when you are submitting plans to committees for their consideration.

The lists are not complete, and are meant as starting points. Consumables are not listed, because they are seldom included in construction budgets and they vary with the curricula.

Another area not addressed is decorative furnishings for walls. The periodic table is just the beginning: display boards, clocks, and mirrors are essential. Murals of scientific phenomena are popular. Be creative. Schools are no longer the drab institutions they once were.

Safety Equipment for Every Classroom

Item	Number per Class	Representative Cost per Unit
Acid cabinet	1	$ 600
Fire blanket	1	$ 100
First aid Kit	1	$ 50
Fire extinguisher ABC	1	$ 40
Spill control center	1	$ 400
Safety shield	1	$ 125
Goggles	29	$ 90
Goggles sanitizer	1	$ 500
Heat and acid resistant gloves	29	$ 200
Aprons	29	$ 350
Safety handbooks	2	$ 250
Safety/chemical inventory software	1	$ 100
Hot hand holder	8	$ 100

General Equipment: Chemistry or Physical Science

Item	Number per Class	Representative Cost per Unit
Electronic balances	8	$2500
Anti-theft locks for balances	8	$ 200
Triple-beam balance	8	$ 800
Auxiliary masses for balances	8	$ 400
Hot plates	8	$1200
Autoclave/sterilizer	1	$3500
Centrifuge	1	$ 300
Flasks/Erlenmeyer 125/250/500/1000 ml	140 per size	$1000
Corks/rubber stoppers for flasks	280 per size	$ 840
Clamps/test tube and extension	40/16	$ 240
Volumetric flasks 100/500 ml	42 per size	$1400
Rimless test tubes (OD × Lmm) (6 × 50) (13 × 100) (18 × 150)	72 per size	$ 100
With corks to fit	72 per size	$ 25
Funnels/short and long stemmed	36	$ 180
Microscale chemistry kits (test plates and spatulas)	8	$ 150
Pipettes/volumetric 1 ml/5 ml/10 ml	24 per size	$ 450
Thermometers	40	$ 200
Spectrophotometer with tubes and lamps	1	$1600
TI calculator-based lab systems	8	$2000
TI calculator for overhead	1	$ 300
Interface probes for calculator-based labs, temperature/pH/micropressure	8 each	$2400

General Equipment: Life Science

Item	Number per Class	Representative Cost per Unit
Electronic balances	8	$2500
Aquarium /40 gallon complete	1	$ 500
Monocular compound microscopes 4x/10x/40x with in-stage condensers	8	$2500
Binocular stereoscopic microscopes	8	$2500
Hot plates	8	$1200
Autoclave/sterilizer	1	$3500
Dissection pans and kits	15	$ 300
Flasks/Erlenmeyer 125/250/500/1000 ml	35 per size	$250
Corks for flasks	70 per size	$ 210
Slides and cover slips	720	$ 50
Slide survey sets	8 per type	$ 160
Volumetric flasks 100/500ml	14 per size	$ 450
Plant grow light/station	1	$ 600
Funnels /short- and long-stemmed	36	$ 180
Pipettes/volumetric 1 ml/5ml/10 ml	24 per size	$ 450
Rimless test tubes (OD × Lmm) (6 × 50) (13 × 100) (18 × 150) plus corks to fit	72 per size	$ 100 $ 25
Petri dishes	80	$ 200
Electrophoresis cell and power supply	1	$ 700
TI calculator-based lab systems	8	$2000
Interface probes for calculator-based labs, temperature/pH/carbon dioxide	8 each	$2400

General Equipment: Physics

Item	Number per Class	Representative Cost per Unit
Electronic balances	8	$2500
Power supplies ac/dc	8	$2000
Optics light bench	8	$3200
Laser/modulated 0.8mW	1	$ 500
Hot plates	8	$1200
Oscilloscope	8	$4800
Photogate timers	15	$1500
Triple-beam balances	8	$ 800
Thermometers	15	$ 75
Spectrophotometer with tubes and clamps	1	$1600
Test tubes and (OD/Lmm) 18 × 150 Corks	72 72	$ 30 $ 15
Volumetric flasks 100/500ml	14 per size	$ 450
Metersticks	16	$ 50
Stopwatches	16	$ 160
Vernier calipers	8	$ 80
Clamps, extension (universal)	24	$ 200
Pulleys	16	$ 50
TI calculator-based lab systems	8	$2000
TI calculator for overhead	1	$ 300
Interface probes for calculator-based labs, temperature/pH/ pressure/light	8 each	$3000

Sample Checklists

Elementary Science

Category	Guidelines	Good	Fair	Poor	Comments
Is there adequate floor space for the students to work safely?	40 sq ft minimum per student for science room; 45 sq ft minimum for multiple-use classroom Sufficient space between desks. 4 ft aisles				
Is the space flexible?	Rectangular room without alcoves				
Is there room for open floor activities and demonstrations?	Room 30 ft wide, minimum Movable student tables Movable teacher's table				
Is there adequate space for the teachers?	Secure storage and desks Space available to teacher during planning time.				
Is the power supply adequate and safe?	Ground-fault interrupters Sufficient circuits and outlets to serve program and technology needs				
Is the lighting adequate?	Directed and diffused to avoid glare 50 foot-candles, minimum per sq ft 75–100 foot-candles at work surface				
Can lighting levels be controlled?	Separate switches for rows of lights Room-darkening shades or blinds				
Is there safe and adequate storage?	10 sq ft per student for teacher's storage and preparation space Secure storage Space for lab and AV equipment				
Is there a good infrastructure for communications?	Telephone for emergencies Network wiring for computers Cable for video communication				
Are there counters or tables for investigations?	Counters 36" high for adults, 24" for grades K–2, 27" high for grades 3–5 Tables 18–20" high for grades K–2, 21"–23" high for grades 3–5				
Is there a water supply suitable for investigations?	1 sink at adult level, at least 1 per 6 students (K–2), 1 per 5 students (3–5), at student's level Swivel and high-arched faucets, deep bowls				
Is there adequate space for displays?	Counter and floor space Shelves and display cabinets Many easily reached tackboards				
Is there space to keep living organisms?	Shelves at windows for plants Grow lights Terrariums or aquariums				
Does the space meet ADA requirements?	At least one wheelchair-accessible counter and sink Accessible safety equipment, doors, and passages				
Are fire and safety measures in place?	Fire and safety equipment, eyewash Adequate fire exits Adequate room ventilation and exhaust fan				

Adapt and expand upon the categories and guidelines in this checklist to suit your program's needs. See Chapters 3 and 4 for detailed suggestions.

SAMPLE CHECKLIST

Middle School Science

Category	Guidelines	Good	Fair	Poor	Comments
Is there adequate floor space for the students to work safely?	45 sq ft min per student for laboratory; 60 sq ft min for combination laboratory/classroom; Sufficient space between desks, 4-ft aisles				
Is there adequate space for the teachers?	Teacher's space with secure storage and desk, not in shared classroom				
Is the power supply adequate and safe?	Ground-fault interrupters; Sufficient curcuits and outlets to serve program and technology needs; Sufficient outlets at lab stations				
Is the lighting adequate?	Directed and diffused to avoid glare; 50 foot-candles, min, per sq ft; 75–100 foot-candles at work surface				
Can lighting levels be controlled?	Separate switches for rows of lights; Room-darkening shades				
Is there safe, adequate storage and a secure place for chemicals?	10 sq ft per student for teacher's storage and preparation space; Separate, lockable room or closet; Space for separation of incompatible chemicals				
Is the preparation space adequate and secure?	Lockable preparation room, preferably at least 8' × 16'				
Is there a good infrastructure for communications?	Telephones for emergencies; Network wiring for computers; Cable for video; Television or LCD projector; Room-darkening shades or blinds				
Are there counters or tables for investigations?	Counters 36" high for adults, 32"–36" high for students; Tables 25"–30" high for students; Movable lab tables or fixed lab stations				
Is there a water supply suitable for investigations?	At least 1 sink per 4 students at students' level, a large sink; Swivel and high-arched faucets; Deep bowls				
Is there space to keep living organisms?	Greenhouse or window shelves for plants; Terrariums or aquariums				
Is there a separate space for small-group and individual student projects?	Student project room with view-window or adequate space arranged to facilitate supervision; Safety equipment and GFI-protected outlets				
Is there space for long-term investigations?	Student project room with holding space for long-term projects; Space for investigations in the classroom				
Does the space meet ADA requirements?	At least one wheelchair-accessible workstation; Accessible safety equipment, doorways, and passages				
Are fire and safety measures in place?	Fire and safety equipment; Adequate exits				
Are there exhaust fans to vent smoke and fumes?	Exhaust fans are vented to outside of the building				
Are a safety shower and eyewash provided where chemicals are used?	Dual eyewash within 25 ft of every workstation if hazardous chemicals are used; Eyewash and shower available for simultaneous use				

Adapt and expand upon the categories and guidelines in this checklist to suit your program's needs. See Chapters 3 and 5 for detailed suggestions.

SAMPLE CHECKLIST

High School Science

Category	Guidelines	Good	Fair	Poor	Comments
Is there adequate floor space for the students to work safely?	45 sq ft min per student for laboratory; 60 sq ft min for combination laboratory/classroom Sufficient space between desks, 4-ft aisles				
Is there adequate space for the teachers?	Teacher's space with secure storage and desk, not in shared classroom				
Is the power supply adequate and safe?	Ground-fault interrupters Sufficient circuits and outlets to serve program and technology needs				
Is the lighting adequate?	Directed and diffused to avoid glare 50 foot-candles, minimum per sq ft 75–100 foot-candles at work surface				
Can lighting levels be controlled?	Separate switches for rows of lights Room-darkening shades or blinds				
Is there safe, adequate storage and a secure place for chemicals?	10 sq ft per student for teacher's storage and preparation space Separate, lockable room or closet Adequate space for separation of incompatible chemicals				
Is the preparation space adequate and secure?	Lockable preparation room, preferably at least 8' × 16'				
Is there a good infrastructure for communications?	Telephones for emergencies Network wiring for computers Cable for video communication Television				
Are there counters or tables for investigations?	Adult-height counters and tables Movable lab tables or fixed lab stations Epoxy resin work surfaces				
Is natural gas or other heat source available?	Natural gas or hot plates 1 service per 4 students Safety shutoff in classroom				
Is there a water supply suitable for investigations?	At least 1 sink per 4 students, 1 large sink Swivel and high-arched faucets, deep bowls Hot (max 120°F) and cold water				
Is there adequate space for displays?	Shelves and display cabinets				
Is there a separate space for small-group and individual student projects?	Room with view window or adequate space arranged to facilitate supervision GFI-protected outlets				
Is there space for long-term investigations?	Student project room with holding space for long-term projects Space in the classroom				
Does the space meet ADA requirements?	At least one wheelchair-accessible workstation Accessible safety equipment, doorways, and passages				
Are fire and safety measures in place?	Fire and safety equipment Adequate exits Adequate ventilation Exhausts vented to outside of building				
Is a fume hood provided where it is required?	Fume hood required if hazardous chemicals are used Fume hood vented to outside of building				
Are a safety shower and eyewash provided?	Dual eyewash within 25 ft of every workstation if hazardous chemicals are used Eyewash and shower available for simultaneous use				

Adapt and expand upon the categories and guidelines in this checklist to suit your program's needs. See Chapters 3 and 6 for detailed suggestions.

Glossary of Construction Terms

ABC extinguisher—A fire extinguisher for use on all general sources of fire: "A" sources (burning paper, wood, trash, etc.), "B" sources (burning flammable liquids), and "C" sources (electrical fires).

Architect—A person licensed to perform architectural services, from analysis of project requirements and creation of a project design to general administration of the construction contract.

Building permit—A permit required by most municipalities before new or significant renovation construction can proceed and is-sued to the owner and the general contractor. Application usually involves the architect's submission of a complete set of design draw-ings and calculations to be reviewed for com-pliance with local building codes.

Casework/Cabinetwork—Cabinets, coun-ters, shelves, and other woodwork.

Change order—A written order to the contractor authorizing a specific change in the work from that described in the original construction contract.

Conduit—Plastic or metal tubing through which wire is pulled for electrical power, telephone lines, data connections, and other uses.

Construction contingency—An allowance in a construction budget to cover the costs of changes resulting from circumstances that cannot be predicted, such as the need to re-move buried trash or deal with unsatisfactory soils. The allowance should be a minimum of 5 percent of the estimated construction cost, and is often greater.

Construction cost—The amount to be paid to the general contractor for construction of the project, including change orders. When a construction manager is employed, the con-struction cost is the sum of all trade construc-tion contracts, including change orders.

Construction documents—The products prepared by the architect and engineering consultants that will be used by the general contractor as directions for constructing the facility. Typically, they consist of drawings, which may include plans, elevations, de-tails, sections, and schedules, and technical specifications that describe the products and construction techniques to be used.

Construction management—A form of project delivery in which the owner contracts with a construction manager to perform cer-tain services during the design phase and to manage the construction process.

Construction manager (CM)—A firm hired by the owner to provide advice on costs, scheduling, and constructibility during the design phase and to coordinate the work of various trade contractors during construc-tion of a project. The construction manager may be a general contractor or a professional consultant.

Contingency fund—A fund additional to the construction budget that covers unforeseen changes in projected costs. *See* Design contin-gency and Construction contingency.

Design/bid/build—The traditional linear process in which the owner hires an architect, who designs the project and assists the owner in obtaining bids for the construction of the project. The design must be completed before bidding and construction take place. During construction, the architect administers the construction contract and observes the work in progress as an agent of the owner.

Design/build—A process in which the owner awards a contract to a firm or group of firms to design and build a construction project for a fixed price. The owner must first prepare a comprehensive and detailed set of require-ments, including a program, usually with the help of an architect.

Design contingency—An allowance in a construction budget that provides for needed items that will be incorporated into the project before bidding takes place, but which are unknown at the time the budget is established. The design contingency should be approximately 10 percent of the construction cost as estimated before design work has begun.

Downlight—A light fixture that aims light downward. Downlights are often recessed into the ceiling.

Drywall—*See* Wallboard.

Dual eyewash—An emergency eyewash that is designed to wash both eyes simultaneously and operates in such a way that the victim has both hands free to hold his or her eyes open.

Educational specifications—The requirements set forth by a school district that guide the architectural design, such as the general size and nature of the spaces for particular activities. The object of educational specifications is to express the needs of the educational program so that the facilities to be designed and constructed will meet those needs.

Engineering consultant—A specialized firm or individual with expertise in a particular area of construction engineering. Typical specialties include civil, structural, mechanical, and electrical engineering. This consultant is usually a subcontractor to the architect.

Epoxy—Epoxy resin, a member of a class of resins used in adhesives, coatings, and castings.

Eyewash—A fixture that provides streams of water to flush the eyes in case of emergency. Often combined with safety shower.

Fiberoptic cable—Glass fibers in a protective sheath used for the transmission of telephone, television, or computer data signals. Fiberoptic cables transmit data much faster than copper wire and can conduct many different signals simultaneously.

Fire marshal—A state or local official whose responsibility is to assist owners and architects in designing facilities that have the appropriate conditions for fire safety. Generally, the fire marshal gives advice and direction to the parties during the design phase and reviews the final construction documents for compliance with local and national fire protection regulations. Consulting the fire marshal early in the planning process of a project can greatly improve the safety of the result and minimize time-consuming design changes when applying for a permit.

Foot-candle (fc)—A measure of illumination on a surface that is equivalent to that produced by one candle at a distance of one foot; equivalent to one lumen per square foot.

General conditions—A term that has two meanings in the context of a construction project: 1. The written requirements in the agreement between the owner and the general contractor that identify the responsibilities of the various parties to the agreement and delineate details such as insurance to be carried. 2. Cost items involved in a construction project that do not become incorporated directly into the project, such as a job-site trailer, dumpsters, and temporary telephone. The general contractor will include a budget for these expenses in the bid.

General contractor (GC)—A firm hired by the owner to build the project. Many general contractors conduct a portion of the construction, such as the concrete work and carpentry, and issue subcontracts to other trade contractors to perform the balance of the work under the supervision and coordination of the general contractor.

Geotechnical investigation—Underground investigation by a geotechnical engineer to predict as accurately as possible the conditions below the ground surface. The results can direct the location of a new building and the design of its foundations.

Glazing—Panes or sheets of glass or other transparent or translucent material, often set in frames or windows.

Grading—The process of reshaping the slope and contours of a building site to accommodate the design of a facility. Depending on the site and the proposed project, grading may be minor or may become a major project in itself, involving blasting to remove rock or importing loads of soil to fill low areas.

Ground-fault interrupter (GFI)—A circuit breaker, usually located in a socket, used to prevent injury from contact with electrical equipment by shutting off power before damage caused by a ground fault can occur. Required in locations where one might be in contact with a grounded surface and an electrical source, particularly adjacent to a water supply.

Grow light—A fluorescent light bulb that emits light conducive to plant growth.

Gypsum—A common mineral used to make plaster and wallboard.

Hazardous materials survey and abatement—Identification of all locations in which hazardous materials used in past construction may exist within the facilities, and a plan for removing or encapsulating these materials so as to eliminate the hazard. In a renovation project, it is likely that some hazardous materials will be removed from a building before construction begins.

Joist—A horizontal section of wood, steel, or concrete framing, spanning between beams or bearing walls, and used to support a raised floor.

Landscaping—Trees, shrubs, and other plantings on a building site.

Lath—A thin wood or metal strip or mesh used to support plaster.

Life-cycle costs—The cost of owning and operating a building through its useful life, including construction, interest on borrowed money, maintenance, fuels, electricity, periodic repairs, replacement of equipment or finishes, and the ultimate demolition of the building. These costs can be reduced by good design and careful selection of building materials and systems.

Lumen—A unit of light emitted from a single source, equal to the light falling on one square foot of surface of an imaginary sphere with a one-foot radius around one candle.

Material Safety Data Sheet (MSDS)—A reference describing the known hazardous properties of a particular chemical and precautionary measures to be taken when using it. The usual sources of MSDS sheets are chemical suppliers.

Movable equipment—Nonexpendable movable items such as tables, LCD projectors, carts, and laboratory equipment.

Off-site construction costs—Costs for necessary construction on the property of others, such as bringing a water main to the site, connecting a sewer main to the nearest public sewer, and road improvements on adjacent roadways.

Program—A listing of spaces required to satisfy the needs of a particular architectural project, including the overall area, dimensions, physical requirements of each space, and the relationship of each space to all other spaces. The program is often developed by the architect through interviews with the users of the facility and becomes the guideline for the architectural design of the facility.

Punch list—A list of incomplete construction items, generally minor in nature, prepared by the architect or general contractor when a construction project is substantially complete for owner occupancy.

Safety shower—A shower fixture for washing chemicals off a person in an emergency to minimize injury.

Schematic design—The initial design phase of a construction project, in which the architect translates the requirements of the program into a physical concept. A schematic design will display in graphical form the various spaces, their relationships to one another, and how they will work together as a building. Drawings of the exterior appearance of the building are also prepared as part of the schematic design.

Shop drawings—Detailed drawings for the manufacture of items fabricated off site. The drawings are generally prepared by the manufacturer for review by the architect.

Site development costs—Costs in addition to the building construction costs, which may include clearing and grading, roads, parking lots, utility construction, and retaining walls.

Site survey—Survey of the existing conditions on the site, showing the location, bearing, and dimensions of the property lines, any easements, the topography of the land, location and elevation of any structures on the site, and the location and elevation of existing utility lines. The architect needs an accurate site survey in order to develop an accurate design.

Space program—*See* Program.

Specifications—A written document, prepared by the architect, describing the materials, methods, and other details of the proposed construction, furniture, or equipment. The specifications complement the construction drawings.

Subcontractor—A trade contractor who has a contract with the general contractor to perform a specific portion of the construction project for the general contractor. The subcontractor is paid by the general contractor.

Substantial completion—The stage in the progress of the work when the work is complete in accordance with the contract documents to the extent that the owner can occupy or use the work for its intended purpose.

Suspended ceiling—A ceiling system suspended beneath overhead structural framing and often concealing heating and air-conditioning ductwork, piping, electrical conduits, and the structure itself.

Trade contractor—A specialty construction contractor who will perform a specific portion of a construction project as a subcontractor to a general contractor. When the owner employs a construction manager, the term may also refer to a firm that has a direct contract with the owner to perform a specific portion of the construction. Examples of trade contractors include roofing, plumbing, and painting contractors.

Troffer—A trough-shaped reflector that holds fluorescent lamps.

Value engineering—An objective, systematic method of obtaining optimal costs for a facility over a specific number of years, considering the costs of construction, operations, maintenance, and replacement.

Wallboard— Interior wall and ceiling surfacing material, generally consisting of gypsum sandwiched between sheets of paper.

Warranty period—A period of time (usually one year) following the final completion of a construction project during which the general contractor must repair deficiencies and correct work that does not conform to the requirements of the contract documents.

NSTA Position Statement: The Integral Role of Laboratory Investigations in Science Instruction

Introduction

A hallmark of science is that it generates theories and laws that must be consistent with observations. Much of the evidence from these observations is collected during laboratory investigations. A school laboratory investigation (also referred to as a lab) is defined as an experience in the laboratory, classroom, or the field that provides students with opportunities to interact directly with natural phenomena or with data collected by others using tools, materials, data collection techniques, and models (NRC 2006, p. 3). Throughout the process, students should have opportunities to design investigations, engage in scientific reasoning, manipulate equipment, record data, analyze results, and discuss their findings. These skills and knowledge, fostered by laboratory investigations, are an important part of inquiry—the process of asking questions and conducting experiments as a way to understand the natural world (NSTA 2004). While reading about science, using computer simulations, and observing teacher demonstrations may be valuable, they are not a substitute for laboratory investigations by students (NRC 2006, p. 3).

For science to be taught properly and effectively, labs must be an integral part of the science curriculum. The National Science Teachers Association (NSTA) recommends that all preK–16 teachers of science provide instruction with a priority on making observations and gathering evidence, much of which students experience in the lab or the field, to help students develop a deep understanding of the science content, as well as an understanding of the nature of science, the attitudes of science, and the skills of scientific reasoning (NRC 2006, p. 127). Furthermore, NSTA is committed to ensuring that all students—including students with academic, remedial, or physical needs; gifted and talented students; and English language learners—have the opportunity to participate in laboratory investigations in a safe environment.

Declarations

NSTA strongly believes that developmentally appropriate laboratory investigations are essential for students of all ages and ability levels. They should not be a rote exercise in which students are merely following directions, as though they were reading a cookbook, nor should they be a superfluous afterthought that is only tangentially related to the instructional sequence of content. Properly designed laboratory investigations should:

- have a definite purpose that is communicated clearly to students;
- focus on the processes of science as a way to convey content;
- incorporate ongoing student reflection and discussion; and
- enable students to develop safe and conscientious lab habits and procedures (NRC 2006, p. 101–102).

Integration of Labs Into the Science Program

Inquiry-based laboratory investigations at every level should be at the core of the science program and should be woven into every lesson and concept strand. As students move through the grades, the level of complexity of laboratory investigations should increase. In addition, NSTA recommends that teachers and administrators follow these guidelines for each grade level:

Preschool and Elementary Level

- With the expectation of science instruction every day, all students at the preschool and elementary level should receive multiple opportunities every week to explore science labs that fit the definition described in the Introduction.
- Laboratory investigations should provide all students with continuous opportunities to explore familiar phenomena and materials.

At developmentally appropriate levels, they should investigate appropriate questions, analyze the results of laboratory investigations, debate what the evidence means, construct an understanding of science concepts, and apply these concepts to the world around them.

Middle and High School Levels

- With the expectation of science instruction every day, all middle level students should have multiple opportunities every week to explore science labs as defined in the Introduction. At the high school level, all students should be in the science lab or field, collecting data every week while exploring science labs.
- Laboratory investigations in the middle and high school classroom should help all students develop a growing understanding of the complexity and ambiguity of empirical work, as well as the skills to calibrate and troubleshoot equipment used to make observations. Learners should understand measurement error; and have the skills to aggregate, interpret, and present the resulting data (NRC 2006, p. 77).
- As students progress through middle and high school, they should improve their ability to collaborate effectively with others in carrying out complex tasks, share the work of the task, assume different roles at different times, and contribute and respond to ideas.

College Level

At the college level, all students should have opportunities to experience inquiry-based science laboratory investigations as defined in the Introduction. All introductory courses should include labs as an integral part of the science curriculum. Laboratory experiences should help students learn to work independently and collaboratively, incorporate and critique the published work of others in their communications, use scientific reasoning and appropriate laboratory techniques to define and solve problems, and draw and evaluate conclusions based on quantitative evidence. Labs should correlate closely with lectures and not be separate activities. Exposure to rigorous, inquiry-based labs at the college level also is important because most teachers develop their laboratory teaching techniques based on their own college coursework laboratory experiences.

Support for Teachers of Science

To give teachers at all levels the support they need to guide laboratory investigations as an integral part of the total curriculum, NSTA recommends:

- Ongoing professional development opportunities to ensure that teachers of science have practical experiences that familiarize them with the pedagogical techniques needed to facilitate inquiry-based labs matched to appropriate science content (NSTA 2006, NRC 2006, p. 150–151).
- Yearly evaluation of the laboratory investigations to determine if they continue to be an integral and effective part of the whole program and the delivery of all content.
- Periodic training in lab logistics, including setup, safety, management of materials and

equipment, and assessment of student practices. Safety equipment and annual safety training should be provided so that science educators are well informed about yearly changes in safety procedures to ensure that students and educators are protected (NSTA 2000).

- Training to work with students with academic or remedial needs, physical needs, and gifted and talented students so that teachers can differentiate instruction appropriately. Assistive equipment, additional personnel, and facilities, modified as needed, also should be provided to ensure appropriate instruction of all students.
- Effective preservice programs that prepare teachers to carry out science labs as a central part of every science curriculum.

Support for Science Labs

To ensure that laboratory investigations are implemented in schools, administrative support is crucial. NSTA recommends that the school administration recognize the instructional importance, overarching goals, and essential activities of laboratory investigations and provide the following:

- An adequate facility where labs can be conducted. At the preschool and elementary levels, this means a classroom with sufficient work space, including flat moveable desks or tables and chairs, equipment, and access to water and electricity. At the middle and high school levels, a safe, well-equipped lab space should be available, with necessary equipment and access to water and electricity. In addition, appropriate facilities to work with students with special needs should be provided. (Biehle 1999)

- Adequate storage space for all materials, including devices and materials in common use that are considered hazardous. (Biehle 1999)
- Funding for yearly educator training on how to manage materials and guide inquiry-based learning during labs.
- A budget for regular maintenance of facilities and equipment, as well as annual costs for new or replacement equipment, supplies, and proper waste management.
- A budget that recognizes additional costs required for field experiences.
- Laboratory occupancy load limits (number of occupants allowed in the laboratory) set at a safe level based on building and fire safety codes, size and design of the laboratory teaching facility, chemical/physical/biological hazards, and the needs of the students (Roy 2006; NSTA 2000). Science classes should have no more than 24 students even if the occupancy load limit might accommodate more. (NSTA 2004) Research data shows that accidents rise dramatically as class enrollments exceed this level. (West et al. 2001) Teachers should not be faced with a Hobson's choice—teach in an unsafe environment or sacrifice the quality of teaching by not doing labs.

Assessment

Assessment, a powerful tool in science education, serves both formative and summative purposes. Not only does it help show what students have learned and the nature of their reasoning, it also indicates what gaps remain in learning and what concepts must be reviewed (NSTA 2001). NSTA recommends the following steps to ensure that laboratory investigations are part of the assessment process:

- Teachers of science, supported by the administration, be given the time and training to develop assessments that reveal and measure inquiry skills—the ability to design, conduct, analyze, and complete an investigation, reason scientifically, and communicate through science notebooks and lab reports.
- Instruction and assessment be aligned so that formative and summative assessments are meaningful and can be used to improve the science curriculum as well as determine what students have learned.

—Adopted by
the NSTA Board of Directors
February 2007

References

Biehle, J. T., L. L. Motz, and S. S. West. 1999. *NSTA guide to school science facilities*. Arlington, VA: NSTA Press.

National Research Council (NRC). 2006. *America's lab report: Investigations in high school science*. Washington, DC: National Academy Press.

National Science Teachers Association (NSTA). 2006. NSTA Position Statement: Professional Development in Science Instruction.

National Science Teachers Association (NSTA). 2004. NSTA Position Statement: Scientific Inquiry.

National Science Teachers Association (NSTA). 2004. *Investigating safely: A guide for high school teachers*. Arlington, VA: NSTA Press.

National Science Teachers Association (NSTA). 2001. NSTA Position Statement: Assessment.

National Science Teachers Association (NSTA). 2000. NSTA Position Statement: Safety and School Science Instruction.

Roy, K. 2006. (Lack of) safety in numbers? *Science Scope* 30 (2): 62–64.

West, S. S., J. F. Westerlund, N. C. Nelson, and A. L. Stephenson. 2001. *Conditions that affect safety in the science classroom: Results from a statewide safety survey*. Austin, TX: Texas Association of Curriculum Development.

Additional Resources

Clough, M. P. 2002. *Using the laboratory to enhance student learning. Learning science and the science of learning*, ed. R. W. Bybee, 85–96. Arlington, VA: NSTA Press.

NSTA Position Statement: Safety and School Science Instruction

Preamble

Inherent in many instructional settings including science is the potential for injury and possible litigation. These issues can be avoided or reduced by the proper application of a safety plan.

Rationale

High-quality science instruction includes laboratory investigations, interactive or demonstration activities and field trips.

Declarations

The National Science Teachers Association recommends that school districts and teachers adhere to the following guidelines:

- School districts must adopt written safety standards, hazardous material management, and disposal procedures for chemical and biological wastes. These procedures must meet or exceed the standards adopted by EPA, OSHA and/or appropriate state and local agencies.
- School authorities and teachers share the responsibility of establishing and maintaining safety standards.
- School authorities are responsible for providing safety equipment (i.e., fire extinguishers), personal protective equipment (i.e., eyewash stations, goggles), Material Safety Data Sheets and training appropriate for each science teaching situation.
- School authorities will inform teachers of the nature and limits of liability and tort insurance held by the school district.
- All science teachers must be involved in an established and ongoing safety training program relative to the established safety procedures which is updated on an annual basis.
- Teachers shall be notified of individual student health concerns.
- The maximum number of occupants in a laboratory teaching space shall be based on the following:
  1. the building and fire safety codes;
  2. occupancy load limits;
  3. design of the laboratory teaching facility;
  4. appropriate supervision and the special needs of students.
- Materials intended for human consumption shall not be permitted in any space used for hazardous chemicals and or materials.
- Students and parents will receive written notice of appropriate safety regulations to be followed in science instructional settings.

—Adopted by the NSTA Board of Directors
July 2000

References

Section 1008.0 Occupant Load—*BOAC National Building Code/1996*

Section 10-1.7.0 Occupant Load—*NFPA Life Safety Code 101-97*

40 CFR 260-70 Resource Conservation and Recovery Act (RCRA)

29 CFR 1910.1200 Hazard Communication Standard (Right to Know Law)

29 CFR 1910.1450 Laboratory Standard, Part Q The Laboratory Standard (Chemical Hygiene Law)

National Research Council (1995). *Prudent Practices in the Laboratory*. Washington, DC: National Academy Press.

Furr, K. Ed. 1995. *Handbook of laboratory safety*, 4th Ed. CRC Press.

Fleming, D., et al. Eds. 1995. *Laboratory safety*, 2nd Ed. ASM Press.

National Science Education Leadership Position Paper. 1997. Class size in laboratory rooms. *The Navigator*. 33 (2).

Number of Lab/Classrooms Required Per Enrollment

Well-designed facilities are the foundation for safe and effective science education.
Based on 24 students per class as per Natural Science Teachers Association and
Natural Science Education Leadership Association recommendations.

Developed by
Dr. Sandra S. West
Department of Biology
Texas State University – San Marcos
San Marcos, TX 78666
sw04@txstate.edu

Student Enrollment	No. of Lab/Classrooms when 4 yrs. of science is required	No. of Lab/Classrooms when 3 yrs. of science is required	No. of Lab/Classrooms when 2 yrs. of science is required
400	4	3	2
600	5	4	3
800	7	5	4
1000	9	7	5
1200	10	8	5
1400	12	9	6
1600	14	10	7
1800	15	12	8
2000	17	13	9
2200	19	14	10
2400	20	15	10
2600	22	17	11
2800	24	18	12
3000	25	19	13

Note: The *Science Lab Calculator* can be found at
http://www.bio.txstate.edu/%7escied/Safety/Safety.html
Click on "Science Lab Calculator"

The *Science Lab Calculator* can be used to determine site-specific needs.

Bibliography

American Association for the Advancement of Science (AAAS). 1990. *Project 2061: Science for all americans.* New York: Oxford University Press.

American Association for the Advancement of Science (AAAS). 1991. *Barrier free in brief: Laboratories and classrooms in science and engineering.* Washington, DC: Author.

American Chemical Society (ACS). 1993. *Safety in the elementary (K–6) science classroom.* Washington, DC: Author.

American Chemical Society, Committee on Chemical Safety. 1995. *Safety in academic chemistry laboratories* (6th ed.). Washington, DC: ACS. (Single copies are available without charge to school science administrators and teachers.)

American National Standards Institute (ANSI). 1990. *Emergency eyewash and shower equipment* (ANSI Standard Z358.1-1990). New York: ANSI.

Americans with disabilities act accessibility guidelines for buildings and facilities. 1991. *Federal Register* 56 (44): 144.

Architectural and Transportation Barriers Compliance Board (ATBCB). 1992. *Americans with disabilities act accessibility guidelines for buildings and facilities.* Washington, DC: Author.

Ballard, R., D. Edwards, M. Kestner, C. Stallings, and W. J. Tucci. 2002. *School science facilities planner.* Raleigh, NC: North Carolina Department of Public Instruction. Available online at *www.schoolclearinghouse.org/pubs/SCIENCE.PDF.*

Baughman, J. Jr., and D. Zollman. 1977. Physics lab for the blind. *The Physics Teacher* 15 (6): 339–342.

Biehle, J. T. 1995. Complying with science. *American School and University* (May).

Biehle, J. T. 2000. Planning the middle school science classroom. *School Planning & Management* (Jan).

Biehle, J. T. 2000. The science resource area in the state-of-the-art high school. *PEB Exchange* 41: 23–25. Available online at *www.oecd.org/dataoecd/52/36/14642267.pdf.*

Biehle, J. T., 2002. Science facilities. *School Planning & Management* (August).

Biehle, J. T. 2006. A five-step approach to planning for technology in new science spaces. *Science Scope* 30 (1): 58.

Biehle, J. T. 2006. Lifetime costs of real capital ownership. *School Planning & Management* (Dec).

Biehle, J. T. 2006. School greenhouse design tips. *The Science Teacher* 73 (8): 58–64.

Biehle, J. T. 2006. Science in structure. *The Science Teacher* 73 (3): 10.

Biehle, J. T., L. L. Motz, and S. S. West. 1999. Designing high school science facilities. *The Construction Specifier* (Oct).

California Department of Education, Science and Environmental Education Unit (CDE). 1993. *Science facilities design for California public schools.* Sacramento, CA: Author.

Collins, B. K. 1985. One person's trash. *Science and Children* 22 (8): 17.

Cooper, E. C. 1994. *Laboratory design handbook.* New York: CRC Press.

Dell'Isola, A. J. 1974. *Value engineering in the construction industry.* New York: Construction Publishing.

DiBerardinis, L. J., J. S. Baum, M. W. First, G. T. Gatwood, E. F. Groden, and A. K. Seth. 1993. *Guidelines for laboratory design: Health and safety considerations.* 2nd ed. New York: Wiley/Interscience.

Fickes, M. 2001. The furniture of science. *School Planning & Management* (Jan). Available online at *www.peterli.com/archive/spm/211.shtm.*

Flinn Scientific. *Flinn biological catalog/reference manual.* 1996. Batavia, IL: Flinn Scientific, Inc. (Contains advice on safety in the laboratory)

Flinn Scientific. *Flinn chemical catalog/reference manual.* 1996. Batavia, IL: Flinn Scientific, Inc. (Contains advice on safety in the laboratory)

Flinn, L. C., III. 1993. Overcrowding in the science laboratory. *Flinn Fax!* 93 (1): 4–5.

Florida Department of Education (FDE). 1992. *Barrier free in brief: Laboratories and classrooms in science and engineering: A school science safety manual.* Tallahassee, FL: Author.

Florida Department of Education (FDE). 1992. *Science safety: No game of chance! A school science safety manual.* Tallahassee, FL: Author.

Florida Department of Education (FDE). 1993. *Science for all students: The Florida preK–12 science curriculum framework.* Tallahassee, FL: Author.

Fox, P. 1994. Creating a laboratory: It's elementary. *Science and Children* 31 (4): 20–22.

General Services Administration, Department of Urban Housing, Department of Defense, and United States Postal Service. 1988. *Uniform federal accessibility standards.* Washington, DC: U.S. Government Printing Office.

Gerlovich, J. A., ed. 1984. *School science safety: Elementary school*. Batavia, IL: Flinn Scientific.

Gerlovich, J. A., ed. 1984. *School science safety: Secondary school*. Batavia, IL: Flinn Scientific.

Governor's Committee on High School Science Laboratories for the 21st Century. 1992. *Look of the future: Report of the governor's committee on high school science laboratories for the 21st century*. Baltimore, MD: State of Maryland, Public School Construction Program.

Grocoff, P. N. 1996. *Effects of correlated color temperature on perceived visual comfort*. Dissertation, University of Michigan, College of Architecture and Urban Planning. (Available from University Microfilms, 1-800-521-3042)

Harbeck, M. B. 1985. Getting the most out of elementary science. *Science and Children* 23 (2): 44–45.

Heintschel, R. M. 1982. *Science in Ohio's secondary schools: A status report*. Columbus, OH: Ohio State Department of Education. (ERIC Document Reproduction Service No. ED 224 708)

Hill, F. 1988. *Tomorrow's learning environment: Planning for technology: The basics*. Alexandria, VA: National School Boards Association.

Jbelly, K. A. 1990. *On providing a safe and effective science learning environment: Safety practices/conditions and accreditation*. Austin, TX: Texas Education Agency.

Justrite Manufacturing Co. 1985. *How to handle flammable liquids safely*. Des Plaines, IL: Author.

Kaufman, J. A. *The Kaufman letter*. Natick, MA: James A. Kaufman and Associates.

Keep, G. D. 2002. Buildings that teach. Educational Facility Planner 37 (2). Available online at *http://sbw.cefpifoundation.org/pdf/BuildingsTeach.pdf*.

Krajkovich, J. G. 1983. *A survey of accidents in the secondary school science laboratory*. Edison, NJ: New Jersey Science Supervisors Association.

Kwan, T., and J. Texley. 2002. *Exploring safely: A guide for elementary teachers*. Arlington, VA: NSTA Press.

Kwan, T., and J. Texley. 2003. *Inquiring safely: A guide for middle school teachers*. Arlington, VA: NSTA Press.

Laboratory Safety Workshop. 1986. *Laboratory safety guidelines: 40 suggestions for a safer laboratory*. Natick, MA: Author. (Available from the organization's website at *www.labsafety.org*)

Laboratory Ventilation (ANSI Standard Z9.5-1992). 1992. New York: American National Standards Institute.

Lackney, J. A. 2002. 12 design principles based on brain-based learning research. Workshop presented at the CEFPI Midwest Regional Conference. Available online at *www.designshare.com/Research/BrainBasedLearn98.htm*.

Lien, V., and G. Skoog. 1983. Survey of Texas science education. *Texas Science Teacher* 18 (2): 5–17.

Los Angeles, Orange, and San Diego County Offices of Education. 1989. *Remodeling and building science instruction facilities in elementary, middle, junior, and senior high schools*. Downey, CA: Los Angeles County Office of Education.

Lowery, L. F., ed. 1997. *NSTA pathways to the science standards: Elementary school edition*. Arlington, VA: NSTA Press.

Madrazo, G. M., Jr., and L. L. Motz, eds. 1993. *Sourcebook for science supervisors*. 4th ed. Arlington, VA: NSTA Press.

Maryland State Department of Education (MSDE), School Facilities Branch. 1994. *Science facilities design guidelines*. Baltimore, MD: Author.

McIntosh, I. B. D., C. B. Dorgan, and C. E. Dorgan. 2001. *ASHRAE laboratory design guide*. Atlanta, GA: American Society of Heating, Refrigerating, and Air-Conditioning Engineers, Inc.

Means Engineering Staff, eds. 2006. *Means building construction cost data 2007*. 65th ed. Kingston, MA: R. S. Means.

Mione, L. V. 1995. *Facilities standards for technology in New Jersey schools*. Trenton, NJ: New Jersey Department of Education.

Motz, L. L. 1999. Think safety first. *The Science Teacher* 66 (6): 10.

Narum, J. L., ed. 1995. *Structures for science: A handbook for planning facilities for undergraduate natural science communities, volume III*. Washington, DC: Project Kaleidoscope.

National Fire Protection Association (NFPA). 2003. *NFPA 30 flammables and combustible liquids code*. Quincy, MA: Author.

National Fire Protection Association (NFPA). 2004. *NFPA 45 standard on fire protection for laboratories using chemicals*. Quincy, MA: Author.

National Research Council (NRC). 1996. *National science education standards*. Washington, DC: National Academy Press.

National Science Teachers Association (NSTA). 1993. *Safety in the elementary science classroom*. Arlington, VA: NSTA Press.

National Science Teachers Association (NSTA). 1993. *Scope, sequence, and coordination of secondary school science: Vol. 1: The content core*. Arlington, VA: NSTA Press.

National Science Teachers Association (NSTA). 2006. Laboratory science (1990 position statement). In *NSTA Handbook 2006–2007*. Arlington, VA: NSTA Press.

National Science Teachers Association (NSTA). 2006. Safety and school science instruction (2000 position statement). In *NSTA Handbook 2006–2007*. Arlington, VA: NSTA Press.

National Science Teachers Association Task Force on Science Facilities and Equipment. 1993.

Facilitating science facilities: A priority. Arlington, VA: NSTA Press.

North Carolina Department of Public Instruction, Division of Science Education. 1991. *Hints on science room design*. Raleigh, NC: North Carolina Public Schools.

North Carolina Department of Public Instruction, Division of School Planning. 1991. *North Carolina public schools facility standards: A guide for planning school facilities*. Raleigh, NC: North Carolina Public Schools.

North Carolina Department of Public Instruction, Division of School Planning. 1992. *North Carolina public schools furnishing and equipment standards: A guide for planning and equipping new facilities and evaluating existing schools*. Raleigh, NC: North Carolina Public Schools.

Rakow, S. J., ed. 1998. *NSTA pathways to the science standards: Middle school edition*. Arlington, VA: NSTA Press.

Reese, K. M., ed. 1985. *Teaching chemistry to physically handicapped students*. Washington, DC: American Chemical Society.

Ryan, K. 2001. *Science classroom safety and the law: A handbook for teachers*. Batavia, IL: Flinn Scientific.

Showalter, V. M., ed. 1984. *Conditions for good science teaching*. Arlington, VA: NSTA Press.

Steele, M. M., P. A. Conroy, and J. A. Kaufman. *There's No Safety in Numbers*. Natick, MA: Laboratory Safety Workshop. (Review of state-by-state rules on class sizes)

Summerlin, L. 1995. *A to Z safety in the elementary science classroom*. 2nd ed. Birmingham, AL: Alabama Science Teachers Association.

Summers, J., J. Texley, and T. Kwan. 2006. *Science safety in the community college*. Arlington, VA: NSTA Press.

Texas Administrative Code. School facilities standards. Title 19, part II, chapter 61, subchapter CC, §61.1033. (Available online at *www.sos. state.tx.us/tac/index.html*)

Texas Education Agency (TEA). 1989. *Planning a safe and effective science learning environment*. Austin, TX: Author.

Texley, J., and A. Wild, eds. 1996. *NSTA pathways to the science standards: High school edition*. Arlington, VA: NSTA Press.

Texley, J., T. Kwan, and J. Summers. 2004. *Investigating safely: A guide for high school teachers*. Arlington, VA: NSTA Press.

Utility PhotoVoltaic Group. 1998. *Schools going solar*. Washington, DC: Interstate Renewable Energy Council, American Solar Energy Society, and Utility PhotoVoltaic Group.

Wang, D. 1994. A working laboratory. *The Science Teacher* 61 (2): 26–29.

Ward, J. 1992. Shopping for science. *The Science Teacher* 59 (6): 28–33.

Ward, S., and S. S. West. 1990. Accidents in Texas high school chemistry labs. *The Texas Science Teacher*, 19 (2): 14–19.

West, S. S. 1991. Lab safety. *The Science Teacher* 58 (6): 45–49.

West, S. S., L. L. Motz, and J. T. Biehle. 1999. Science facilities by design. *The Science Teacher* 66 (6): 28–31.

West, S. S., S. J. Westerlund, A. Stephenson, and N. Nelson. 2003. Conditions that affect secondary science safety: Results from 2001 Texas survey, overcrowding. *The Texas Science Teacher* 32 (2).

Young, J. A., ed. 1991. *Improving safety in the chemical laboratory: A practical guide*. 2nd ed. New York: Wiley/Interscience.

Young, J. A. 1997. Chemical safety, part I: Safety in the handling of hazardous chemicals. *The Science Teacher* 64 (3): 43–45.

Young, J. A. 1997. Chemical safety, part II: Tips for dealing with laboratory hazards. *The Science Teacher* 64 (4): 40–41.

Young, J. A., W. K. Kingsley, and G. H. Wahl. 1990. *Developing a chemical hygiene plan*. Washington, DC: American Chemical Society.

INDEX

timeline for, 11, 13
using recycled materials in, 95
Construction contingency, 131
Construction costs, 13–16, 131
off-site, 133
Construction documents, 131
Construction management, 131
Construction manager (CM), 4, 13, 131
Construction procurement process, 17
Contingency fund, 16, 131
Cooling of greenhouse, 91
Costs, 13–16
change orders and, 15, 131
construction, 13–16, 131
off-site, 133
construction contingency, 131
contingency fund, 16, 131
design contingency, 132
of equipment, 125–127
estimates of, 8, 16
life-cycle, 133
location of science facilities and, 7–8, 69
prioritization and, 16
project budget, 14–15
of projections systems, 125
site developmental, 134
value engineering, 16, 134
Council for State Science Supervisors, 29
Courtyards, 93–94
Curriculum
facility design and, 9
house model, 7–8, 55, 69
integrated, 19–20
grouping facilities for, 55–56, 70
in high school, 70
in middle school, 55
review of, 5–6
of secondary courses, 21, 69
standards-based programs, 19
use of greenhouse in, 89–90
Curriculum coordinators on planning team, 3, 4
Curriculum subcommittee, 4, 6

D

Darkening classrooms, 49, 52, 64–65, 82–83
Demonstration tables, 61, 78
Design/bid/build process, 131

Design/build process, 131
Design contingency, 132
Designing science facilities, 9–13
ADA checklist for, 106
addressing school board, 10
communicating with school board, 10
for elementary school, 45–53
evidence to support recommended design, 9
for high school, 69–88
for middle school, 55–68
presentation to school board, 10, 13
roles of consultants, 9
roles of science education leader, 9–10
evaluation, 10
information and communication, 9–10
planning and coordination, 9
promotion and representation, 10
schematic design, 133
time required for, 9
Digital data video streaming, 22
Display space
in elementary school, 48, 52
in high school, 79–80
in middle school, 62, 63
Distance learning, 23, 24–25, 107, 109
Downlight, 132
Dry-erase boards, 48, 62, 79
Dual eyewash, 132

E

Earthquake-prone areas, 40
Educational specifications, 132
Electrical generators
solar, 94, 99, 111–112
wind, 94, 99
Electricity in classroom, 33–34, 49, 63, 80–81
Electronic marker boards, 26, 49, 63, 80
Electronic security systems, 26
Elementary school science facilities, 45–53
checklist for, 128
multiple-use classroom, 46
space requirements and room design, 45–46
specialized science classroom, 46–53
computers, 50, 52
display space, 48–49, 52
furnishings, 47, 50
lighting and darkening rooms, 49–50, 52

preparation and storage areas, 52–53
sinks, 47, 51
storage, 47–48, 51–52
teacher's space, 52
utilities, 49, 52
work space, 47, 51
Emergency exits, 33
Emergency shut-off controls for utilities, 34, 49, 64
Energy conservation, 94, 99
Engineering consultant, 132
Epoxy, 132
Equipment, 3
for chemistry or physical science, 126
for life science, 127
manufacturers of, 17
movable, 133
for physics, 127
planning for purchase of, 125
safety equipment, 126
Exhaust fans, 38, 49
Eye protection, 39
Eyewash station, 35, 132
dual eyewash, 132
for students with disabilities, 105

F

Facilitating Science Facilities: A Priority, ix
Facilities for Secondary School Science Teaching: Evolving Patterns in Facilities and Programs, ix
Facilities subcommittee, 5
Family and consumer science, 56
Fiberoptic cable, 132
Filtering software, 23–24
"Finger" lab station design, 59, 72–73
Fire marshal, 132
Fire protection, 39
Fixed lab stations
in high school, 72–75
in middle school, 57, 59–60
Flooring materials, 100–101, 108
Foot-candle, 132
Formaldehyde-free wood, 95
Fume hoods, 37–39, 81–82
for students with disabilities, 105
Funding, 8, 13–14
Furnishings, 3